MARY CLIMBS IN

MARY CLIMBS IN

THE JOURNEYS OF BRUCE SPRINGSTEEN'S WOMEN FANS

LORRAINE MANGIONE AND
DONNA LUFF

RUTGERS UNIVERSITY PRESS
New Brunswick, Camden, and Newark, New Jersey
London and Oxford

Rutgers University Press is a department of Rutgers, The State University of New Jersey, one of the leading public research universities in the nation. By publishing worldwide, it furthers the University's mission of dedication to excellence in teaching, scholarship, research, and clinical care.

Library of Congress Cataloging-in-Publication Data

Names: Mangione, Lorraine, author. | Luff, Donna, author.
Title: Mary climbs in : the journeys of Bruce Springsteen's women fans / Lorraine Mangione and Donna Luff.
Description: New Brunswick, New Jersey : Rutgers University Press, 2023. | Includes bibliographical references and index.
Identifiers: LCCN 2022048836 | ISBN 9781978827189 (cloth) | ISBN 9781978827202 (epub) | ISBN 9781978827219 (pdf)
Subjects: LCSH: Springsteen, Bruce—Appreciation. | Women rock music fans—Psychology. | Rock music—Psychological aspects.
Classification: LCC ML420.S77 .M32 2023 | DDC 782.4216609—dc23/eng/20221019
LC record available at https://lccn.loc.gov/2022048836

A British Cataloging-in-Publication record for this book is available from the British Library.

Credit lines for song lyrics are listed in the Permissions section

∞ The paper used in this publication meets the requirements of the American National Standard for Information Sciences—Permanence of Paper for Printed Library Materials, ANSI Z39.48-1992.

rutgersuniversitypress.org

For all the women fans who shared their journeys
with us with honesty and passion

LM: In honor of fan friends Martha Cook, the most
prescient and creative, Cathy McKay Zarbo, the
most fun and passionate, and Lisa McCann,
the most reflective and mystical

DL: For Gareth, Ellen, and Nathaniel, my
companions on the most important journey

CONTENTS

MARY CLIMBS IN

Introduction

On a mild autumn day, two strangers sat in a sunny, suburban living room watching the documentary *Springsteen and I*. Lorraine, a professor of psychology, and Donna, a sociologist working in health care, had never met before, though their paths might easily have crossed earlier. They had presented separately at The Glory Days Springsteen Symposia, organized by a team of scholars and fans (led by Mark Bernhard, Ken Womack, and others) that took place at Monmouth University in New Jersey and, as a result of connections made there, they had both been invited to join the editorial advisory board for *BOSS: the Biannual Online Journal of Springsteen Studies*. Lorraine and Donna jumped at the chance to cowrite a review of the fan documentary, *Springsteen & I: "Friends since . . ."* and thus began a camaraderie and collaboration.

As Springsteen fans ourselves, we had varying experiences of comments and jokes about our fandom over the years, sometimes assuming it to be something that we should have outgrown or that was fueled by sexual fantasy, but those stereotypes did not reflect our own experiences, those of women fans we knew, the commentary by women at the conferences, or writings by women fans in both fiction and nonfiction (e.g., Bishop 2019; Edelman, 1996; Iver, 2019; Mason, 1985; Powers, 2016; Wurtzel, 1994). As we talked together and reflected on our own experiences, we felt so much of what it meant for women to be Springsteen fans remained underexplored.

It started with sharing our own stories with one another.

Lorraine grew up in Connecticut, a place where Springsteen occasionally gave small, intimate concerts—sometimes in high school gyms! Alas, she was an early skeptic toward her friend Martha who had "climbed in" right away, as she and her younger brothers teased Martha with witty names for Springsteen. Although her older brother had introduced her to many rock groups (as with many women in the study), his tastes veered toward the more esoteric—Emerson, Lake, and Palmer, Pink Floyd, and the Moody Blues—not Springsteen. Yet the connection with Springsteen's work was fermenting, quietly, under wraps, a bit buried. While not growing up on the Jersey shore, there was enough about small-town living, beach, community, shared Italian American Catholic ethnicity, New York City family from the Lower East Side, the Bronx, and Brooklyn with strong attachment to the New York Yankees to help Lorraine finally resonate with the world evoked by Springsteen. Her own journey started in earnest in the later 1970s, intensified with her first concert in Kansas City near where she attended graduate school. It was perhaps most of all the psychologist in Springsteen that spoke to the psychologist in this author, and that cemented the connection. How could it be that his music so mirrored the theories, research, and clinical work that she was studying? How did he understand so much of the human psyche? It feels fitting that her first concert was filled with songs from *Darkness on the Edge of Town* and *The River,* two intensely psychological albums, as well as all the dancing, shouting, and arm waving. She has acknowledged that Martha was light years ahead, opening the door for her to climb in.

Donna's journey as a Springsteen fan began at age sixteen in Britain. In the backseat of her father's car, she heard "Hungry Heart" blast from the radio. She asked her father to turn up the volume and her younger sister to quiet down. As she listened, she understood she had a hungry heart too.

As for many British youth of that time, music was a defining part of Donna's identity. Growing up in Birmingham, England's second-largest city, a musical cauldron and a routine stop on tour itineraries, she went to concerts often. Just a few months after hearing "Hungry Heart," Donna got tickets to see Springsteen on the British leg of *The River* tour. Her first impression was that everyone in the audience was old: who are these people? But what she saw and heard on stage reflected her own yearnings—the promise of a bigger, more alive life. She saw herself in both the protagonist and the girl in the Springsteen songs.

Decades later, and through her move to live in the United States, Donna remains a Springsteen fan. The realities of life, and of life in the United States, have proved more complicated, of course, than her youthful romanticism—the gap between dream and reality that Springsteen's music has long explored. But, through the contradictions and her ever-growing feminism, Springsteen has remained an unlikely life guide. For Donna, Springsteen is like a trusted friend who is always a little way ahead of her, illuminating stages on the journey. His music showed what lay ahead and, remarkably, how she would feel about it.

The idea of transforming our personal fan relationships to include research about fans, in addition to obsessing over music and concerts, came gradually through our participation in The Glory Days Springsteen Symposia and from that viewing together of *Springsteen & I*. As a psychologist working in an academic setting to educate and train doctoral students becoming clinical psychologists, and a sociologist working in health services training and research, we bring differing backgrounds to our work together, and to the research that formed the basis for this book. One of us frames the world in more individual and small-group interactions and the other in larger group and society-level phenomena. Both views have contributed to our understanding of Springsteen and his female fans.

As women, writers, and academics, much of our scholarship and interest had focused on women, always curious about what happens in women's lives and between women and men, from the women's point of view. It seemed almost natural to explore how women fans view Springsteen and his work, specifically as women and about women. Among many excellent pieces of Springsteen scholarship, one stands out as an impetus for this book: Daniel Cavicchi's (1998) groundbreaking work on Springsteen fans, *Tramps Like Us: Music and Meaning among Springsteen Fans,* the first in-depth exploration of the experiences of Springsteen fans. However, Cavicchi did not specifically explore gender in the fan experience and noted that work remained to be done about women fans. This is the challenge that we claimed. Cavicchi's work inspired us to search further to see how fandom and Springsteen had evolved over the decades and what fandom held for women.

Cavicchi's groundbreaking work and Robert Coles (2003), who articulated the magnitude of Springsteen's work to fans in his compelling narrative account, *Bruce Springsteen's America: The People Listening, A Poet Singing,* laid the foundations for our study. *Springsteen and I* moved the conversation further forward by depicting the experience of some women fans, but these are individual experiences, chosen (we assume) in part for "dramatic" or "cinematic" effect, rather than representing women fans' perspectives more broadly. Five years after our initial survey, we read Gina Barreca, noted author and professor of English, and a contributor to the Springsteen seventieth birthday compilation *Long Walk Home* (2019), in describing her own fan experience, ask a similar question to one that motivated this project: "Why do so many of us, not only American women but also those from around the world, find Springsteen's music compelling?" (p. 163). It appeared to us that this question was still alive and waiting for more answers.

Watching that documentary together sparked conversations between us that we continued through conducting a survey of women fans, poring over the results, publishing a book chapter and an article based on some of the results, conducting a second survey, and finally writing this book. We hope to move the wider conversation about Springsteen fans forward by focusing on women's experiences. We hope you will join us for the ride.

CHAPTER 1

Women Fans of Bruce Springsteen

Why Listen to Them and What Might They Tell Us?

His music and influence have no doubt made me into the person I am today. Over the years, I have not just listened to his music—I have metabolized it.

It is commonplace to say that an album, a song, or a musician's work is the soundtrack of one's life, and soundtracks of our lives are undoubtedly important. But soundtracks remain outside us, a background to the central events of our lives. To metabolize suggests something more profound—a taking into your very core, transforming and being transformed in the process. It is striking for this fan to describe their engagement with Bruce Springsteen in this way. What is it about Springsteen and his music that can inspire this kind of intense connection? And is the quote even more interesting when we know that the fan is a woman? We wanted to find out more about what being a Springsteen fan means for women and what impacts it has on their lives.

Saying anything new about Bruce Springsteen is a challenge. The year 2020 marked 50 years since his first album. In those years, Springsteen has gone from Jersey Shore music scene legend to international icon, with increasing cultural stature and influence. He has been widely honored, awarded, quoted, and debated. His live concerts have become the standard against which other performers are judged, and his music catalog has spanned stadium rock anthems to spare, acoustic ballads that draw on folk, country, and blues traditions to create something uniquely his own. Springsteen, now a septuagenarian, shows no sign of slowing down or moving into complacency or retirement. Instead, he continues to widen the boundaries of what a rock star can do, most recently with his memoir, groundbreaking and Tony Award–winning Broadway show, debut as a movie director, and support for fans and New Jersey throughout the coronavirus pandemic.

Throughout this remarkable and wide-ranging career one facet has remained a constant: the devotion of his audience. Though the audience itself has grown, the intensity of the devotion has remained a consistent and noted feature, from old fans to new. Commentators have argued for a quasi-religious dimension to Springsteen fandom (Cavicchi, 1998; Cullen, 2005; Symynkywicz, 2008; Woge, 2011) such that his audience is almost a secular religious community, with a level of devotion and ritual with few parallels among other music fans (The Grateful Dead, Dylan, and Phish are possible comparators, see Swirsky, 2014). Consequently, his fans have become worthy of study in their own right. As with Springsteen, can there be more to say about Springsteen fans? The answer, we argue, is a resounding yes.

So what is there to say? We explore something that we perceived as missing in previous works on Springsteen fans: a nuanced understanding of the particular and relational nature of fandom for women. Women have featured heavily as characters in Springsteen's work and among his fan base, yet little has been written about how women fans see themselves and his work. Our perspective on this question is unique—our work brings a psychology lens to an exploration of fandom that can deepen our understanding of women's felt, lived experience of being a Springsteen fan. Based on an unprecedented analysis of the perspectives of hundreds of women fans, our work examines themes that emerged about relationship, meaning-making, healing from a range of issues or life events, personal growth, creating the self, identity formation, and the power of groups and community as central to the fan experience, and it illuminates the ways in which Springsteen fandom is for many women a developmental "journey" that helps to shape their lives.

As writers Cohen and Sawyers noted in *Long Walk Home*, their edited volume commemorating Springsteen's 70th birthday, Springsteen recognized that his music belongs to his listeners and that people turn to it not to find out about him, but "to find out about themselves" (Cohen & Sawyers, 2019, p. 3). For many women fans, as we will explore, Springsteen is on that journey of self-discovery with them, thus the book title which brings together a compelling image from "Thunder Road" and the journey taken together. Many women resonate and identify with Springsteen, feeling heard and understood through his music. They feel they have a relationship with him and are involved in an ongoing process of personal growth accompanied by his work and presence. They are active co-creators of that fan relationship rather than being a solely receptive audience.

Others have asked why Springsteen's music is so personal for many people and why it attracts so many fans (Cohen & Sawyers, 2019), but few have asked in what *particular* ways it resonates for *women* fans. In an age where gender is both an increasingly mutable category and a political flashpoint, the devotion of women fans to a male rock star can seem, on the surface, questionable or concerning. Further, especially early in his career, some commentators criticized Springsteen for his use of lyrics like "little girl" to describe women and argued that his work supports sexist or patriarchal views (Alterman, 1999; Delmonico, 2011; Palmer, 1997). Yet fans often hear and see things differently than academic critics. We wanted to explore how this "problem" of Springsteen's writing on women, past and present, seems to fans.

To answer our questions, we needed to hear directly from women fans themselves. In 2014 we conducted a large, international survey of Springsteen's women fans. We explored their answers in a book chapter, journal article, and conference presentations (Mangione & Luff, 2018, 2019). In 2021 we created a second survey to explore reactions to Springsteen's work in the intervening years, his legacy, and the evolving role of fandom in their lives. Our analysis of the rich and complex responses from both unique surveys forms the foundation for our conception of women's fandom of Springsteen as a personal, relational, and developmental journey.

Why Study Fans?

As we reviewed academic writings on fandom, questions arose for us, as they might for others: Why study fans? Why is this important? What does it mean to be a fan? And, specifically, what does it mean to be a rock fan? Is being a rock fan the same as being a sports fan or a fan of video games? Are those fandoms the same as being a "Bruce fan"? As the word derives from "fanatic" what does that say about societal views of "fan"? Are those of us who are Springsteen fans actually "fanatics"? Finally, when there are other, perhaps seemingly more consequential things to study, why is this topic important?

A basic reason to study fandom is that it is a significant part of our culture and our humanity and therefore worth understanding in depth. Any casual look at social media platforms, a newsfeed or newspaper, or television reveals the magnitude of fandom in our lives. Fandom of many kinds—sports teams, social media personalities, films, and music among them—seems to provide something important to individuals and groups, perhaps something that they cannot get elsewhere. Fandom is central to many families and individuals, to how people connect, participate in intense emotions/battles/dramas, and create and share in a culture. It is sociological in its societal manifestations, and anthropological in that fans have existed over the years and across cultures. Psychological aspects are abundant given fandom's role in people's lives and psyches: What is it that fans do, and why do they do what they do? Where does it fit in their lives and who they are? How does one become a fan, and what makes one stay a fan or become a "diehard" fan?

Wolff (2018) describes the fan/academic dilemma and controversy in a way that resonates with our thinking by explicitly addressing the tension between academics' views of fans and fans' views of themselves. Wolff argues for and acts on including fans in the discourse, letting them self-define what it means to be a fan, and incorporates his own research with fans on Twitter. Our work here similarly does not seek to define fans and what they are about, but to let them self-define who they are and what their fandom means to them. That is what this book explores—how women fans of Bruce Springsteen understand the nature of their fandom and what they do with it: how they live it out, what it means to them, how it shapes who they are.

Whole schools of psychology and psychotherapy devote themselves to themes we explore in this work: feelings, identity, meaning, purpose, healing, personal growth, loss and other existential issues, and relationships. We look more deeply at these experiences in exploring views of women fans. The foundational importance of relationships—from family relationships to friendships to sexual and romantic relationships—and attachment in people's lives and well-being, from childhood through old age, weaves throughout this work. We explore the significance of meaning in life, including how people find and create meaning, and what happens when life feels empty and meaningless. Another emphasis is the task of identity development, figuring out whom one is and where one finds a place in the world. In some chapters, trauma, social justice, marginalization, and diversity, particularly socioeconomic diversity, emerge. Loss, grief, and mortality on an individual or societal level figure too as universal experiences at the heart of our existence. We could not delve into Springsteen fandom without addressing the value of community, shared experiences, and engagement. Many of Cavicchi's themes around the meaning of Springsteen's work and the communal experience are echoed here.

Our framework for this book draws heavily on relational aspects of psychology and psychotherapy, broadly speaking: a common factors and relational approach to psychotherapy (Safran & Muran, 2000; Wampold, 2001, 2010); existential psychology (Bruner, 1993; Frankl, 2006; Markman et al., 2013; Overholser, 2005; Yalom, 1980); relational-cultural theory (Jordan, 2018; Jordan et al., 2004); and attachment and development throughout the life span (Bowlby, 1980; Wallin, 2007). Psychological themes in Springsteen's work framed Mangione and Keady's discussion (2007) on how relationships can transform people and their experiences, particularly around suffering, loss, and disconnection. These theoretical approaches were not developed with Springsteen in mind of course, but their power is such that they allow us to see things about him—and the fans who love him—that we otherwise could not see.

What Does It Mean to Be a Springsteen Fan?

Why are people able to remain fans of Springsteen over decades, so that some fans feel that they "grew up with" him and he has been a companion for life? Musical groups or performers come and go, and fandom vacillates, but Springsteen's longevity, presence, and nearness to fans are hallmarks of his career. He also attracts new, sometimes younger, fans. It must be more than just glamour or celebrity status, two huge markers of success in our culture, that brings in new fans and nurtures old fans. Perhaps he continues to connect with so many fans, and to mean something significant to them on a personal level, because of two changes in society's relationship to popular music that Springsteen embraced.

The first is social relevance, in that Springsteen, from the early days, engaged with diverse genres of music that question and examine our culture and our relationship to that culture. His version of rock and roll looked incisively at the world, at individuals and relationships and social and political context. He commented on society and issues of social justice as they were becoming more clearly front and center in American popular culture.

The second reason Springsteen was able to connect is personal relevance, the ways in which he explicitly addresses the internal world of personal meaning, identity, developmental questions, and crises, searching for the self, and foundational relationships. Springsteen's work has always focused on uncomfortable realities and often sad or tragic moments, as well as the fun, the easy, the joyful. In this way his work connects with the interests of psychology.

Of course, Springsteen was not the first or only musician to address social or personal relevance, to step into the psychological realm. Many versions of popular music were moving in that direction in the 1960s and 1970s, and some had always cohered around societal reflections and critique (folk music, protest music, Joe Hill, Joan Baez, Bob

Dylan) or around the complexities of personal relationships (the blues, all the love and loss songs, Frank Sinatra, Ray Charles), and certainly the Beatles and John Lennon, among others, inhabited both realms. Yet Springsteen elegantly intertwined the societal and personal with hard-driving rock and roll and all-night celebrations in concert, tossing the mix high into the air and deep into the psyche. Something emerged synergistically, paying homage to those coming before him yet bearing his own stamp. What made Springsteen special is that he fused those explorations with other dimensions of everyday life—including the pure joy of party music and dancing.

The emergence came as more traditional places for people to find meaning and take a moral stance on society's ills were foundering or outright disappearing, as families, churches, shared traditions, and belief systems faced challenges, something heard poignantly on "Independence Day." The song, which is explicitly about fathers and sons, also addressed how an uncritical handing down of expected personal identity for the individual, or at the societal level of shared values and meaning, no longer worked. The need and desire for people to create the architecture of their own values and identity have grown along with Springsteen's attention to these issues, adding to the resonance some fans feel in listening.

The Need for Women's Voices

As we have previously noted (Mangione & Luff, 2018), differences in fan experience based on gender cannot be presumed; however, many commentators have argued that female music fan experiences are different than male experiences, not least that women's music fandom is more often derided or sexualized (Anderson, 2012; Cline, 1992; Duffett, 2013; Hill, 2016; Larsen, 2017; Rhodes, 2005; Wise, 1984/1990). Digesting works in fan studies contributed to our thinking and helped formulate our questions. In reading prior work on women fans, many of the criticisms of portrayals of female fandom resonated with us in relation to Springsteen fans. These included a lack of investigation of women's experiences as distinct from those of men, stereotypes of Springsteen's masculine appeal as related to women, and an idea that some kind of problem or pathology exists with women fans of male rock stars. Depth and a specific point of view seemed missing in considering fans and fandom in relation to Springsteen and women. As fans and as scholars, we felt a gap in the voices that were heard and the understanding that resulted. Overall, the gendered experience of Springsteen fandom remained underexplored or only partially understood.

We set out to uncover what draws women to Springsteen, how some women have been fans for decades, how the relationship with Springsteen and his work is perceived, what role his work plays in their lives, what it is like being a newer or younger fan, and how women feel about Springsteen's apparent relationship with and attitude toward women in his work. These are the essential topics in our surveys and in this book. In respecting these issues as important to women, and prioritizing women's voices and perspectives, we locate our work within a feminist and qualitative research framework.

We wanted to understand fan attraction in all its levels and manifestations, beyond stereotypical assumptions. Fandom for women has traditionally been thought to relate heavily to sexual and romantic fantasies toward the rock star, though some feminist writers have argued for a variety of motivations in women's fandom (Cline, 1992; Gray et al., 2007; Hill, 2016; Larsen, 2017). We wondered about the larger meaning of attraction in both initial and ongoing connection to Springsteen. This work aims to draw out the multiple dimensions of women's connection to Springsteen to offer a broader perspective on becoming and staying a fan. Cohen and Sawyers (2019) comment that their book "does not claim to represent every Springsteen fan" (p. 5), and of course neither does this one, but the goal was to enlarge the pool of commentators. We want women fans to have their say here, and have it heard, shared, enjoyed, and mused upon, just as Cavicchi (1998) and Coles (2003) had done years before. We still resonate with Coles's title that includes *the people listening,* wanting to listen to women who have listened so well to Springsteen.

Our work adds to a growing body of work on and interest in diverse experiences among Springsteen fans. In a section specifically on gender and sexual identity, Wolff's (2018) collection includes commentary on feminist theory (Moss, 2018), heterosexuality (Hubbs, 2018), and queer identity (Casio, 2018), all of which launch questions about women in his work. Another article examines the multifaceted role of the character Mary in Springsteen's work, often a theme in essays on Springsteen, drawing on religious and cultural imagery and meaning (O'Donnell, 2018). Within this mostly academic volume, notably in the section on gender and sexual identity, is our chapter (Mangione & Luff, 2018) and Casio's (2018) giving voice to women fans.

In *Long Walk Home* (Cohen & Sawyers, 2019), commentary on women in Springsteen songs, fans, and personal experience by Barreca (2019), Bishop (2019), and Adler (2019) is included. Bishop's writings of Springsteen and the magic in rock and roll would likely resonate with many women in our study. As the editors of that volume have noted, so much has been written about and by Springsteen, but "what remains to be examined is the impact he and his art have had—and will continue to have—on audiences in the United States and across the globe" (Cohen & Sawyers, 2019, p. 6). We agree that that is where the conversation needs to head.

How to Listen—What We Did

So how were we going to find out more about women fans? We felt like anthropologists engaging in an ethnographic study of a distinct but complex culture, and we, who had been part of that culture, were now stepping back and observing through research. Given our background disciplines, we favored qualitative research methodology to explore personal experiences in depth, yet the typical small number of participants in qualitative research would not reflect an extensive fan base. We decided on a survey with mostly open-ended, reflective questions, and hoped that participants would write from their hearts and speak their minds. We constructed questions from reading prior work on Springsteen fans and from a few interviews with a sample of women fans, contacted through our networks and representing a cross-section of fans in some respects (age, longevity, international and U.S. fans, race and ethnicity). Analysis of these interviews helped in constructing survey questions.

Creating a survey to hear women's voices was a joyful task as we imagined women telling their stories. After basic demographic questions, such as age, location, and length of fandom, the survey delved into the music and the man. We asked women for their perspectives, feelings, thoughts, and values, and they answered—in large numbers. Hoping for 100 respondents, we contacted the well-respected fan site Backstreets.com to see if we could publicize our survey on their site. Within a week or so we had a thousand respondents and were simultaneously overjoyed and overwhelmed! It was moving to us that so many women wanted to respond and took our questions seriously, yet the scientist portions of our psyches wondered how to do justice to such rich information. Part of that information is included in a chapter for the book, *Bruce Springsteen and Popular Music: Essays on Rhetoric, Social Consciousness, and Contemporary Culture,* edited by William I. Wolff (2018), and in an article (Mangione & Luff, 2019) in a special issue of *Interdisciplinary Literary Studies* marking the anniversary of *Darkness on the Edge of Town,* edited by Eileen Chapman and Kenneth Womack. Given the large number of enlightening responses from so many women, the idea for this book, and a follow-up survey, was born. We invite readers to share in the experiences of women fans who participated in the studies, and to reflect on the role of music and Springsteen in their own journeys through life.

GATHERING THE DATA

We hoped the first survey would answer these questions: What is it that women fans get from Springsteen's music? Why is his music important to them, and in what ways? How do they feel as women about him? How do they feel about his perspectives on women? Do they have a relationship with Springsteen? Of the 1,158 respondents, 908 answered demographic questions. Of these 908 women, 602 were from the United States, representing 44 states and the District of Columbia (including 105 from New Jersey), and 306 were from 24 other countries. These other countries were: Argentina,

Australia, Austria, Belgium, Brazil, Canada, Denmark, Finland, France, Germany, Greece, Hong Kong, Ireland, Italy, Netherlands, New Zealand, Norway, Portugal, South Africa, Spain, Sweden, Switzerland, United Arab Emirates, and United Kingdom. Of all respondents, 66% were aged 45–64, but the overall age range of fans was 15–88 years. Fifty-one percent had been a Springsteen fan for 30–39 years, 9.5% for 9 years or less. Ninety-six percent had seen Springsteen perform live at least once.

We fielded the second survey in 2021 to gather responses to specific recent Springsteen activities and works and garner ideas regarding his legacy. Of the 742 individuals who took part in the second survey, 434 women completed demographic questions. Of these 434, 43.32% were aged 55–64, but ages ranged from 18 to older than 75. Of the 434 women that completed the survey, 299 respondents were from the United States, including the District of Columbia (with 31 from New Jersey), and 134 from 22 other countries (all included in the countries listed earlier from the first survey). In terms of longevity, 47.70% of respondents stated that they have been a Springsteen fan for more than 40 years, but the range was from 1 to 39 years.

There are inevitable limitations to our surveys in that respondents were a self-selected sample who had internet access and were comfortable answering an online survey. In the first survey, we did not ask about dimensions of diversity, such as race/ethnicity, religion, or sexual orientation. A sample is always a sample, not representative of all fans everywhere, but still we gathered a wide range of opinions.

FIGURING OUT THE DATA

To analyze data for this book, both authors read all the survey responses and generated initial themes and then refined these in discussion together. The resulting main themes are represented by our chapters. In choosing representative responses to include, we worked continuously in the collaborative practice of qualitative analysis to best embody participants' thoughts and feelings in order to communicate to readers. There were always more eloquent responses than could be included. We did not substantially edit women's responses other than for confidentiality when there was potentially identifying personal information, or where a small change in punctuation or grammar made a response clearer. We added quotation marks around the songs and italicized the albums they mentioned.

Fans' responses were not monolithic. Women held different views about Springsteen and his work. Springsteen's fan base gathers a multitude of people under one tent, allowing for individuality of experience and beliefs. Understanding that broad appeal adds to understanding of fandom by exploring the tensions between received ideas about fan identity and fans' self-perception. Divergent views included, for example, fans who were extremely "in love" with Springsteen, those who criticize some aspects of his music/persona yet remain fans, and those who stated specific reasons for their fandom. What offers unity is that most women fans seem to be on a developmental journey through their fandom. For some their fandom is life-saving and essential, for others it is joyful and fun, but they all seem to be finding or creating meaning through their experiences as a Springsteen fan.

Walking the Path with Springsteen: Where Are We Going?

So how did we meld all these facets: the magnitude and longevity of Springsteen's career, the deeply felt commentary by new and long-term women fans, as well as our academic and personal perspectives? How do we make sense of the feelings, thoughts, reflections, beliefs, activities, and opinions of so many "experts" on themselves and on Springsteen? How do we let women fans speak as unique purveyors of individual experience, while acknowledging substantial points of similarity along with definite differences?

The journey of our book will lead readers on a narrative arc through Springsteen fandom and universal human processes and situations. In chapter 2, "'The Ties That Bind': Becoming and Staying a Fan," we explore the critically important beginnings of fandom and how such fandom continues, delving into survey answers that address questions such as the following: How did the connection with Springsteen start? What was going on for the women when it started? Who else was involved, such as family or friends? Was it sudden or gradual? We address a question that reappears throughout this work: Do you have a relationship with Springsteen, and if so, how would you describe it? The idea of a "relationship" with someone one has never met, or has met fleetingly, feels germane to our time of fluidity in roles, the cult of celebrity, the pandemic and isolation, social media, and ever-breaking news, in which the world feels so close and yet so far.

The complicated question of Springsteen's view of women, what fans think it is and isn't, and what it means and does not mean, is addressed in chapter 3, "'Hey Little Girl': Women on Springsteen and Women," where we show how women fans understand debates about the issue of Springsteen's writing on women in relation to themselves, and they offer some unexpected and thought-provoking perspectives. Differences and juxtapositions among fans illustrate ways in which fans are divergent in their perspectives on Springsteen's writing on women.

In chapters 4, 5, and 6, we examine why and how Springsteen speaks to women fans, the core of this work. We look at the meaning his work holds to understand what women do, internally, with their experiences. The question of community looms large around Springsteen and fans, a sense of "we are in this together." In chapter 4, "Springsteen as Friend or Family Member," we explore critical notions of Springsteen's authenticity, a sense that he struggles as we struggle, of Springsteen as a regular guy who feels familiar rather than occupying a pedestal. We discuss what live performances, including connection to the E Street Band, have meant to fans, both individually and in community.

In chapter 5, "Teacher of Life, Guide of the Spirit," we see how Springsteen takes on a role as teacher, mentor, or guide for some women, his music and performances helping them with questions and concerns in life. As Cohen and Sawyers (2019) noted, Springsteen's work resonates in part because his writing helps people "address the issues they are facing" (p. 3). We all face choice points, times of uncertainty, and moments when another voice, maybe one that has traversed that terrain already, can illuminate the way forward. Some women find this voice within Springsteen's work. Spiritual questions resonate deeply with some fans, and seeing Springsteen as a spiritual guide has been an unexpected gift.

Chapter 6, "Walking the Path Together through Darkness," confronts the difficult times that some fans have experienced, and the role that Springsteen has played in their times of darkness. Many have turned to his music/performance for a deeper or ongoing level of guidance, support, insight, and comfort. His music can be both a refuge and therapy in the darkest parts of women fans' journeys, creating a profound sense that they are not alone through hard times.

In the final three chapters, we consider expansion, both in terms of geography and of Springsteen's role in the world, what his legacy might be, and our reflections on immersion in Springsteen's work and the powerful commentaries from these surveys. Springsteen as an international phenomenon, even while remaining an iconic New Jersey musician and expanding into new roles and genres, are discussed in chapter 7, "From New Jersey to the World."

At a certain point in life, thinking about legacy, what one is leaving behind, how one will be remembered, strikes a chord for many people. In his memoir, Springsteen hopes that he will be "an ancestor" for his family (Springsteen, 2016), but it is likely that his legacy will inspire future artists (Cullen, 2019) and be carried by his fans, as illustrated in chapter 8, "Twenty-First-Century Legacy," which explores what can be learned from younger fans from the first survey and fans from the second survey, regarding what might carry into the future, as both Springsteen and his bedrock baby boomer fan base age.

Finally, if "Thunder Road" is an invitation to the journey, and Mary has indeed climbed in, where are we now on that journey after this study? Chapter 9, "Further on up the Road," our last chapter, discusses what this exploration adds to our understanding of women fans in general, Springsteen's fans in particular, and Springsteen's work and appeal. We offer our personal perspectives on the Springsteen journey through our views on "Thunder Road" and this experience for us as fans, researchers, and writers.

As we invite you now to climb in for the ride with women fans, one woman captures some of the excitement and intensity of the journey ahead*:

> It has been a long, wonderful journey and I hope it continues.... I take a lot of heat about being as big of a fan as I am, but I am a fan all the same and proud of it. I crossed the border once for a show and the border guard asked me about my license plate and I told him it was my favorite Springsteen song and he said I was the 5th personal plate through to the show on his watch. He said you guys are nuts and have a good time at the show. Well said and no offence was taken by me because it is true. We are a unique group. Thank you for this opportunity.

*For authenticity, all responses retain most of the original spelling, punctuation, and styling supplied by the respondent.

CHAPTER 2

"The Ties That Bind"

Becoming and Staying a Fan

We have a contract—an emotional contract.
He's there for me. I'm there for him.

BEGINNINGS ARE FUNDAMENTAL and foundational. The moment something starts to germinate lays the groundwork for all that is to unfold. Springsteen has been relating that for decades through the recounting of creation stories of the band in his live shows. In one version, he carefully set the stage, then called on earlier spirits and muses, such as the gypsy who knew what he had to do and how to do it. In another version, he invokes the bear in the swamps of Jersey terrifying Clarence and Bruce as they made their way through darkness. Springsteen has also stressed the idea of continuity, staying together over time, as manifested in a lifelong conversation with fans through his music, performance, and public statements. As Springsteen puts it, "I guess you would call it a conversation with your fans that's always renewing itself. I've been dedicated to that my whole life" (Santelli, 2013, p. 428). His views suggest that fans join him on an open-ended journey which, however it starts, propels them into a continuing connection. Here we explore how women fans first entered this "conversation" with Springsteen through descriptions of those starting points, as a basis to consider the ongoing meaning of the journey.

Women fans clearly delineated a time, and sometimes a place, in which they first heard or heard of Springsteen's music and how it affected them. While many of them had a "moment" which won them over to Springsteen fandom, that moment took several different forms. Daniel Cavicchi (1998) spoke of that moment using the religious idea of conversion. He chose the word "conversion" purposefully and drew parallels between the experience of becoming a Springsteen fan and the experience of religious conversion: "Stories of becoming a fan are personal narratives that center on a 'conversion' or significant change in one's attitude and behavior toward the music and image of Springsteen. I use the word 'conversion' deliberately; fans often talk about introducing someone to Springsteen's music as 'converting' them" (p. 42). Cavicchi describes some fans' conversion as similar to psychologist William James's classic description of the self-surrender experience for some Christians, "in which a person, after a great deal of frustration and unhappiness, gives up the will to change and then suddenly is converted" (p. 43). While this idea of conversion may not describe every woman's response about intense experiences that "hooked" them, it captures something essential.

Writers from other disciplines have noted the profound significance of beginnings and first connections. Creation myths throughout cultures and history, described by Joseph Campbell (1988), remind us that how things begin sets the stage for what is to come. These are stories, told by all cultures, that dig at the heart of how the earth was formed, humans originated, and gods or goddesses had a hand in such endeavors, making possible a whole civilization. Campbell (1949/ 1973) also wrote about the journey of the hero who is called to leave everyday life and enter a more arduous path. This journey frequently begins with a call, often unexpected and sometimes unheeded, and the subsequent journey includes helpers along the path of learning and challenges.

Psychology, from various theoretical perspectives, also tells us that what happens early in relationships, the beginning stages, are critical, especially for the deepest relationships in our lives, and they provide the foundation for what unfolds over time. Both attachment theory and psychoanalytic theory, with their accompanying clinical work and research, emphasize the critical nature of the early years for development throughout later life. A child's caretakers become models for later life, just as a child's attempts to understand the world set the stage for lifelong learning. Early attachments and interactions really do matter. In this case, interactions and attachment are with a body of work and a particular artist/performer, but they resonate in powerful ways with psychological perspectives. And, at least in some cases, these experiences happened early or at a critical juncture in women's lives. While most fans in this study did not encounter Springsteen as children (though some did), we suggest that the beginning of the fan relationship is especially significant and lays the foundation for what follows.

Another experience that seems to matter in adult development is the "coming of age" period of a person or an "age cohort" as described by Robert Knight (2004, Knight & Pachana, 2015) in his framework for understanding older people called contextual adult lifespan theory and a related psychotherapy approach. He discusses the significance and consequence of what was happening in the culture as people grew up and entered adulthood, a time period that can influence a person's whole life. This is especially important to understand in working with and relating to older adults. "Knowing the historical period in which the client was an adolescent and young adult can be helpful in understanding the social milieu in which that client's first adult identity was formed" (2004, p. 144). Springsteen's music was part of the culture and many fans' lives as they negotiated adulthood. Springsteen also comments on major cultural forces and events during that coming-of-age time, which may have influenced the bond with him and his work for years to come.

In this chapter we look at women fans' first experiences with Springsteen and consider how this connection continued over time across varied life trajectories. We delve into answers to the opening items on our survey about becoming a fan to address questions such as, How did the connection with Springsteen start? How was the connection made? What was going on for the women at the time? The specific questions we asked were these: Can you tell us when you first heard/discovered Bruce Springsteen? How did you first get involved with Springsteen's music?

How Did It All Begin?

Discovering Springsteen's music did not happen in an interpersonal vacuum for most women; rather, it was intertwined with family, friends, and romantic partners. Relationships with significant others were a catalyst for their involvement with his work. This was notable given how important the idea of "relationship" was to become for the women in their ongoing interest. Springsteen has spoken about being in a relationship with his audience, describing the "relationship I've built up with my audience" as "outside of my family [it] is the most important relationship in my life" (Strauss, 1995, p. 172).

For women fans, their introduction to Springsteen and his music often happened across generations, within families, something perhaps uncommon in rock music fandom, certainly in the early decades of his career. Learning about Springsteen sometimes coincided with a significant event or time in their lives, such as a crisis or searching for something of meaning. What happened next, during or after that first encounter, varied from a quick and decisive attachment (similar to conversion or the "call" to the hero's journey) to a more slowly dawning bond. The following pages explore different ways in which that connection took hold.

Who Made the Introductions?

We saw it all in fans' responses: mothers, fathers, brothers, sisters, friends, boyfriends, girlfriends, and even an aunt or cousin. Being introduced to Springsteen's music was often through a close family member or friend, someone either deliberately "teaching" the woman about Springsteen—sort of inaugurating her into the fan society—or from being around the music that her brother, parents, or college friends played. Perhaps, in the years before *Born in the U.S.A.*, the fact that Springsteen's work was not typically played relentlessly on commercial radio gave these introductions the feel of a personal invitation. It didn't just happen to everyone on the block.

STARTED LISTENING AS A CHILD

In recent Springsteen concerts, performances of "Waitin' on a Sunny Day" feature a young child chosen to sing along with Springsteen on stage. A parent's letter about a child's late arrival at school due to a Springsteen concert made the local newspaper ("Late to School," 2016). Introducing a child to Springsteen has a long history. "My father brought home *BORN IN THE U.S.A.* on vinyl. I was 4 years old. It was 1984. I've been addicted ever since." "My parents introduced me to his music from an early age. I can recall listening to him at the age of 3."

Moms were involved. This British fan adds fun times with her mother and dancing: "I was seven when *Born in the U.S.A.* came out, and my mum loved the album. She would play it all the time and I would dance around and sing along. When I was fifteen, I listened to the album again, and then I found some old Springsteen albums on a school trip (*Wild, Nebraska, Greetings*)." Another fan regrets part of her response to her mother's introduction. "My mom worked for a company and brought home a cardboard cutout of Bruce on the cover of *Darkness on the Edge of Town*. I said "Who's this?" She then introduced me to the album. I've been hooked ever since although I'm really pissed I trashed the cutout!"

Dads get involved in early introductions too: "Since I can recall, Springsteen music has been the soundtrack to my life. When I was very little, my father used to play it all the time, this was my very first contact with Bruce. Throughout my teenage years and early adulthood, his presence increased and the meaning of his music also changed. But, basically, my father was the decisive factor." Another fan speaks to making that connection one's own: "My dad is a big fan of him, ever since I was a little girl I have heard him play Springsteen's music. I grew up with his music in my life, and when I was 15, I started listening to Springsteen's records of my own interest. Now 22 years old and I have already been to nine concerts. There is so much joy and love that fills my heart from the memories I've experienced when I've been to Springsteen's concerts." Memories from childhood can often remain for a lifetime. The music becomes part of their foundational experience and can grow over time as relationships surrounding the music evolve. Early experiences have a way of intertwining with identities and fundamental ways of understanding the world. Early attachments tend to stay with us and can provide a blueprint for later relationships throughout life.

Brothers introduced many women to Springsteen in a way that fits both the annoyance of and looking up to brothers. "My brother is 4 years older than I am. He was 15 and I was 11. He was blasting *Born to Run* in his bedroom for days and days. I got so annoyed, I went in and said, "Give it to me." I took it in my room to listen for myself. And I was blown away. I took down all of my Frampton and Andy Gibb posters. It was the beginning of intense, lifelong fandom." "Grew up with my older brother and cousins. They all listened to The Boss. I looked up to them when I was very young and it was only natural that I adopted their music. When I became a youth I started to dig deeper in to his records and became a bigger fan than they ever were." Sometimes, though, it was a sister who escorted the young girl into awareness. "My sister turned me on to *Born to Run* and I found my spirit in his characters and stories and tremendous power in his music."

Being a Bruce fan can flower into a family enterprise, with family bonds and Springsteen bonds intertwining such that it may be hard to tell where one begins and the other ends. This robust thread of familial involvement is revisited in later chapters.

FRIENDS

Given the importance of peers in shaping interests and tastes, especially in adolescence and young adulthood, it was not surprising that friends were important in these introductions. The sharing of music in adolescence can intensely cement attachments, carving out individual and collective identities. Many women expressed the give-and-take and value of friendships. "I used to dance to "Hungry Heart" with my two closest friends in college, at the local dive bar—that song still bonds the three of us after all these years." "I was a junior in high school and was at a friend's house hanging out during Christmas break. We would always listen to music there, usually Led Zep or Neil Young. One night he put on *Born to Run*. As we were listening to it, the song "Tenth Ave Freeze Out" really grabbed me. I had heard some of Bruce's stuff before, but I'm not sure if I had ever heard that song. I went home and grabbed my sister's BTR album and then grabbed *Darkness* from my brother. That was the start of everything." Vivid images of kids hanging out together. . . . This is what adolescents do and how they teach each other about the world, their lives, the hurts and joys, and relationships.

SIGNIFICANT OTHERS

Love, closeness, and connection between romantic partners can encourage the sharing of music that captures both of them. The dawn of romantic relationships is often a time of solidifying interests and tastes, including music, that will become part of their identity as a couple. It may also teach each person about the inner worlds of their partners. A woman who found Springsteen in the 1980s preferred a different genre of music until she heard her boyfriend talk of his love for Springsteen. Understanding Springsteen was, at first, a way for her to understand her boyfriend. "Actually because of someone I was in a relationship with. I had heard and sort of liked a few songs, but Bruce wasn't really on my radar. I tended to listen to more folk, singer-songwriter type music rather than a lot of rock. I had been dating someone who was a big music fan, and we had a lot of shared tastes. He had shared a lot of music with me, but not Bruce. I remember him being really excited about Bruce having a new album coming out, which was going to be *Born in the U.S.A.* and talked about how much he loved Bruce. I guess I bought the album trying to figure him out. I liked it and then basically worked back through the catalog and became a big fan. The fact he liked Bruce so much did tell me some things about the man I was dating. The relationship did not work out, but my relationship with the music has lasted." Falling in love with Springsteen could be wrapped around falling in love romantically—the rush and excitement enhancing each other. Some fans concisely showed the connections. "When I fell in love with my new man I fell in love with Bruce because he loved him." "I fell in love with him and a girl who was already a Springsteen fan. (I'm a lesbian)."

Attachments with key people, and a musician, can be validating as young people consider what speaks to them and what does not. Fan experiences might mirror Springsteen's early years of figuring out music, bands, and friends on the Jersey Shore, often spoken about in concerts. Adolescents are searching for something, and part of it, maybe, can be found in a record. Rousing music and a passionate performer might express what others in their lives cannot.

And I Was Hooked!

For many fans, the phrase "and I was hooked" summed up the compelling, immediate connection forged in one intense experience with Springsteen's music, usually coming at the beginning of discovering Springsteen, but sometimes years of casual listening passed until that moment hit. The image of being hooked is powerful—a fish gets hooked and there is no going back, one speaks of getting hooked on drugs, and songs have a hook that catches the listener, drawing them in. Probably many songs and performers have this power. Being hooked points to the capacity of Springsteen's music to pull people in and address some vital part of them. The *Born to Run, Darkness on the Edge of Town,* and *Born in the U.S.A.* albums were particular catalysts. One can ask why something feels compelling to someone—is it a time in their life, does it resonate with something specific, or is it just a particular sound? Given "the call" to enter the hero's journey, how and why does a creative art "call" a person? What does that mean for someone?

"Meaning-making" is a term from psychology (Kegan, 1982) used especially by existential and social constructivist psychologists, as well as some schools of educators (Ignelzi, 2000), that is interwoven in our discussions of women fans and Springsteen. It speaks to the critical role of how people understand and construe their experiences and their world. The importance of meaning-making in psychology and human development stems partly from Viktor Frankl's early work arising out of his Nazi concentration camp imprisonment, *Man's Search for Meaning* (2006)—a mainstay of existential and humanistic psychology. In it, the fundamental importance of how one construes events, experiences, and emotions (even such extreme ones as he and others experienced in the concentration camps) is emphasized over the actual events themselves. Who we become as people stems from what we do with situations and events of our lives, how we make sense of them and find meaning. Existential psychologist Irving Yalom (Overholser, 2005; Yalom, 1980) takes themes of existential philosophy and situates them within psychotherapy, and Jerome Bruner (1993), a cognitive psychologist, saw meaning and narrative as central to our humanity. Markman et al. (2013) updated the study of meaning in psychology through multiple perspectives on meaning, its loss, and reconstruction. McAdams's (2013) work, emphasized here in chapter 5, showed how meaning is made through narrative storytelling. "As autobiographical authors, life meaning becomes instantiated in the stories of our lives—internalized and evolving narratives of the self that explain who we were in the past, who we are today, and who we hope to be in the future" (p. 173). Lastly, Robert Neimeyer et al.'s (2014) eloquent work on grief and loss rests on the importance of meaning and meaning reconstruction. The centrality of the creation of meaning in life frames this study and women's responses to Springsteen. "Being hooked" suggested something formidable that spoke in untold and perhaps unconscious ways to women as they sought meaning, continuing to anchor their ongoing fandom. Meaning-making in conjunction with early and ongoing attachment creates longevity and commitment.

Fans described the immediacy and power of connection: "It was 1978, I was outside my home and my brother had 'Prove It All Night' screaming from his Camaro . . . and I instantly asked, 'Who is THAT'? And my brother replied 'Bruce Springsteen.' And from that second on was an INSTANT fan. I remember my heart sinking to my stomach when I heard his voice." Sometimes another artist brought a woman to Springsteen. "Heard Patti Smith singing 'Because the

Night' and became totally obsessed with her and her music. I loved the song, it would almost make me weep, the riff, the lyrics. . . . I was a teenager going through all the teenage confusion and loving the idea of being in love. I looked at the credits and saw it had been written by her and some Springsteen guy. I checked him out. Patti was 'chucked'—actually more 'sidelined' because I still adore her and her music, her delicious voice—Bruce had the guitar, the look, the lyrics, the pose. He had the band, the songs. I was hooked."

For some the hook came from a single song. "Jungleland" spoke to a few on an almost visceral level, the power and intensity coming through, whether in concert, alone in a room, or driving a car.

> At 13, I borrowed *Born to Run* from my sister who had gotten it along with *Born in the U.S.A.* as birthday gifts. BIUSA was in heavy rotation in the 80s and I wasn't too into it at first. BUT, BTR was more "new" to me. The first time I heard "Jungleland" and actually listened to the lyrics took me to another place. I was reading the *Outsiders* by Hinton at the time, and could picture the fight between the Socs and the Greasers when Bruce sang "The midnight gang's assembled and picked a rendezvous for the night." So much action in a 14-minute song. . . . It blew me away and I was hooked.

Sometimes one finds oneself in a song. "I first heard the words 'barefoot girl sittin' on the hood of a Dodge drinkin' warm beer in the soft summer rain' and every hair on my arm stood up. That is pure street poetry, I thought." And maybe the listener identifies with that barefoot girl.

"Thunder Road" had a similar power to captivate. "I was 14 and a boy mentioned in school that he liked Bruce Springsteen. I had never heard of him but went home and looked thru my older sister's records and found *Born to Run*. Put the LP on the turntable and heard piano and harmonica to 'Thunder Road' and I was hooked. 37 years later I am still a Bruce Springsteen fan!" She noted how intertwined music and lyrics are, how instruments influence and excite with a life of their own.

Major moments in life, family relationships, and a song can coincide. "From birth. I'm 22 years old and there is a home video from the day I was born in which my father sang an amended rendition of 'Pony Boy,' where he changed the lyric to 'pony girl.' I've been hooked ever since." The hook also came with the darker albums. "Borrowed *Born in the U.S.A.* album from my friend's older sister. I was 14 and it was 1984. The album was on tape and I played it over and over loving the clarity and power of all the tracks. I remember learning all the words to the songs. I then searched for other Springsteen albums and found *Darkness on the Edge of Town* in my local record shop on sale for £3.65. Next was *Nebraska* and I was hooked." Many fans joined with "Born in the U.S.A." in the 1980s, the worldwide hit that propelled him to international superstardom. "I found a cassette tape of *Born in the U.S.A.* in the basement and tried it out. I fell in love instantly." And sometimes life is forever changed from an album: "I was 15 when the *Born in the U.S.A.* album came out and my life as I knew it was over."

Maybe there was something, a sense of openness, a yearning, a hunger, a question, and upon hearing Springsteen, part of that question was answered or some of the hunger was sated. We are reminded of "conversion" experiences as we hear of intense responses to the music and how life took on a different meaning, glow, or feeling from that moment forward. Many people search their whole lives for some moment, some experience, such as this.

"You Have to See Him Live"

"You have to see him in concert! Then you will understand" was an oft-heard refrain. Given how monumental Springsteen's live shows are to his fans and his reputation, many women specifically stated that live shows were the experiences that cemented their identity as fans. Does Springsteen become more alive, more real, once seen interacting with an audience? Does he then exist in some interstitial realm between "just like us" and rock-and-roll star? In an interview, Springsteen stressed the literal meaning of being in "concert" to explain the connection he seeks with the audience: "The word 'concert'—people working together—that's the idea" (Percy, 1998, p. 231). Perhaps this commitment to working together is in part what makes Springsteen concerts so legendary. A sense of community feels real and tangible as fans gather before the show, sharing stories, and in the thick of the music, sharing their passion.

Certainly, the magic and intensity captured some fans, whether really liking him or indifferent beforehand. "I had been listening to his music since I was a baby but when I went to a show all changed! A very strong connection between me and Bruce started." "I first saw him live in Boston in 1975, after a suggestion from one of my high school teachers, who was from NJ. The live performance was amazing, and he had such a connection with the audience, that he felt like a friend." For this woman, the analogy was more celestial. "As with many other people, I really didn't know Bruce when I went to my first concert—Nov. 30, 1980. However, four hours later . . . I was completely changed. My roommate at the time thought I had seen Jesus Christ that night. . . . I came home so exuberated by the concert."

Sometimes years of casual interest predate that concert. One can wonder why this fan made it to a concert, finally, as it proved to be a turning point. "I first heard his music when I was a kid and *Born in the U.S.A.* came out. For the most part, I was only a fan of his hits that I would hear on Top 40 radio. I finally saw him in concert during the Wrecking Ball tour and it was by far the BEST concert of my life. Turned me into a hard core fan for life!" For an international fan (and her mother), seeing Springsteen started almost routinely. "I went to a concert of his in Germany. My mum and I bought tickets just because of our general interest in rock music. We had never seen Springsteen before, we only knew a couple of songs from the radio. I think we're hooked ever since." The route to Springsteen was sometimes circuitous, and a live show was the necessary change agent. "I heard 'Hungry Heart' on the radio as a little girl and liked it. Years later I liked songs that came out on the *Born in the U.S.A.* album as well as 'Philadelphia' and 'Secret Garden.' I liked the 'Dancing in the Dark' video, but I did not really connect with him and become a fan until I saw him live for the first time in 2003 on The Rising tour. It changed my life. It was only then that I was exposed to the music he made before *Born in the U.S.A.*, which is some of my favorite music."

This woman was a serious fan for many years but seeing him live intensified the "hook." "A boyfriend had the *Darkness* album in the late seventies, and I liked it okay and bought a copy for myself. Another boyfriend had the BtR album and 'Thunder Road' was his go-to music for any time he needed a lift. And I really liked that track, but when I first heard 'Candy's Room' from a decent stereo down the dorm hall in 1980—I was smitten. I bought all his albums as they were released from that point onwards. I did not see him perform live until 2000, however—due to geography and other life circumstances, after which time my appreciation and obsession deepened." For other women, an introduction from a significant other combined with a concert. "My partner has been a diehard Bruce fan from the '70s and as such I had to 'endure' his passion once we started living together. However, I bought my partner 'surprise' tickets to go and see him as he had only seen him once live and thought he would appreciate him live and since then our journey with Bruce began!" "In the latter part of '75 my husband brought home the album *Born to Run* and said 'listen to this.' I put the children to bed, put the headphones on and listened . . . again and again. He then managed to get tickets to the second show at London's Hammersmith Odeon. We went and it was and remains simply the best show I've ever been to." This fan had a long journey, including some difficult times, until finally the concert cemented her fandom. "A friend lent me *Born to Run* when I was in graduate school, and I listened to it obsessively while working on some academic papers, but I didn't really connect the album to its author. I just liked the album. . . . When I finally got to see Bruce live, it changed my life, and now here I am, reading 'Backstreets' at work and filling out academic surveys about my fandom."

Springsteen's live performance, typically with the E Street Band, has been heralded by critics and writers. It connects fans to something larger and more alive. It can change everything. A few women noted that before seeing Springsteen live they had not understood his appeal. "My husband was given tickets to the 2012 Washington DC concert. Before seeing Bruce live, I did not see his music as anything extraordinary." "Through my partner, who I thought was exaggerating the impact of the music, the emotion of the lyrics and the quality of the sound. I went to see the Rising Tour in Paris and was completely blown away." His performance was not disembodied or intellectualized; rather it seemed to fill them with a new experience of life, themselves, or the music, something that can stay with a person, residing somewhere inside and quietly nurturing her, and for many fans, compelling her further into fandom.

When Did Fans Join the Road Trip?

What does it mean to have "grown up" with Springsteen from his early days with his scruffy beard and beguiling invitations, or to have found Springsteen later, perhaps as the voice of comfort after September 11th or as an artist from rock history? While most respondents had been fans for years, we also heard from those (about 10%) who "discovered" Springsteen more recently. Whether they were younger women coming of age, or older women who hopped in the car later, newer fans seemed to share first experiences similar to those of longer-term fans.

Newer fans gave similar responses about learning about Springsteen from family and friends, especially dads, while growing up. This young fan tells that story with specific songs. "My father first introduced me to the music at a very young age listening to the lighthearted tunes of 'Santa Claus Is Comin' to Town' and 'Waitin' on a Sunny Day,' and 'Out in the Street.' When he drove me to school he would play these for me. Slowly as I became older I put more and more Springsteen music on my iPod and I have been a fan ever since." Another fan in the 25–34-year-old group, introduced to Springsteen by relatives, was "smitten" at a concert. "I moved in with my aunt and uncle after college and they were super fans. They brought me to my first concert. We had GA tickets and were lucky enough to get right up front. During the concert, Bruce bent down and let us strum his guitar during 'Thunder Road,' and then during 'Girls in Their Summer Clothes,' he changed the lyrics to 'hello beautiful girls!' I became smitten ever since. I had heard his music before, but never REALLY listened to it until then. Since then, 'The Rising' and 'Tunnel of Love' have really helped me through many life events, including my recent divorce." Sometimes connection comes from a serendipitous event, as with the handful of women who heard Springsteen on *We Are the World* and connected.

A few international fans joined more recently, perhaps as his international audience and touring have grown. "My aunt invited me to see Springsteen's show, in 2012 in Paris, Bercy. At this time, I only knew a few songs, like 'Hungry Heart' or 'Born in the U.S.A.' I was very impressed by his performance, the way he sings onstage and so on. . . . It was my first rock show, so I really appreciated it. I went another time, in 2013 in Paris Stade de France, and, there too, I felt in love." An older recent fan from South Africa writes of songs that first touched her. "I heard the little song 'Tomorrow Never Knows' from *Working on a Dream* on our local Afrikaans radio station here in South Africa. It touched something in me, so I went to YouTube and from there to the lyrics. After I heard 'Thunder Road' and 'Dancing in the Dark,' too, and became aware of the depth of the lyrics, I was hooked."

We heard about times when everything came together to create a moment that felt like it was meant to be, like that lost piece of a puzzle that completes the whole picture, something that may not happen often in most people's lives, so the singularity of these times stands out, as this young southern European fan stated. "My mother is a fan and showed me his music. As I was growing up I did not understand it, but when I went to a show in 2012, it changed my life. IN that moment, I understood it, I understood his music. It all made sense. That is how I became a real fan. That was no better time for me to become a fan, I would not get it in any other moment of my life." Such moments of understanding are rare.

Sometimes history intervened. Springsteen's music played at a school assembly would probably not have happened in the early years, but his response to September 11th changed that. "'Into the Fire' from *The Rising* album was played during a school assembly. I liked the song so sought out more by Springsteen. It wasn't until my parents bought me his 1973–84 collection that I listened more seriously, and when his *Wrecking Ball* album and tour were announced I had to get myself tickets. After that I became a much more serious fan." September 11th was instrumental for this older fan. "Heard his *Rising* album after 9/11 and I was hooked. Then I started listening to and watching earlier work." When remembering how lost, confused, and stricken this country, and much of the world, was post 9/11, it is not surprising that this album fostered a deeper connection. It is said that an inspiration for *The Rising* album was when, in the aftermath of 9/11, a fan shouted across a parking lot at him, "Bruce, we need you!" Whether this story is true or metaphorical, Springsteen's music indeed offered support.

Other newer fans had personal life-changing events turning them into fans. "It was last year, watching his Rock in Rio show on TV. I just knew a few songs and I liked them, but did not know his music that much. After Rock in Rio concert, I just fell in love with his songs. They filled my heart with hope and faith again, after my father passed away a month before the show." For long-term fans, albums such as *Greatest Hits* may not speak to them, but to newer fans such a compilation contributed. "I've always liked his hits that played over the radio. Especially 'The River' and 'Dancing in The Dark.' This made me buy the *Bruce Springsteen & The E Street Band: The Greatest Hits* in 2009. I heard the album and suddenly I liked Bruce even more, but I still wasn't any big Bruce fan yet. It wasn't before a night in 2013 it happened. I sat alone at my bedside and browsed through Bruce's music on YouTube and suddenly I heard 'I'm Going Down' and 'Atlantic City.' I REALLY enjoyed those tracks and listened to Bruce the whole night and BANG! I turned into a Bruce Springsteen maniac!;)"

"Maniac" or just an ardent fan, we hear the intensity of connecting. Something clicked, came together, made sense. Given the developmental stages and tasks across the life span, initial experiences, and bonding mean something different at different times of life. Women become Springsteen fans from a variety of backgrounds, generations, and musical experiences. However, a similar quality exists in most stories of first connections—something about his music and performances touches them deeply, and their lives or perspectives shifted dramatically.

He Was There When I Needed Him

How is it that sometimes when a person is in greatest need, help just seems to appear? Is this help always available yet the person is more open to it under certain circumstances? The idea of Springsteen being a helper, and accompanying women on their life journey, is a major theme throughout this book, and especially in chapters 5 and 6. Springsteen has acted akin to a guide or teacher, and for some, this role goes even deeper; several fans feel they owe their life itself or their mental health to his music. Here we briefly look at help that arrives when one is in need for women whose Springsteen journey started with such help.

"I was in a violent, demeaning relationship and I was sitting in my car at the drive-in movies, considering suicide, when 'Born to Run' came on the crackling speaker hanging from my car window. I wanted to know what happened to the character and his Wendy. Enough said." "I was suffering from severe depression and in the hospital. On the radio came 'Point Blank.' In there is a line that says 'shot between the eyes, point blank.' It said how I felt, nonexistent, see-through, barely there, of no consequence to anyone. From that moment on I used Bruce to heal me, no matter what the hurt. All these years later, I owe him my life."

The arts have always included possibilities to heal, support, and inspire people. Many find comfort or inspiration in an amazing piece of literature or a stunning painting. Religion and psychology promote the conversation and practice of healing, supporting, and inspiring also. Rock and roll, as Springsteen has "testified" on stage, can similarly open doors in the psyche and affect people's lives. Many fans commented on starting or deepening their connection to Springsteen at a turning point, needing help and finding it in his music.

Another was helped to mourn her brother. "My older brother would play it. He passed away when I was 13 and thus music helped me mourn." This fan credits him with helping end an addiction. "When I needed it, it appeared. I was totally immersed in the women's movement and listening almost exclusively to 'women's music,' old

Beatles and John Lennon. I needed to quit smoking before I turned 40 and I needed 'just a little help.' Bruce must have heard my call for help, cuz he came dancing into the dark of my needy self and kept me not having that one cigarette. I listened to BitUSA (vinyl back then) over and over as I screamed crying while growing up again without lighting up. He dragged me through. I owe my life to him."

People in pain and isolation often search for something or someone to hold onto, even a reason to keep trying and to stay alive. Sometimes they find a friend, sometimes a family member, sometimes a psychotherapist or a crisis hotline. Springsteen's music was that something for many women fans, a healing connection further explored in chapter 6.

Learning Bruce

What does one do after "conversion"? Cavicchi (1998) discusses activity after the transformation: "Fans describe a subsequent period of exploration. Like religious converts who intensify their participation in the activities of the religion with which their conversion is associated, fans describe a period of exploration after converting in which they intensify some previous musical activity, such as listening to recordings or buying collectibles" (p. 44).

For some women, the conversion moment ushered in a process of learning Springsteen's work. This solidified the original connection and excitement and added to their commitment. They sort of "caught up" on Springsteen and "studied" what they missed by not knowing about him (or not even having been alive) earlier. It is one thing to like a performer, and another to immerse oneself in the artist's work and life with the intent to know and feel it more profoundly, as some women describe. The immersion period (which can last a lifetime!) seems imperative for some fans.

> "Dancing in the Dark" was released in 1984 and I loved the song. A couple of years later, aged 12, I went out and bought the single, but when I got home I found that someone had switched the records and

the 7-inch vinyl inside the "Dancing in the Dark" sleeve was "Born to Run" with "Meeting Across the River" as a B-side. At first I couldn't believe it was the same Bruce Springsteen, but I only owned that one single and so I was stuck with it and after listening to it a few times I fell in love with it. That's when I started saving up my pocket money to buy the albums. I could afford a new album every two months or so, giving me plenty of time to appreciate each piece of Springsteen's back catalog. Some records I loved instantly (*The River*), some took me a while to get into (*Darkness*—I would force myself to listen to each album for a few days before passing judgment). *Nebraska* was the only album I didn't like.

What Keeps a Fan Devoted?

Our survey asked the following: Do you think you have a relationship with Springsteen as a fan? How would you describe that relationship? Personal attachment to Springsteen was essential to many descriptions of their fandom, yet evident distinctions also surfaced. While many women gave a resounding "yes" to the question of relationship, a small subset said no, and many equivocated over what that meant or what type of relationship it actually is. Women fans' attraction to Springsteen ranged from sexual attraction and romantic fantasies to a sense of a buddy or a friend to a more spiritual mentor, but their fandom typically seemed built on some sense of relationship, broadly defined. Discussing relationship here lays a foundation to an elaboration of "relationship" in subsequent chapters.

To understand this kind of relationship that may exist between people who have never met, we turn to psychoanalytic theory and therapy, and its evolution over decades to a greater emphasis on relationship (Safran et al., 2018; St. Clair & Wigren, 2004), as contributing to the framework for our study. The concept of internalized relationships from the object relations school of thought is helpful. Scott Rutan (Rutan et al., 2014) and Bonnie Buchele (Buchele & Rutan, 2017), clinicians and scholars whose writings on object relations and group therapy speak to internalized relationships, inform our work. Object relations theory is situated within an acknowledgment of the inherent importance of relationships for all human beings. "Object relations theory begins by assuming that people are born seeking and needing relationship" (Buchele & Rutan, 2017, p. 536) and "an innate goal of life is to find meaningful relationships" (p. 537). In discussing group therapy, Rutan et al. (2014) speak of relationships: "We maintain that the ability to enter into cooperative, loving, interdependent relationships has always been a sign of psychological maturity and health. This is particularly so today. Indeed, one quick but accurate indicator of mental health is the degree to which individuals allow themselves to know how important others are to them" (p. 1).

Another stream of psychoanalytic thinking and therapy, self psychology, created by Heinz Kohut, adds to this discussion of relationship through the concept of the self-object, defined as "the person used in the service of the self or experienced as part of the self, especially with regard to fostering esteem and a sense of well-being" (St. Clair & Wigren, 2004, p. 209). Self-object needs, including mirroring, idealizing, and twinship needs, are ways of viewing and relating to important people in one's life (self-objects). An "extended immersion in these transferential states" helped one "to gradually develop a more reliable sense of vitality or well-being" (Mitchell & Black, 2016, p. 161). Self-object needs start early but last throughout life because they are fundamental to our humanity. Perhaps Springsteen acts as a self-object for some women, providing a function for the self either through mirroring a sense of specialness, importance, or vitality leading to self-esteem, seeing the other as powerful and creating a feeling of goals to strive toward and of life making sense, or feeling the similarity to others through a shared sense of humanity (T. Ellenhorn, personal communication, August 2021).

This idea of a "relationship" with Springsteen also brings in the concept of mutuality from relational-cultural theory (Jordan, 2018). In an early paper, Judith Jordan (1986), who would go on to delineate a school of therapy from this perspective, describes mutuality in a relationship. While we do not suggest that fans have this level of mutuality with Springsteen, these concepts give a sense of what the relationship might feel like to some fans.

> In a mutual exchange one is both affecting the other and being affected by the other; one extends oneself out to the other and is also receptive to the impact of the other. There is openness to influence, emotional availability, and a constantly changing pattern of responding to and affecting the other's state. There is both receptivity and active initiative toward the other.
>
> Through empathy, and an active interest in the other as a different, complex person, one develops the capacity at first to allow the other's differentness and ultimately to value and encourage those qualities which make that person different and unique. When empathy and concern flow both ways, there is an intense affirmation of the self and paradoxically a transcendence of the self, a sense of the self as part of a larger relational unit. (p. 2)

Relationships as fundamental, serving important needs, and a sense of mutuality, mark the starting point for looking at women's thoughts about their relationship with Springsteen. As we read through and discussed the responses, our analysis suggested different understandings about the fan "relationship" that felt critical. As we outlined in prior work (Mangione & Luff, 2018) we wondered about the following: Is the connection to Springsteen as a person, or to his music, or to the fan community? Does a sense of connection equal a relationship or are they different? Is the relationship perceived as one-sided or mutual in any way, and if so, how? Are empathy and concern included, and is that possible with someone whom one has never met? Is lust/romantic attraction involved or not? How important is it to actually meet the man, and does meeting constitute a relationship? While many fans felt they definitely had a relationship with Springsteen, they navigated these questions and nuances. With those who rejected the idea of a relationship, we saw attempts at understanding the connection they did have, focusing on the one-sidedness of fandom, respect for his privacy, or only knowing his public persona. Many of these fans, however, seemed as avid as those who claimed some kind of "relationship."

So What Is a Relationship with a Rock Star? The Paradox of the Intimate Stranger

Most women fans elaborated upon the relationship they felt they had, or didn't have, with Springsteen, and what it meant to them. For this younger fan, being years apart in age didn't matter, and she benefited from his experiences and developmental milestones as she has reached them. Her tone of love and respect was found many times over in women's words.

> Other than my family and a couple close friends, my relationship with Bruce and the band is the longest of my life. It doesn't have anything to do with any sort of cosmic connection, but I think his awareness of the world has evolved with my own (although 40 years apart) so that when I needed the connection in high school and college, I could listen to his albums that he made when he was young. I can listen to his albums about being an adult and a working-class citizen now and appreciate them more. I understand, now that I'm married, his work about relationships and the struggles there. I know how much he and the band appreciate us, the fans, because they give us everything every single time we see each other. And that translates back. I'll give him everything I have when I see him, because that's how I can show them how much I care and how much they mean to me. So I'd describe it as a mutual love and respect, and one that we both cherish and can't get enough of.

Here the use of "mutual" feels both genuine and significant.

Another woman describes an emotional contract with Springsteen, while acknowledging limits on where it begins and ends. "We have a contract—an emotional contract. He's there for me. I'm there for him. I have no desire to date Bruce or kiss Bruce. I want his marriage to Patti to keep going and keep both of them happy. I need Bruce to keep making music. Sometimes, I fantasize that I might meet Bruce somewhere—

a record store or a boardwalk. I always wonder what I might say. I don't think I would really say anything. How do you thank someone whose music has been your life?" Being near Springsteen helps cement the idea of a relationship for some women. "It is an ongoing conversation (as Springsteen himself has stated) through the music. Also, due to the fact that I have been in the front row during quite a number of shows, Springsteen has started to recognize me. I've been fortunate enough to get to talk to him (briefly) on a couple of occasions." The relationship can hold shared passions and identities. "Respect and mutual love of rock 'n' roll music. Growing up Italian and Catholic."

For these fans, the relationship exists unequivocally. "I think that Bruce puts a lot of thought into his next album as where is he going to take us next. Sometimes it works and sometimes it doesn't. I think that Bruce is the only artist that really thinks about his fans when it comes to putting out music. For example, we needed Bruce after 911 and he was this with 'The Rising.'" "I definitely do. As a younger fan, I'm part of the next generation of Springsteen fans and I think that's very important. He has had a huge impact on my life even if he doesn't know it. I just wish I had the chance to tell him that." "My relationship to him is that we have been there for each other. I support him by buying his records and going to his concerts. He supports me by always doing his best to put out great music and perform great in concerts." Longevity and consistency are important. "He has been a constant throughout all the changes life brings." "I definitely have a relationship with him as a fan. Here's a guy I feel like I can relate to, yet, if I met him I would lose it. He's helped me through both happy and tough patches in my life, and I feel like I owe him." The understanding of feelings is foundational. "He can put into words my feelings . . . there is no situation I have faced that I cannot think of an appropriate Springsteen song. He has been with me through many difficult times." Springsteen exists as part of an internalized and very alive matrix for many fans.

Other fans were more circumspect, offering a nuanced and questioning perspective on the nature of their relationship with Springsteen. "This is a hard question to answer. When I see Bruce live he always tells us how important we are to getting where we are going, that he can't get there without us. I always feel that connection in a live performance, which is very different from any other musician I have seen live. Even though I don't know Bruce except through his music, I guess I would say that I do have a relationship with him." Others see the relationship as important but not mutual.

> It's one sided—since I've never met him—and he doesn't know me. So—of course I have a one-sided relationship with him! Our lives have paralleled in some ways. We got married (his second time to Patti) around the same time, had kids almost the same time. So, his writings/music has followed my life. Politically we agree. He's always there for me when I need him—whether it's on Sirius or a CD or a YouTube video. Whatever I want. Whenever I want. Whatever time I want him there. A BFF who doesn't know I exist! However, there is nothing like a live Bruce concert. Nothing. He makes you feel that he came to play for you—and only you! Had to add that!

Another fan ponders:

> Fan is such a strange word. I guess I'm a fan. But my "relationship" to Bruce goes so much deeper. There have been so many special times in my life that he and his music have made an impact. I couldn't list them all. My family and friends would say I'm a fan. I have the usual posters, pictures, mementos as I'm sure thousands of others have. I get so uptight when tickets go on sale. I have never bought tickets from a scalper and have not missed a tour. It hasn't been easy. I always think one time my luck will run out. It's almost like a "fix." . . . I need to see him (and the E Street Band) live to rejuvenate. I have to have the new albums right away so I can read the words . . . play it often, think about it.

A perceived sense of admiration plays into this response. "Yes, as an admirer, I do. I like to think of myself as a storyteller so my bond and relationship with Bruce is a real one. It's a give and take relationship. It's based on the admiration I feel for him. He also admires us, he identifies himself in us, I have seen it in his eyes." The importance to each other, the felt connection, the similarities in life choices, yet also the one-sidedness, are palpable, as is questioning what "fan" means, suggesting a multifaceted internal structure known as the relationship with Springsteen.

Yet it is important to hear from those who would not use the word "relationship," and who see inherent barriers between a rock star and fans. "I have a relationship with his music and with my friends who are also passionate about his music. I don't think I have a relationship with him personally, though he has been a constant throughout my life." For this woman, the reality of the situation precludes a relationship per se. "I am not sure it is possible to have a relationship with someone you have never met and obviously he doesn't know me. However, I do follow what he does, I check out his website, Backstreets and Badlands (UK-based site) at least weekly, listen to his music most days and think about him a lot!" For some, the vastness of his fan base makes the idea of a personal relationship impossible. "All Springsteen fans think they have a relationship with him. They think they can walk up and start a conversation with him and relate to him—me, I think I'm one of a million in his eyes." There are also "quiet" fans out there. "No, I think I am one of the quiet ones. I don't know everything about his life. I admire him as a musician and how he conducts his life but I don't know him." The contrast with typical relationships stands out. "Not really. Relationships are hard. Being a Bruce fan is easy." Given all this, we wondered about one-word responses: "Strained!" "Imaginary?"

Within a spectrum of answers, the personal nature of the connection, a sense of "mutuality" that ebbs and flows, and the felt closeness all challenge traditional notions of a "relationship." Many female fans feel a deep and nuanced relationship with Springsteen and his work, including some who disavow a typical relationship. Perhaps "connection" is a better word to use. His music provides a space and mechanism for identity creation, meaning-making, and community that can challenge, nurture, and inspire fans, keeping them connected long after their introduction. Chapters 4, 5, and 6 explore dimensions of that abiding relationship further. For some, the relationship includes all his fans, or embraces a spiritual sense. "I do think he has a relationship with all of his fans on some level. I think he realizes that it's like a following of some kind. I always feel like I've been to church when I walk out of a show. That's a huge effect to have on people." Yes, it is.

In a world in which artifice abounds, the perception of Springsteen as authentic forms the basis for connection to him and his music. He seems to understand the complexity and significance of who he is to others, as Springsteen expressed in Strauss (1995), "I think every fan creates an image of you in his or her head that may not be totally accurate. I think the pressure to be grounded—and for fans to feel like you're speaking to them—is good. That's what I want to do" (p. 176) and in Percy (1998), "At your best, your most honest, your least glitzy, you shared a common history, and you attempted both to ask questions and answer them in concert with your audience" (p. 231).

After the Beginnings . . .

Beginnings happen in many ways. Some beginnings are defining moments that can lead to intense connections and new opportunities. But the power of beginnings can also fade—relationships full of promise end. That which sustains fandom over time is intriguing: how Springsteen's music continues to speak to women's lives and growth, nurturing something like a relationship.

Given this impact in women's lives, we turn next to Springsteen's ways of speaking about and to women in his music and how fans have responded. In rock music, a traditionally male forum, women can often be and feel marginalized, unheard, unseen, stereotyped, or idealized. We hear directly from women about their experience of Springsteen's writings about women.

CHAPTER 3

"Hey Little Girl"

Women on Springsteen and Women

> I think his music uses derogatory or stereotypic images of women/femininity in a way that is inherently critical and therefore conveys an underlying respect that is empowering or enfranchising.

NOTHING IS SIMPLE, straightforward, or easy about relationships between men and women in the twenty-first century. Women have gained, and not gained, equality in the workplace and ascendancy to leadership positions, the fruits (some harvested, some withering on the vine) of the many phases of the women's movement over more than a century. The complexity of these relationships has surfaced and deepened in the last few years as women have emerged to publicly tell their stories about sexual harassment and assault by men, stories boiling over in their transparency and intensity, stories that have been silenced for decades. Distrust, apprehension, broken promises and dreams, betrayals, and criminal actions have swirled in the public consciousness, no longer relegated to back rooms, the silence of humiliation, and hush deals.

Sound bites and news headlines can help to mobilize and motivate, to create community and open conversations about who is heard and included. They raise questions about what is and is not possible, but without delving. Can a person from one gender, in a world where the very notion can be a question, meaningfully speak to a person from another? Is there a bridge across that gulf? The archaeologist image floats to mind, piecing together remnants in some vast layered topography of a mysterious culture of male–female relationship.

It is complicated to explore the role that a man—especially a male rock star—can play in women's lives, and even more so in relation to the gendered aspects of his work. Springsteen's all-too-male persona from the 1980s and his use of words such as "little girl" can make one wary, even queasy. Given that the music industry has become increasingly female dominated and expressive of female experience in recent decades (Rhodes, 2005; Challis, 2015), and given the, at times, overwhelming male energy among concert audiences, why do some women persist in driving down their own lane of "Thunder Road"? What would women fans say about views of women and male–female dynamics within Springsteen's work, including possibilities of stereotyping and sexism?

What Did Springsteen Just Say about Women?

Words can take on different meanings and engender an array of responses, at different times and according to the context, which is often the case with gender relationships. What we say, and how we respond to what others say, is socially constructed, reliant on the norms and conversation of the times to create meaning. To treat our conversations otherwise, as fixed truth and unwavering meaning, would be to deny the world in which one exists, and, using a Springsteen image, deny the possibility of the transformation he sometimes invokes, such as redemption or even resurrection.

Our exploration of women fans' relationship with Springsteen occurred against a background of popular and academic debate about Springsteen's writing on women, discussed in detail in a previous book chapter (Mangione & Luff, 2018) and revisited here. Some commentators have been critical, for example, questioning his repeated lyrical use of "little girl" to describe women and suggesting that Springsteen's image and work contain patriarchal and sexist attitudes (Alterman, 1999; Delmonico, 2011; Palmer, 1997). Others have disagreed, arguing that Springsteen depicts the real struggles of men and women in relationship, reflecting complexities of contemporary gender and heterosexual relations, but his writing is generally supportive of women (O'Donnell, 2017; Pardini, 2012; Zitelli, 2012), even feminist (Barreca, 2019). Others have argued that his work plays with fixed notions of gender and sexuality (Smith, 1992), offers "a possibility of something that looked like equality for all expressions of gender" (Adler, 2019, p. 158), and can speak to queer experience (Casio, 2018). Given that Springsteen's career has now spanned 50 years, "in which the place of women in rock and pop music as independent artists and as fans has changed dramatically" (Mangione & Luff, 2018, p. 114), we were interested in what women fans of all ages and length of fandom made of his writing on women.

In this chapter we show how women fans understood the "problem" of Springsteen's writing on women in relation to themselves. Overall, fans dismissed ideas of Springsteen or his work as sexist, but they held nuanced perspectives. Many spoke of an "evolution" in his writing on women and on heterosexual relationships over time, an evolution that mirrored their own journeys and the social changes of the past 40 years. Fans stressed the importance of understanding Springsteen as a "realistic storyteller" as some critics have done (Santelli, 2012), who depicts real women's, as well as men's, lives. Further, they discussed the ways in which they have personally felt supported *as women* by his work and his performance, including their sense of his relationships with women in the audience and in his life. Yet others did identify and challenge sexism in his work, and as we know, the minority voice can often express something necessary to be heard. We illustrate minority or divergent perspectives, including positive appraisals of his "heteronormative" writing from lesbian, queer, and feminist women, and responses addressing sexism in his work.

What Did Women Say About Springsteen and Women?

Aware of debates about Springsteen's writing about women, we asked women fans about feeling supported or alienated *as women*. Our hope was to find what fans think and feel, whether or not they were aware of critiques of Springsteen's writing on women, seeking responses from their own experience and appraisal. We asked three sets of questions:

1. Has there ever been a time when you felt supported as a woman by Springsteen's music or performance? If yes, please tell us in what ways you felt supported.
2. Has there ever been a time when you felt alienated as a woman by Springsteen's music or performance? If yes, please tell us in what ways you felt alienated.
3. Springsteen has sometimes been criticized for speaking about women in sexist or stereotyped ways in his music. What are your thoughts about this?

Responses in each area, support, alienation, and sexism, follow.

Supported as a Woman?

"Support" is a vague word, open to interpretation, and indeed women interpreted it differently. "As a woman" is also open to interpretation. We did not want to define these terms for women; rather, we wanted them to self-define in their answers what support and being a woman meant to them. A portion of the respondents did not respond to this question, perhaps due to survey fatigue or the ambiguity of the question. Among those responding, about half exclaimed a resounding "Yes," that they had felt supported as women. The range of that support shows the many routes that Springsteen fans take in interpreting his work. However, a smaller portion stated that they did not feel supported, and another portion felt supported but not as women per se or wondered about the meaning of the question. This variety of responses is portrayed in the following sections.

YES, SUPPORTED AS A WOMAN!

Respect and Understanding

Springsteen was seen by many as respectful and appreciative of women. "He appreciates, understands, and is supportive of women, and it comes through his music." "I've felt that Bruce has been very honest about his own perceptions of women, and his respect for women shows in his honesty." "He consistently writes about women in respectful terms. Women are rarely sex objects. They are characters, fully formed. The 'secret garden' idea is also incredibly important for my identification with him as a woman. He does not just see women as means for his pleasure, he sees women as a puzzle meant to be unlocked through love."

Beyond a sense of respect, many women talked about feeling understood. "Springsteen is one of the few male rockers who can write about women in a realistic, compassionate, and respectful manner. As a woman, his music reflects my own life and experiences." "I think Bruce really understands women, and loves us, and knows the words to say, in both song and in his onstage chatter, to let us know he enjoys us, loves performing for us, and that he feels for us much of what we feel for him. I don't get that sense from any/many other performers." "His lyrics reflect his understanding and enjoyment of women and an understanding of the challenges they face in the world."

From Mother to Sister to Wife to Daughter: The Women in His Life

Several fans referred to Springsteen's relationship with the women in his life to express the respect and understanding they felt from him. Any long-term Springsteen fan is aware of his mother, Adele, who has joined him on stage, danced with him, admonished him, and basked in the glow of appreciation from the crowd. This was not lost on women fans, many of whom commented on such relationships as evidence of respect for women. "These relationships have definitely helped him understand women and respect them." Others echoed this sentiment. "He clearly loves women—his mom, his sisters, his wife and his daughter. You have to love a man who brings his mom on to stage to dance with her." "Springsteen's performances where he is with his mother and/or he speaks about her [are] awe inspiring. You can feel how much he cherishes her and appreciates her as a strong role model."

Patti's involvement with the band was seen as evidence of support of women. "I've always seen Bruce's relationship with Patti as a real positive for women. He's talked about how she's taught him how to behave in a relationship." "When he brought Patti into the band. At first it was just as a backup singer, but the onstage presence of a woman was inspiring, and the way he worked her into arrangements of songs. And he's actually sung songs that are about a woman's point of view, something many guys would be much too macho, or much too worried about not being macho, to do." In recent years, Springsteen has written about the role that his relationships with his mother and Patti play in the evolution of his understanding of masculinity and relationships (Springsteen, 2016). In the 2021 podcast, *Renegades,* with Barack Obama, Springsteen spoke of Patti's love giving him faith "to risk parts of myself I had never risked before," that she "was trying to define for me a broader sense of maleness and masculinity, a freer sense" (Obama & Springsteen, March 29, 2021, No. 7). Though it took him time and work to get over a sense of embarrassment, handed down from his father, at "simply having a woman at my side" (Obama & Springsteen, March 22, 2021, No. 6), he realized that he needed Patti's assistance in changing himself to have the full life and family he wanted. Clearly some women fans understand how important the special women in his life are, notice how he interacts with them, and sense their impact on him.

The Women in His Songs

Who are the women in his songs, what are they doing and feeling, and how does he portray them? The theme of strong female characters ran through many responses. "I don't know if Bruce is a feminist per se, but he's pro women. He seems to support strong women in his songs." "I have felt supported by Springsteen's music in the way he depicts women in his songs. They are independent, smart, hardworking; admired and desired by men yet respected (and those who are disrespected do something about it). Women in Springsteen songs are strong enough to leave a situation they don't like, tough enough to stick it out when they know they're with the right person, beautiful and charming enough to make a man stay up all night trying to fight their feelings, and easy-going enough to enjoy laid-back nights and the simplicity of dating a good man."

Relationships between men and women are noted as supportive toward women. Fans commented on each partner's role. "I guess the most poignant one was listening to him on stage sing 'Back in Your Arms,' such a plea for forgiveness. It reminds me of the power women have in their relationships. When he sings 'Girls in Their Summer Clothes' I feel beautiful and light. But, when he sings 'I'll Work for Your Love'—well, doesn't that say what every woman wants to hear—woman need to know their love IS something that should be worked for and not lightly either." "In 'I'm Goin' Down' he appears to support a woman's sexual satisfaction in a relationship. In 'Thundercrack' he calls the woman his partner, and that's an early song in which he demonstrates his attitude that relationships are partnerships. Also, in 'For You' there's an example of him 'asking' a woman to do something, and not telling her to do it (the Format covered that song and the singer changed that line to telling)." "The lyrics of 'I'll Work for Your Love' come to mind, as does 'Drive All Night.' I don't think of Bruce as a writer of love songs because his narratives and themes are so complicated, but there are songs and pieces of songs that resonate with me, both as a feminist and as a woman worthy of love."

While Springsteen songs examine relationships, they also speak about inner strength and confidence. "The females in 'The River' or in 'Atlantic City' make me feel like I'm not alone. I've been those characters and felt the feelings described in the songs. And I've felt supported by the quiet beauty and grace that he gives these women who may be in a difficult situation. I've clung to the hope that Springsteen provides these characters—the possibility for escape and change. But also the admiration of just going through a realistic life—it's hard, and getting by is a feat in itself. I think Springsteen gives that to me. His music tells me things are ok. And I'm ok with that. I don't need anything more." "All of his songs really come back to the core of being and all the emotions you can have with yourself, your family, your relationships, your work, even. But that all the women in his songs are somehow beautiful. That's empowering."

One fan described women characters as "round," eloquently conveying a common response. "Springsteen's women are round, and seem cast by someone who truly loves and admires and honors women. I can't think of (or imagine) a single lyric that cheapens a woman or women. To the extent that I can put oneself in the place of any of the women in any of Bruce's songs, they make me/women feel admired, sexy, and, above all, part of the story—part of everyone's story. A man who announces that 'you ain't lived till you've had your tires rotated by a red-headed woman' is not objectifying, but swooning with delirium over the sexual power of his woman." "I always felt Bruce endowed a certain dignity on women who were down on their luck, as in 'I Wanna Marry You,' and I respected that. At times, I have felt like one of his characters, but always reminded myself to 'walk tall, or don't walk at all.'"

Female dignity isn't always connected to male rock music. Several fans compared Springsteen's writing with that of other musicians, and the music industry as a whole. "Women play strong, meaty, substantial roles in his music and in the band, and he isn't shy about it. It's refreshing in a male-dominated industry." "Unlike a lot of his contemporaries, many of the songs about women or lyrics about love and women are far from misogynistic. Many of his songs deal with men trying to prove themselves worthy enough for the women they love. He's the classic good guy from the wrong side of the tracks trying to prove himself worthy of his woman's love."

Not a Beauty?

A small set of responses on support cohered around that famous line from "Thunder Road." "'You ain't a beauty but hey that's all right' for me . . . is a great line for me as a woman." "I have always felt supported as a women by Springsteen music and performances. He writes how you feel. Think of one of Bruce's most beloved songs, 'Thunder Road,' 'You ain't a beauty but hey you're alright.' That is telling every girl alive you do not have to be beautiful to be loved or cherished. Do young girls today get that message???" "The line that always sticks with me is: 'you ain't a beauty, but hey you're alright. And that's alright with me.' Sadly, such a simple sentiment is revolutionary to a girl who was abused and called fat and ugly on a daily basis. And as a message to all girls in the world, you don't have to look like a supermodel and starve yourself, there are guys out there who are ok with who you are and will want to be with you. There are many other ways, having women in the band, speaking out on women's issues, but that line is so incredibly important." When one thinks of the negative self-esteem, eating disorders, and other mental health issues abetted by our cultural obsession with a constricted view of beauty and self-worth, it makes sense that this line speaks to some women as countering messages of beauty conformity and consumerism in music.

Lesbians and Bruce

Lastly, in discussing "support" a small but vocal cadre of fans, self-identified as gay, commented on where and how they feel supported, with some noting his support for the LGBTQ community more broadly. "As a lesbian I felt supported when he included gay/lesbian couples in his 'Tougher Than the Rest' video. Especially at that time in America." "I feel and think supported as a woman in all his songs. Respected, admired and valued. Well . . . not only am I a woman, but I'm gay. A few years ago—when NJ was grappling with same-sex marriage—Bruce put something on his website that reached out to those of us 'gay brothers and sisters' I believe is part of it . . . and well, he just got elevated even higher by that point."

Springsteen's gestures toward and respect for people with diverse identities was appreciated. "In recent years, I think Bruce has made it a point to try to write from the point of view of people unlike himself: women, gays, soldiers, etc. I don't know that this really makes me feel 'supported,' but I do appreciate the fact that he does this." "I did like it when I was at a concert and someone had a big sign at the back that said 'Lesbians Love The Boss' and he pointed at it and said, 'I love you too!'"

NOT SO SUPPORTED, OR STUMPED ME ON THIS ONE!

While there was more than a handful of "No" or "Not really" answers, and even a few "Never" responses, meaning they did not feel supported by Springsteen as a woman, many responded with a question of their own or a qualification. In fact, the very first response we read let us know that interesting comments were forthcoming. "Not really. I actually think Bruce can seem a bit chauvinistic at times, BUT I think he acknowledges that tendency."

We found many such responses that sculpted their "no/not" answers to address and enhance the complexity. "Hmmm—not really. I think he writes from a man's point of view. Except for maybe a few songs—'The Wish,' 'Tougher Than the Rest,' 'JESUS WAS AN ONLY SON.'" One woman responded with "stumped me on this one," while another said, "I'm lost in this question????" These fans may have been speaking for those who said they did not understand the question or know how to answer or had never thought in this way before. We appreciated feedback from the fans about our work, and heard some definite criticism of this question, something not seen with other questions. "This is a weird question to me. His music is very important to me, but I don't think the reason it is important is any different from that of a male fan. So I guess the answer is no, I've never felt supported 'as a woman' but I feel supported all the time 'as a person.'" We stand behind the importance of our question and are glad we asked it, seeing the depth and breadth of responses, including naming it as weird. It is important to acknowledge the disconnect between the focus on gender and gender issues for some commentators and fans—certainly not all people think in gendered terms, even if the academic and political worlds often do. This was a reason to ask fans directly about their experience of Springsteen's work and women. We found women's comments about not experiencing Springsteen as supportive, or not in terms of gender, striking in the ongoing cultural conversations about gender. This less gendered view is often not verbalized or is contentious within academic debates.

Some responses pointed to ideas of a common humanity. "I'm not necessarily sure if just by being a woman. I think it's much more humanistic than by gender identity." "All the time . . . his music crosses over both genders. . . . I don't look at it as his music as supporting me as a woman, I look at it as supporting me as a human being. I would hope that he would think the same thing and didn't write to a specific gender." "Not specifically as a woman. More as a member of the human race. Man or woman I think his stories of hope and redemption resonate with all of us." "I can't say that I felt supported as a woman specifically by Springsteen. . . . Because I feel Springsteen speaks to all of his fans—men, women, children. He talks about all times, hard times, good times, bad times, times we all have. And those times relate to all of us whether we are men or women. I have never tried to relate it to being a 'female' fan. . . . I am just a fan." "So far I did not think about that. What I like is that the audience at his concerts are as many men as women, Young, old, everything. I feel supported in a way that has nothing to do with being a woman, but as a human being in general by the message: Don't be afraid to live your dream."

This more universal framework, that we can hear and respond to something based on our shared humanity, seems to have fallen out of favor in many political arenas, yet many fans continue to find something of great value in an experience of common humanity. At this point in time, it feels almost radical, and really critical, to highlight such possibilities, and to imagine they may be underreported in a society where that is not the dominant narrative. "Support for one gender or another in a musical performance or piece is asking a bit much of the performance or piece. I think over time, his message has been on track and positive for all people, all human rights, and that he is deeply supportive of equality."

THERE'S MORE TO THIS QUESTION . . .

Other women brought in their identities, or parts of who they are, in talking about support. "Umm, that's harder. I'm actually VERY feminist and have worked in the domestic & sexual violence field for over 20 years. I know of some very specific Springsteen content I dislike, but I can't specifically recall stuff I specifically like/appreciate/support as a woman (other than a lot of widespread, non-gender-specific social justice stuff)." "Not particularly that I can name, but I love Bruce's personal and political views regarding women, gays, and the working mom & pop." "I feel supported by his music as a human being—not necessarily as a woman. I do appreciate his support of gays and lesbians—initially with 'Streets of Philadelphia' and later as he publicly supported gay marriage. Once in concert—while singing 'American Land'—he offered a shout out to a group of lesbians—that was kind of cool. Also—he once took a sign on stage from a woman which said, 'This lesbian has Better Days when she hears Bruce.' Then he, of course, sang Better Days." "Bruce has always respected his audience. From not panicking about a bomb threat to catching him in the audience, he trusts us and we trust him. Respect. So yes, as a woman, I have felt that respect. But I think gays and blacks and even Republicans can feel the respect too." "Specifically as a woman? I never thought about it. As a person and as an American, both patriotic and disillusioned." "I am a Vietnam-era veteran, and his work with them made me feel supported." Myriad aspects of identity, mentioned here, paint a picture of an interconnecting web of ways that fans felt "supported" by Springsteen's work, and highlight how overgeneralizations of women fans can miss this diversity.

From a different angle, one woman spoke to her career in broadcasting that affected her perception of a lack of support for women.

> Interesting question. Maybe when Bruce talks to the guys from stage about fucking up a good thing has felt supportive, but I don't think I can pull this specific thread out of the canvas for myself. If anything, as of recently, I feel Bruce could be more supportive of women. For example, I'm a broadcaster, and I have been acutely aware of how few women have interviewed him. Chris Phillips's interview book has 2 women-hosted interviews out of 30 in the book. Recently, they did a preview listening party at a record store and did a promotional video

from it, and though the camera panned to show two women in the room, neither of their comments were used so it was all men. Clearly not representative of Bruce's fan base.

Alienated as a Woman?

Analyzing responses to this question was probably the easiest and quickest of the entire survey. Many women skipped this question, and the vast majority said no, never, or not at all. It makes sense, of course, that devoted fans of any artist would not endorse alienation. However, the few substantive answers about alienation deserve attention, especially as we purposely used the word "alienate," which invites a stronger response than just not liking (although some fans responded in those ways). Very few fans love everything an artist does; we wanted to hear the depth of any criticism. While a few women wrote about a particular alienating song or incident, including his politics and the male energy in the audience, to which they just couldn't relate, certain themes stood out across several responses: sexualized songs, infidelity, and specific lyrics.

OVERT SEXUALITY: "JUST DIDN'T NEED TO GO THERE"

Certain lyrics and songs were not well-received by some women. In particular, "Reno" and "Red Headed Woman" were criticized for explicitly sexual lyrics. Common to these responses was the idea that the explicit lyrics were unnecessary, that there was no "need to go there." "Oh yea—he played 'Reno' live at the Tower Theater (Philly)—and I was sitting next to a guy who attended alone. I didn't feel alienated—just uncomfortable. I think I understand 'Reno' from an artistic point of view—I just have not re-listened to it." "I really don't like the song 'Red Headed Woman' and feel it is demeaning to women and embarrassing to his wife." "Uhm, 'Red Haired Woman.' Just didn't need to go there." "'Reno.' Can't understand." "'Reno'—it just creeps me out." "I admit his overtly sexual songs like 'Red Headed Woman' made me slightly uncomfortable. I'm no prude, but that one stretched the boundaries of good taste IMHO." Springsteen hit negative notes with these songs for some fans, perhaps summarized as a perceived disrespect for women and a breaching of certain boundaries.

Sometimes Springsteen's behavior on stage was received poorly.

> His statements during concerts in recent years about the band and he "stimulating your sexual organs." A concert does not do that. It is a very strange remark, it looks alienated from reality, or as if he got carried away by the overload of relatively young female attention for him as an old man.—Also, the way he interacts with female fans in the front rows when his wife Patti is not on stage. For example, when she is with the band he often picks women of his own age or children for "Dancing in the Dark." When she is not on stage, he chooses the younger woman and also flirts a lot more with the women in the front rows.

Other fans commented on feeling alienated because of rumors about Springsteen's personal life, rather than his work or performance, particularly stories of cheating on either his first or second wife. "Not as a result of his music or his performance, but I felt alienated in the mid to late 80s when he had an affair with Patti, got divorced, and then split up the E Street Band. He lost me for several years." "Not by his music—but by his actions. Reading that he may have cheated on Patti really turned me off." We report these responses not to comment on the truth or otherwise of them, but to note that for some fans, a sense of disrespect toward women on or off stage had an impact on their connection as fans.

IT'S IN THE WORDS

Lyrics beyond "Reno" and "Red Headed Woman" were not well received by some women, even lyrics that other women felt were supportive. These included the line from "Thunder Road" about not being a beauty that elicited mixed responses. Springsteen gets a pass on "alienation" per se from this fan. "Yes dislike, but alienated no. As a 20+ year feminist there's a LOT of popular culture that I have turned my back on as a result of feeling alienated, but I suppose that because I love Springsteen's music SO MUCH, this is just one (literally the one and only instance) where I tolerate some sexist/misogynistic lyrics." Rape culture is invoked in this description of lyrics, but also tempered by her connection to Springsteen.

> Some of the lyrics to Springsteen's songs do sound a little sexist when taken out of context. For example, referring to a woman as a "little girl" in "I'm on Fire" or singing, "I'm pulling you close, you just say no / You say you don't like it, but girl I know you're a liar / 'Cause when we kiss, fire" in "Fire" strikes most educated listeners as patronizing and embracing male dominance and rape culture. But I don't see these as reflective of Springsteen's personal beliefs as much as the working class characters in his songs. Maybe I'm just making excuses for sentimental reasons; I want to continue to love Springsteen due to my associations with his music and my childhood and my love of my father. But I do think it's important for savvy listeners to pay attention to mixed messages in song lyrics, and to voice their opinions when they feel offended or alienated.

The way Springsteen sometimes describes women dismayed fans who hoped for more from him. "Back in the late '70s and early '80s, he was always referencing the women in his songs as 'little girl'—that was a little annoying. He seems to have grown out of that." "Sometimes I hear lyrics that rub me the wrong way—I love 'Rosalita' but, as with Wendy and Sandy and Mary and Janey and the many other women he writes about, it rankles me that he calls and/or treats them as 'girls.' I usually chalk this up to poetic license and sociocultural norms, but they often remind me that Bruce is essentially a 'guy's guy.'" "A few songs on *Devils and Dust* . . . not my favorite portrayal of women." A Danish fan who had written in a previous response that she would like to see Springsteen discover feminism, given the passive nature of women in his songs, elaborated. "This continues to this day. That recent video he directed himself, for 'Invisible Game,' even that allows only a passive role to the females. Again it's a pity. He has such passion and power, he is in such a position to influence people. I love what he has done in terms of race/ethnicity, and I wish he'd have done the same for women."

Does he need to say "Daddy"? Why does he do that? "This is such a small thing. There are some songs that he refers to himself as 'daddy.' For whatever reason, that terminology makes me uncomfortable. I don't think he longs for someone younger, so why use that word when many others would work." "I don't think so. Looking back on lyrics like 'Hey, little girl is your daddy home,' they might seem kind of creepy. But at the time, in our youth, they didn't seem that way."

While this line from "Thunder Road" is often mentioned as supportive, another side exists, often so true of art and our reactions. "Only one lyric insults me and that is 'you're no beauty but you're alright.'" "Thunder Road 'you ain't a beauty but hey you're alright'—only Bruce Springsteen could say that and get away with it. I'd climb in."

These comments on alienation, although sparse in a fan survey, give glimpses into the negative press among some critics of Springsteen's views of women.

NOT ALIENATED BUT LET ME EXPLAIN . . .

Notwithstanding these important examples of alienation, the vast majority simply answered no to this question. However, some further described their "no" answers. For this person, a sense of gender fluidity was important. "Never felt alienated. As a matter of fact, when I sing his lyrics sometimes they allow me to slip from one gender into the other" (Mangione & Luff, 2018, p. 124). And for another woman, being a fan is when she is most herself. "Never ever. It's the only time I belong. I fit in I'm just me. A soul in a body no one's mother daughter sister cousin etc. Just me and all the other souls we get it."

This fan refers to the idea, mentioned earlier, that Springsteen ultimately speaks to the human experience. "Alienated is not something I've felt. But I don't think he speaks to the 'female' experience in the way he speaks to the 'male' experience and the pressures of masculinity and duty. Yet I don't really expect him to. To me, he does a fine job of speaking to the human experience, and I choose to see his work through that lens, which in my opinion is the important one."

In their responses, some women directly addressed—and dismissed—Springsteen's use of "little girl" and other language that has concerned critics and some fans. "NO. It has never bothered me that he uses phrases like 'little girl.'" "Nah, he has evolved like we all have. I don't mind him singing 'hey little girl' but wouldn't allow it from someone in real life." "Never. Although I am not fond of the 'little girl' used so often in his older music. But one can understand it in the context of the time." A fan from Sweden comments as an onlooker to American culture. "Not really, just the typical way of Americans, calling women 'baby' and 'little girl' ('I Wanna Marry You' . . .) but that has changed as he's matured."

This woman states unequivocally what she has seen and heard. "Never. I have never once seen a woman pranced around in next to nothing during a concert. Never heard him call women 'bitches' and 'hos.' I have never once listened to his music and immediately felt objectified the way I do when I hear a lot of music nowadays."

These answers led into considering a question that has dogged Springsteen over the years.

Is He Sexist? Does He Stereotype?

We asked directly whether fans see Springsteen's work as sexist or stereotyping. Academic writers and music critics have expressed this concern, but, imagining that this may not be shared by many women fans, we were not surprised at the overwhelming response of "No, he's not" in various forms. However, some women did acknowledge a level of sexism in his work. The directness and honesty of the responses, again, offered insight into the nuanced ways of thinking among fans about gender, sexism, artistic expression, and culture.

SEXISM? STEREOTYPES? NONSENSE!

The word "nonsense" was used six times in response to this question, "ridiculous" was mentioned thirteen times, and "rubbish" was used too—strong responses to our question. The tenor of most responses was no, that is not who Bruce is or what Bruce does. Many women simply said that they had never heard this criticism before, or that they didn't feel that way. Some other brief responses along this line were just as emphatic. "Bullhockey. He simply appreciates women." "Never thought about it, and never heard anything about it either." "Crazy talk. He's simply reflecting life as it really is." "I am a woman who knows her mind and has a strong sense of self. I do not think his music is derogatory to women." "Those critics are misreading his lyrics. And I say this as an academic feminist." "I have found his music to be everything opposite of that statement." Some women compared Springsteen to other artists in refuting the criticism of sexism. "If I were to list some artists that have songs that criticize and are sexist or stereotype women I would not think of Bruce Springsteen. If you listen to the radio for 10 minutes you will know what I mean."

"I CAN UNDERSTAND WHY"

Some women fans did see sexism or stereotyping in Springsteen's music, but typically there were caveats in their responses. "They are generally right. He is old school rock and roll. Guitars, cars, girls—all 'things.' However, he also sings about relationships and emotions and other things where women are human. And his songs about fighting against the powers that be apply to women as much as or more than men."

One fan was more concerned about overall representations in his music.

> I think women in his songs are well portrayed overall and maybe more so than people give him credit for, but I also think he severely underrepresents them (i.e., the women he talks about don't seem worse represented than the men, there just aren't nearly enough of them). I actually struggle with it a bit, because this is something that I relate to a lot and I don't feel excluded, but I also know that it never seems to be aimed at me. (I also think his complete exclusion of any orientation other than heterosexual is offputting, but that's a different problem).

Other fans noted some stereotyping of women but felt this problem extended to male characters. "I think Bruce generalizes both women and men. I think it is less of a problem with Bruce than with most other artists." Another agreed but felt that men at least always had the central role. "I agree that some of the representations are stereotypical. Women are often girlfriends or wives in his songs. Men are not exactly a wide variety of characters, but men (with the exception of the Pete Seeger covers) are always the narrator, and thus the voice most connected to the listener is always male."

"IT IS EVOLUTION"

A common theme among women who did see sexism or stereotyping was to note an evolution over the years as Springsteen has matured and as our culture has grown in understanding of sexism in society. Youth, the early years of rock and roll, and relationships that change people were all noted as facets of this evolution. Springsteen's work was contextualized within a time, a place, and an industry, with importance placed on evolving to reflect a different set of values.

Women fans focused on Springsteen's age at the time of writing lyrics that some consider sexist or stereotyped, noting both his youth and the zeitgeist of the times as powerful influences. "Young performers use the language of the time—one should not criticize actions from the past—no evidence of this in his current work." "Back in the 50s and early 60s that was the typical way of referring to women (like for instance 'I'm on Fire . . . Is your Daddy home') and Springsteen grew up back in the 50s. It's only in his early writing he is using terms that could be interpreted as sexist." "Those songs were written when he was quite young, and most young men at one time or another will voice sexist views, he has gained wisdom with age." Some women noted commonalities in Springsteen's growth over time with their own development. "I never felt Bruce has written sexist comments about women. We change as we grow older, and as we grow up our perspectives change. His journey has been just like the rest of us. A learning experience, that helps us along the way." "It's never bothered me. Bruce was referring to the person he was at the time over the years. The man he grew into seems to be a hell of a feminist."

Others commented on the wider context of the music industry, noting that it has not historically, or even currently, been known as a bastion of gender equality. They noted patterns, and occasional growth, in the "language of rock" over time. "Most likely the result of the era he grew up in and the sexism in the music industry in his early career." "I understand this criticism. I think in part that tendency was a product of his youth and his early musical influences. His female characters have become increasingly empowered over the years." "His turns of phrase such as 'Little girl' and 'Baby' are part of the rock vocabulary and I don't take it personally. You could say he stereotypes men when he writes about working-class guys coming home from the factory and wanting to go out drinking and beating people up. It's a way of casting categories to get at the bigger picture."

> I don't see it that way. He just talks about characters. You could say he has stereotyped men too, e.g., some guy down on his luck for some reason, looking for redemption. How many songs does that describe? He does use "baby" or "girl," etc., and I've heard people say they don't like that. But honestly, he's 65, and he is very much connected to the older musicians who did the same thing. I grew up with a lot of people who spoke the same way. I consider myself a feminist so if I heard something that sounded sexist, I am sure I would dislike the song and it would stand out in my mind for that reason.

Some fans mused in depth about where Springsteen's attitudes had come from, how they had changed in his writing, and what influences people as they grow.

> He's written plenty about women as objects—of affection, of salvation, of redemption—so the criticism has some validity. But I also think he's evolved over the years, and the women he writes about now tend to be more fully realized than the ones he wrote about in his early career. Janie in "Spare Parts," the anonymous woman who lost her love on 9/11 in "Counting on a Miracle," the wife in "Devil's Arcade" whose husband came back from Iraq, damaged both physically and mentally . . . there's a lot more depth to these characters than to Puerto Rican Jane, or the barefoot girl in "Jungleland," or Rosalita."

> "Cars and girls"? The only song I have really felt uncomfortable with is "You Can Look (But You Better Not Touch)." The whole song bothers me, but Dirty Annie in the last verse is a particularly passive female character. I think Springsteen's writing has improved over the decades and "Tunnel of Love" is probably the turning point where he began to treat female characters as equal in importance to male characters. I think this is partly down to Springsteen's life experience and partly down to him becoming a better writer and more able to portray female characters.

Fan comments about an evolution echo Springsteen's own public comment on the ways that his masculinity and relationships with women have evolved. In *Renegades: Born in the U.S.A.*, podcast conversations with Barack Obama, Springsteen reflected on the limitations of the American masculinity he grew up with, the ways in which it hampered understanding between men and women. He talks about the American ideal of the "alpha male"—an image of power and domination—and how he had succumbed to the lure of that masculinity for a long time, but ultimately, he saw how destructive that archetype was in keeping him from "knowing my true self" and having the kinds of relationships he wanted. Springsteen notes, "That archetype is a closed man," not revealing of his feelings, and how he had to get rid it to have partnership and a family that is nurturing and allows room to grow (Obama & Springsteen, March 22, 2021, no 6).

Interestingly, one fan acknowledged the importance of evolution while also admitting to a comforting nostalgia about traditional roles.

> I support a family of four. I work at a place that I've been at for 25 years. I've worked my way up in my job to run the department. I have a great relationship with my children. I have no self-confidence issues. I enjoy that my husband is a stay-at-home dad . . . and have been happily married for 26 years (except for the Bruce vs. Stones discussions). Although it takes a lot to offend me, I'm quite surprised at myself that I actually enjoy the stereotyped references to women. I think maybe it's because it causes me to recall fondly the very male role of my

grandfathers toward my homemaker grandmothers. Both sets of grandparents had very loving, supportive relationships, but all four were without choice. The men worked outside the home, and the women raised the children and kept the home. Because I am not without choice, I feel like I can enjoy those nostalgic characteristics that are sometimes portrayed in Springsteen's music.

REAL PEOPLE: "IT'S HONEST MUSIC"

The idea of Springsteen as a realistic storyteller (Santelli, 2012), that his work depicts real people and real situations, conveying a folkloric authenticity (Cantrell, 2017), has been commented on over years by fans and academics. Women fans here noted that if something sounds sexist or stereotyped, maybe he is reflecting reality, writing about what he sees and hears as a realistic observer of the world and people. "Like I said, he has never offended me . . . he is telling us a story from a man's point of view very often. It's honest music and honest song writing is all." Another respondent noted, "Springsteen writes about real people, men and women, in real situations. If those real people have stereotypical attributes, so be it."

Again, as reality evolved so has his writing. "I think he speaks about women in the context of the times in his music. He relates stories about 'real' people as he sees/saw them at different stages in his life." "I've always been sensitive to sexism. I consider myself a feminist. Stereotypes in the songs are reflective of society, the cultural context of the settings, and his particular background." Some fans particularly noted honesty and realism in writing about relationships with women. "He is one of those artists who write 'adult' love songs, about 'real' relationships, with 'real' women." "I think he is very supportive of women and generally portrays them in a sensitive and realistic manner. Women have many roles in society, and he is not worried about addressing them in his songs."

Relating to women in his songs is motivational for this fan. "I can often relate to his characters in his songs so I feel inspired to either be these women or to escape from what he sees as that woman." The act of making his music one's own comes across here. "I don't see it.

[sexism]. He's telling stories about real life. Some of his characters may come across toward women in a negative light, but it's part of the bigger story Bruce is telling. And one thing I really like about his songs is that you can make it yours, your own interpretation. He isn't coming out and telling you how to interpret it." This final comment, drawing on a line both loved and criticized, brings this question back to personal experience. "I don't think so. Who else could possibly utter the words 'you ain't a beauty but hey you're all right' and have a stadium full of women of all ages scream and applaud. 'Nuff said."

Gender and Springsteen: Not One Easy Answer

Clearly most women who responded feel supported by Springsteen as a woman and a human being, do not feel alienated as a woman, and do not agree with the view of him as sexist. There seems to be a very strong sense of traveling together around gender evolution and a shared understanding, even if the specifics of his work were sometimes uncomfortable or multilayered. Although there may always be a thread of controversy around some of Springsteen's writing on women, at least for some commentators and fans, it feels like a complicated but evolving aspect of his work, reinforcing the journey metaphor of Springsteen fandom. Given the psychological framework of personal growth, change, and meaning as central to this exploration of Springsteen fandom, it would be wrong to freeze anyone at one point in time and thereby define that person or their path. This psychological framework fits with the idea of evolution, context, history, and development, a framework espoused by many respondents. It does not fit with a practice of pronouncing judgment in the present, based on current rules or norms, over past possible faults. In many ways the women's views echo the concept of redemption that is so central to much of Springsteen's music. For Springsteen, while judgment may be real, so is redemption; the fan community is a train filled with saints and sinners—including the driver.

We greatly respect the women who volunteered comments about times they felt disappointed in or alienated from Springsteen due to his behavior or songs—it takes insight to see the shortcomings of someone so admired and honesty to name them. The ability to see flaws yet not turn one's back on someone is central to any important relationship. A certain level of allowing others to be imperfect, lowering the pedestal, contributes to relationships in general. A sense of balance shines through many fan responses, trying to understand their own experience of Springsteen in comparison with what "others" might have said. If a search for meaning and understanding is a major pursuit as human beings, many of the women were certainly wrestling with the meaning involved in Springsteen's writing about women and their relationship to it.

Many women found a common humanity beyond gender in Springsteen's work. "His message transcends gender to me" (Mangione & Luff, 2018, p. 124). Could it be that Springsteen, as he and we journey on, has tapped into both the ongoing complexities *and* a potential for evolution in male–female relationships, one in which connection and community, so often described as missing in our current world, remain possible? And where identification and bonding can cross gender barriers, even with understanding that some gulfs may exist, that a "Leap of Faith" and an open imagination might be needed?

Natalie Adler (2019), writing in *Long Walk Home* tells us, "But in the same way you can know that you are gay before you know what it means, from a young age, I recognized Bruce Springsteen as the butch mother of my hungry heart. Perhaps this is why, as a queer woman, I have never felt left out of his music" (p. 156).

Gina Barreca (2019), also from *Long Walk Home*, ends her narrative emphatically, which some fans might echo. "Of course Springsteen is a feminist. The women in his songs have always been human beings, with their own souls, wishes, nightmares, and achievements. They're not there for decoration or blind devotion; they're part of the music and a vital part of Springsteen's world. They're equally tough and equally vulnerable, as able to make their own decisions and chart their own courses as any man. And, like any man, they are able to fail" (p. 169).

CHAPTER 4

Springsteen as Friend or Family Member

> I feel I know a lot about him through books I've read and his music—he's my friend, my brother, my poet, and my Hero.

RELATIONSHIPS WITH FRIENDS AND FAMILIES, those we love—most of the time—and with whom we can be our true selves—most of the time—those with whom we can lose contact, either emotionally or physically, and yet reconnect—most of the time—such relationships are foundational and precious in our lives, often even when they might be conflictual or difficult. Certainly, friends and family occupy different roles in terms of bonding, history, and connections, yet both share a basic weightiness and rootedness in most people's lives. Sometimes we look up to and learn from our friends and family, sometimes they do the same with us. We can't hide even when we might want to, at least not for long; a realness and intimacy exist that offer the chance to be authentic. Some families are "givens" from birth, whereas others are "chosen" to be in those familial relationships, perhaps especially if some break with family has occurred. What does it mean to be such a friend or family member? Psychologists, sociologists, novelists, poets, and memoirists have written about these core relationships for centuries, but such closeness might not come to mind when writing about fans of a rock star. Yet, women fans repeatedly talked about Springsteen in these ways. Springsteen himself, in the 2020 convocation at Boston College, as students began their year in the pandemic, emphasized the centrality of friendship and family, words that resonate with this chapter.

Some themes in psychology feel relevant to seeing Springsteen as friend or family. Lillian Rubin, an academic researcher and psychotherapist who interviewed hundreds of people for her classic work, *Just Friends: The Role of Friendship in Our Lives* (1990), spoke about how friends help us grow, develop, and navigate ourselves and the world. Blieszner and Adams (1992) describe the history and basics of friendship research, focusing on friendships across the age span and different phases of life, gender and friendships, and the structure of friendships, speaking to their importance. Research focused on "emerging adults" in their late teens and twenties (Demir et al., 2019) has explored how important it can be to share positive events with friends and how it can lead to happiness. In general, Demir et al. (2011) comment, "Decades of empirical research have shown that having friends and close friendship experiences (overall quality, supportive, and intimate interactions) are essential predictors of happiness" (p. 983).

Relationships with family and friends are connected to mental health (Lee and Szinovacz, 2016) in both positive and negative ways. Friendships are deemed valuable yet can often be hard to cultivate (Miller, 2014), with health risks that may accompany a lack of friends. It makes sense that mental health professionals ask about support systems, friends, and family, during intake interviews. Researchers have explored the creation and impacts of friendship from many angles. Hartup and Stevens (1997) researched the development of friends over the life course and how that changes. Feminist researchers (Galupo and Gonzalez, 2013) looked at cross-identity (gender, sexual orientation, and race) friendships through the lens of "three general friendship values (trust and honesty, respect friend as person, there when needed) and three cross-identity salient friendship values (similar lives and experiences, similar values, nonjudgmental)" (p. 779). Siebert et al. (1999) studied friendships in people who were preretirement to look at the impact as we age, finding that friendships can help mitigate negative identity connotations that can go with aging. A comment by Bowker et al. (2006) about kids in middle childhood struck us, given the age at which some women started their relationship with Springsteen. "Previously, researchers have found that the salient characteristics of friendship in middle childhood are companionship, recreation, validation, caring, help, and guidance" (p. 685). This description by Harley et al. (2012) speaks distinctly: "Friendships are voluntary relationships where individuals have to commit time and effort in order to develop mutual and personalized interest and concern. . . . Factors such as trust, intimacy, and commitment are therefore important in the development and maintenance of friendship" (p. 1292). Aspects of friendship interweave in the relationship many women fans have with Springsteen and his music.

Similarly, psychologists have studied families for decades, their central role in the structure of societies as well as their problems, which can be addressed through family therapy. Bengston (2001) discusses the evolving nature and structure of the family over the last century, yet differing forms of family remain strong and salient even with such change. Walsh (2012) focuses on diversity in family forms as norms change, including topics such as culture, disability, single parenting, socioeconomic status, lesbian and gay families, and spirituality. Monica McGoldrick and colleagues (2005) published three editions of the groundbreaking *Ethnicity and Family Therapy*, providing rich descriptions of various structures and customs, encompassing new ethnic groups and their "variations" on family practices and values. Bigner and Wetchler (2012) speak to diversity regarding LGBT families and couples, offering affirmative therapy models for different families. Family is still seen as a bedrock of human development and relationships.

Attachment theory in psychology, mentioned briefly earlier in this book, that started with John Bowlby and Mary Ainsworth with mothers, babies, and small children in the mid-twentieth century, posits that early human attachment is basic to growth, development, and well-being throughout the life span. Family is where people start to become the person they will be throughout their lives. An oft-quoted description by Bowlby (1980) makes this clear: "Intimate attachments to other human beings are the hub around which a person's life revolves, not only when he is an infant or a toddler, but throughout his adolescence and his years of maturity as well, and on into old age" (p. 442). Attachment theory has strongly influenced theories of development, loss and grief, trauma, and psychotherapy (Cassidy & Shaver, 2016; Wallin, 2007). The necessity of attachment figures in life does not abate after childhood (Mikulincer & Shaver, 2016). Attachment theory's focus on the centrality of relationships frames this research.

The defining features women fans describe in their relationship to Springsteen as friend or family member include realness and authenticity, not hiding behind a façade, at least not for long; familiarity and sharing basics such as background or worldview; and being together through good and bad times and ups and downs of the relationship itself. Women fans' sense of Springsteen's authenticity, of his struggling as they struggle, feeds into a sense of identification rather than idealization often associated with fandom. Springsteen feels familiar rather than occupying a pedestal; fans feel that they know his beliefs, values, and emotional wrestling, which reflect their own lives because he is like them. He is a companion on a similar journey—they are "making sense" of life's challenges together. Although Springsteen's authenticity has been critiqued, and authenticity is a thorny topic (Cantrell, 2017), many fans see him as a "regular" guy to whom they can relate.

Friends and Family in a Community

Friends and family tend to exist within a community, be that a small group of friends, as expressed in the phrase "friend group," or embedded within a larger system, such as a workplace, neighborhood, town, extended family, ethnic group, military unit or veterans' gathering, or church. In a community, one can feel "we are in this together" and are there for each other. Fans expressed many striking ways in which community affected their relationship with Springsteen, often dovetailing with viewing him as friend or family. Being part of a devoted fan community is critical to the connection for some women. This includes friendships with fans and participating on listservs and fan site discussions, but especially the community at concerts. Springsteen's live performances with the E Street Band have reached legendary status in the rock world. Women's responses discern what they have meant to them emotionally and spiritually. The lens of group dynamics, the power of the group, and the charismatic leader frame these experiences.

A group is more than the sum of its parts, in that groups can take on a life of their own to become something palpable and more than a collection of individuals. Writers in psychology, such as Brabender et al. (2004), Rutan et al. (2014), and Yalom and Leszcz (2020) speak to that element of "groupness" in a way that is suggestive of how some women fans saw the group that collects around Springsteen, and groups have been noted in Springsteen's songs with their passion, containment, and commitment (Mangione, 2012). When in that group, fans are more than individuals in the company of others. They are part of a new structure and new community.

Further, although Springsteen hasn't always recorded or performed with the E Street Band, undeniable connectedness and camaraderie appear musically and personally when they work together. Numerous women noted the band's significance, particularly in concert, and how Springsteen's connection to the band adds to their attraction. What the band signifies to fans—the nightly message about friendship and connection—increases their loyalty and sense of familiarity, friendship, and family. The beginning and evolution of the band have been abiding themes in concert, and now with the loss of Clarence Clemons and Danny Federici, those losses have been memorialized onstage also.

So let's hear about friends, community, and family.

Are We Friends?

We never asked specifically about friendship, not wanting to narrow responses or validate our hunches; instead, we hoped to see what would emerge from fans. We asked about "relationship" as a more general and inclusive term, and central to so much that psychologists, especially clinical and social psychologists, think about, research, and live out: Do you think you have a relationship with Springsteen as a fan? How would you describe that relationship? Among the variety of responses, many women used "friend" to describe that relationship. From one- to two-word descriptions, to whole paragraphs, we heard about Springsteen as a friend or, in some cases, not a friend.

While a few women simply said "friend," typically there were qualifiers, such as "an untouched best friend," "an invisible friend," or "a long-time, trusted friend." The idea of friend creates the foundation that is then elaborated. Not knowing him personally didn't seem to faze fans. "We became friends almost 30 years ago though he doesn't know me personally." Others echoed this idea. "I sure do (have a relationship with him), he is a part of my life as a friend who gives me comfort, makes me happy and . . . he just belongs to me! Although I know, he doesn't know me and doesn't even know I exist." "He feels like a friend to me, and I feel like I know him." "I feel a special connection, like he's a friend who is always there."

The music is central, certainly, for all fans, and for some it is the heart. "Every new album is like a letter from a friend." Others sought to describe complexity. "In a way I consider him a friend that I need to hear from every day. Through his music I feel that I know his thoughts on life and his dreams. It's not a personal relationship since I don't know him personally. But it's definitely a love, but to the music first." Friendship intersects with performances, including a sense of reciprocity stated many times. "Sure, he is one of my very best friends I have never met. I am one (of millions) who make up the other half of the equation. Springsteen needs an audience—the audience needs Springsteen." "He has had a lifelong conversation with us fans. When I am at a live show I feel like I'm seeing old friends up there on stage that are putting everything they have out there on that night for us. Bruce, as the leader, has made sure that we know we are as important to him as he is to us." "He's like an old friend I get to hang out with whenever I see him in concert."

Reciprocity or mutuality is basic to friendship. A friendship can't be bought or bartered for or be one-sided. Giving and getting something of value must exist for both people. This fan expresses that sense well. "I think Bruce has a reciprocal relationship with his fans through his music and especially at his concerts. He expresses his deep appreciation of his fans through words and actions (I mean how many performers can actually put on such lengthy and exhausting shows night after night, year after year?!) If that's not love, what is?!"

NOT REALLY A FRIEND, BUT . . .

A few women differentiated "friend" from their relationship with Springsteen, as he was important but not in the friend category, or their friendship was solely with his music rather than with him. "I am a fan, not a friend, not anything more than a fan. I don't need to see him off stage, don't need to know about his family life, or his personal life." Another woman shared that clarity and saw value in distance from him but with a wish attached. "I think there's something special about getting to be a Springsteen fan, something that is enhanced by distance and the ability to put him on a pedestal. While I don't think anyone's perfect, I kind of like not knowing his human quirks, and admiring him as sort of superhuman. That's something that can only be achieved as a fan, not a friend. That being said, I'd be ecstatic at the opportunity to meet him."

Some women went in a different direction that wasn't mentioned often—the boyfriend or lover. "Hmmm not really. I have a lot of respect for him, he's handled his life admirably (he is my imaginary boyfriend ha-ha)." "I always say that I've had a 30-year one way love affair." Some fans described his normalcy and friendliness even if not a friend per se. "He has a relationship with all his fans when he's on stage. I am very aware that relationship is NOT a friendship, but when I have been lucky enough to meet him he's been amazingly friendly. But it's still a fan/star relationship. I love the stories of him turning up unannounced at folks' flats or on the Kerry campaign trail. That's proof he's a normal soul." The "relationship" with a performer, even one as seemingly "regular" as Bruce, is complicated, just as many relationships are sometimes hard to define.

For many women, the "friend" was Springsteen's music. "I most definitely have a relationship with his songs, his reaching out to help others. His music has been a friend, a lifting of spirit, a joyful experience, a map to self-discovery, a musical journey I carry with me through 40+ years. I am grateful for this relationship!" "My relationship with him is his music, and when I'm deep into an album, it's like being with my best friend."

WHAT MORE DOES THIS FRIENDSHIP MEAN?

The layering and complexity amplify as some women offered a richer description of friendship. Two themes stood out: Springsteen as the guy with whom you would like to share a beer and hang out, and Springsteen the intimate friend there for you over the years, no matter what, sharing your deepest thoughts and feelings. Let's have that beer first!

Share a Beer and Talk

The image here is striking in its understated sadness. "That Friend I have never shared a beer with." Another woman, who prefers wine, sees that act of sharing as an act of intimacy. "I am feeling very intimate to him. Sometimes I think, I know him. He is like a friend of my own. I could drink some glasses of wine and laugh with him and see a movie in the film theater." This woman recognizes that not everyone feels the way she does and defends him as one might a friend.

> I adore him. If there is something in the news about Bruce I absolutely watch it or click on the link. I follow his Twitter feed and Facebook account. Anytime you have a conversation about music I am always going to bring up Bruce; people ask about the best concert they have ever been to and I always talk about Bruce. Some people

> don't like Bruce, and they try to say he is arrogant or not a good singer or should stick to things he knows about, and I defend him. I don't know Bruce, but I feel like I do. He opens up to us in his music and is very open about himself. I completely respect his privacy and his family and am not a stalker type of person that unfortunately celebrities must deal with, but I really enjoy listening to his music and learning about him. I like to think that we could be friends and hang out and have a beer.

That sounds like elements of a friendship, perhaps shading into idealizing as one might with some friends.

In this final comment, a beer has turned into Christmas Eve dinner: "I know I do (have a relationship)! Ask anyone of my friends. They don't want me to drive, because they know that E-Street Station will be on my radio! I've been to many concerts, and just want to go to more and more and more! He's my friend, I wish I would run into him at beach or at the mall. I probably won't, but it doesn't hurt to hope! I'll gladly have Bruce over for Christmas Eve dinner!"

Going Deeper into Friendship

Beyond social elements of friendship, the camaraderie and hanging out together, many women voiced a psychological, emotional element to their perceived friendship with Springsteen. This included sharing in significant emotional and spiritual life experiences together, and the value of someone always being there for you. The consistency over time is sustained despite long stretches between concerts and even between albums, like friends who live across the globe and only visit occasionally. Friends are seen as critically important, resonating, helping, and reflecting each other along the way, sharing in each other's growth and development. They are doing this with a sense of equality and reciprocity, as a "friend" rather than teacher, guide, or therapist, as explored in the next chapters.

This fan describes how Springsteen is there for her. "The raunchiness of his voice. The way he is able to express my own emotions much better than I can and so helps me to understand life and cope with its ups and downs I feel like he is a friend who I can always turn to, and his music has been like therapy in difficult times. When I see him come on stage at a live show I have to fight back the tears as I love him and his music so." Finding a kindred spirit is common in thinking about close friends. "I found a kindred spirit about searching for the meaning of life . . . the country. . . . the world . . . how it affects all of us as one and together. With *The Rising* album it showed me we are connected and we all need each other." Springsteen is there in tough times. "I think of him as a friend. I can always turn to his music to see me through whatever life throws at me."

Facets of friendship are expressed briefly but intimately here. "I feel like he is my best friend who speaks for me and knows what I am thinking and expresses his music the way I feel inside—I often act like he is my best kept secret to family and friends who don't 'get it'—their loss." "I feel connected to him as a human being, as a friend I can turn to in hard and happy times, and as my favorite performer ever." "As a friend. He's always been there for me—his music has amped up my happiness and eased my pains. What more can you ask of a friend?" "Bruce has always felt much like a long-time, trusted friend: there as a guiding force and to lend support when times are tough and also there to help share in and spread the joy when life is good!" "His music is like a friend, a steady crutch to lean on." "I admire him as an artist, and I feel a deep connection with him. He's part of my life since I was 10, he's like an old time friend or family for me. His voice is so familiar that it's comforting in the hard times, it warms my heart when I'm sad and make me scream with joy when I'm happy. He (his music) is always here for me. His love never let me down and never will."

These comments don't describe casual friends, but ones with a history of trust and caring, present during challenging times and, through his work, sharing his own challenging times. One fan delves into this multilayered experience in detail.

> An interesting question. At times I think of Bruce as a friend I don't know, he always has words to suit my mood, to buoy me up when I'm

> feeling down, to remind how good my life really is, that really compared to so many others I have it easy. He reminds me that I am not alone, there are others out there and God too should I choose to turn to him. At times his voice is like a virtual hug, at others a stiff reprimand or a gentle coaxing, and then there is the music that encourages you to sway, to dance, to pump your arms in the air, to rock and roll and live life.

Even a reprimand is accepted from this friend. This fan wrote in symbolism that could come from Springsteen lyrics. "At times he's my friend, my anchor, my brother, my angel. My relationship just gets deeper and deeper and more meaningful."

Longevity was central to the relationship for many fans. "When I see him in concert it's like visiting an old friend. Now when I go and he plays music from years ago I recall what was going on in my life when the music came out, or when I saw it performed years earlier. It's like a high school reunion, or 'this is your life' retrospective." This long-term friendship can survive over distance. "Bruce, his music, the E Street Band are part of my everyday life since 1984. It's like he is a distant friend who you never see, but is always there for you." "Like that friend that you only hear from once in a while. But, when you hear from them you don't want them to go away. However, when they go away you know that something new will be coming you just don't know when or how." This can happen in life depending on where and how one lives, with friends going away, the uncertainty of it all, especially in our mobile world. However, Springsteen feels like a friend they can count on to return.

THE COMPLEXITY OF FRIENDSHIP

Many fans acknowledge how complicated having such a meaningful relationship with someone they had never met can be, commenting on whether it mirrored, or didn't, the reciprocity of other friendships.

> I feel like he is my friend, my best friend actually, the one I can always rely on. Of course, it is a one-way friendship, but there are ways in which I can give back. I hope that, one day, I can thank him. He is

> my hero, my role model. I really think he is beautiful and hot, but my "relationship" with him isn't based on that, just in the ways he moves me and makes me understand the world I live in. I could say he is a father figure, but finding a father just as beautiful and sexy as I think he is, is just too creepy. He is Bruce and that is all I need. My friend, Bruce.

Despite abundant Springsteen lyrics, sometimes another rock musician helps define the relationship.

> It's a give and take. Like all good friends you need to be honest with each other. You need not share his politics, like every song, agree with a marketing decision, and he gets that. And sometimes we don't want to hear what he has to say, but he's going to say it anyway. His fans are just as much a part of the show as he is and he "proves it all night." (Can't believe I forgot that on my list of favorites. I used to rehearse that song waiting for the bus in case he ever sang it to me.) But he is always there when you need him and knows just what to say. (To quote Bob Seger . . . he's your oldest and your best friend. If you need him, he'll be there again.)

For someone easily idealized, this woman can forthrightly say she doesn't always agree with him yet the friendship continues.

This next woman speaks soberly yet could end up tongue-tied if she and Springsteen ever met. "He is a sort of hero, a constant and consistent feature in my life. I can trust him to produce music that I will (generally) like and want to listen to and to entertain and provide good value in concert. I just get the impression he is a good man overall and like a 'friend'—I feel I 'know' him (but not that he knows me, obviously), though I suspect if I ever got to meet him, I would be tongue-tied and gibbering." Self-reflection about the reality of the "friendship" contextualizes it. "I think of him as the guiding force in my life. I think of him as Bruce, so obviously I think of him as a close, important friend. But, I don't think I'm delusional about it. I understand that this relationship is one-sided."

Springsteen has echoed the complexity, the give-and-take, the long-term nature of friends, and their immense value. When asked about friendship at Boston College, he replied, "They've enriched my life in ways that I couldn't have imagined. In any friendship, you're going to fight, you're going to love, you're going to argue, you're going to hate this about the other guy, he's going to hate this about you. But my band and I, we held the value of our friendship higher than of our personal grievances or disputes. So 45 years in, now we receive the grace and the benediction that lifelong friendships can bestow upon you" (Springsteen Boston College, 2020). While women fans' "friendship" with Springsteen may not include all those interactions and feelings, his views speak to the heart of friendship that many fans understood.

Finally, this fan spoke about connection and offered a moment of laughter with her comparison, laughter that baby boomers reading this book might share. "I do in the sense that he makes and performs music, and I listen to it and attend his shows. Bruce has stated that he thrives on the energy of his audiences, and in some sense, I contribute to that. But I don't feel there is an individual relationship. But, as mentioned above, the first few times I saw him, I left feeling as if he was my friend, as if we had some kind of personal connection. The only other person that made me feel that way in my life was Captain Kangaroo!!:)"

Community: What Brings People Together?

About ten years ago Lorraine was contacted by a young undergraduate researcher who was writing a music and modern life course paper on fans that had long, robust relationships with bands, with an ongoing community of sorts. Of course, the contact with Lorraine was as a Springsteen fan, suggested by one of the student's faculty members, but clearly other bands have had strong, committed communities of fans. Her unpublished work included fans of Bob Dylan, Grateful Dead, and Phish (Swirsky, 2014). She situated her work within the context of modern American culture that, overall, has tended to become more secularized over the years and less focused on community, something written about extensively by Robert Putnam (2001, 2020). That framework is relevant here in looking at the meaning of the fan community, another aspect of friendship, for women fans of Springsteen.

It seems that a layer of love, intensity, and commitment gets transferred to the fan community, especially at concerts, where feelings radiate out and gather up everyone in the room. In some cases, the fan friendship and community mediate the relationship with Springsteen, and in others they supersede the relationship. In an age when many traditional groups may not feel as fulfilling as in the past, groups that resonate deeply can take on greater meaning. Clinical, social, and organizational psychologists have extensively studied groups encountered in life as well as psychotherapy groups, looking at how groups function, group dynamics, development, influence on members, and leadership issues and tasks, typically emphasizing the importance of relationships within groups (Parks & Tasca, 2020; Rutan et al., 2014; Tasca et al., 2020; Yalom & Leszcz, 2020). Although Springsteen audiences are not therapy groups, five "therapeutic factors" or conditions that support the goals in group therapy (Yalom & Leszcz, 2020) have relevance here: instillation of hope, universality, development of socializing techniques, imitative behavior, and group cohesiveness. Instillation of hope begins even before the actual group begins; "universality" refers to realizing that others share one's experience and feelings; "development of socializing techniques" refers to social skills and social behaviors; "imitative behavior" refers to members learning from watching and listening to others; and "group cohesiveness" refers to a complex factor defined as "the attractiveness of a group for its members" (p. 76). These factors are basic to the functioning of a psychotherapy group and, we would suggest, have relevance to many women's experience of the Springsteen fan community.

Also important in group therapy research and clinical writing (Brabender et al., 2004; Yalom & Leszcz, 2020) is the "group-as-a-whole," noting that the group exists as a group, not just as a collection of individuals (a concept originally noted by Wilfred Bion from the Tavistock tradition in England). The group, as an entity, can feel compelling to members, echoing what some Springsteen fans say about their fan community. The question of powerful or charismatic leaders has been addressed over decades by psychologists (Ashkanasy & Tse, 2000; Jones, 2001; Riggio & Riggio, 2008; Rutan & Rice, 1981). While positive and negative details of such leaders are beyond the scope of this chapter, Springsteen seems to possess some attributes of a charismatic leader, such as abundant personal energy and the interactional encounter between leaders and followers.

A few fans noted the lack of a direct relationship with Springsteen but a strong relationship with fans. "I'm certainly a fan. And I have a strong relation to his music. The fan forum in our country has brought me together with many other people thinking the same way. I've also met many great people from all around the world on gigs. I've found new friends, whom I otherwise never met. But a relation to Springsteen? I don't think so. I love his voice and music, but actually I don't know the man behind it, just the music and the picture I've built up myself." For one woman, the fan community had become the driver of her fandom. "My relationship with him really only exists in the presence of other fans, especially at a show. Even when I listen to him by myself, I just long to be in an arena with my closest friends who are fans." Feeling that someone is a decent human being owing to their fandom forms a foundation for community-building. "I don't think that I have a special individual relationship with him, any more than we all have our special individual relationship with him. Does that make sense? I've built friendships from a base of us both being Springsteen fans—it gives a solid and commonly understood starting point about the kind of people we are. It's a bit like already having a mutual friend to recommend you as a decent human being to another decent human being."

Not having a sense of a direct relationship with Springsteen doesn't seem to lessen the intensity of fandom and community. "Ha! I think that Bruce gives to his fans every time he steps on stage. He's never disappointed. Would he recognize me?! Not likely. I have relationships because of him . . . friends and family that share the passion. We've built memories together." "I don't make the mistake of thinking I have a relationship with him, per se. But I do see myself as a proud member of the E Street Family and it's a relationship I take seriously. I will be thrilled to be an audience member as long as Bruce is willing to play. I support his causes and bring food to support food banks, which he has at his shows." Such responses illuminate the community created by fandom, the coming together from many backgrounds around the world. This is not just about one man in the spotlight, but a cascade of connections.

MULTILEVELS OF COMMUNITY: IT GOES WAY BEYOND HIM

Some fans see their relationship to Springsteen and the fan community going further than concerts or music. Being Bruce fans can be a basis for friendship. "I think his fans are important for him and so I feel important. I feel a connection to other fans and so to him. I knew people and are friends with them only because they are also Bruce fans." Fan communities can take on a life of their own, including philanthropy and caretaking. "Springsteen fans are a great community. We have made friends all over the world through his music and 'we take care of our own,' raise money for charities, etc." "The connection to his music, his lyrics, the powerful energy of his live shows, and the lucky experiences where I have met and talked to him are all contributions to the relationship I have with him as a fan. I have met so many people, made lifelong friendships, and have been part of organizations that I would never have experienced without being a fan of his, so it goes way beyond just him." "I have been on E Street Radio and involved in the Bruce fan community, so my relationship is with Bruce and the E Street community. I have donated tickets to fans in need and met many friends through Bruce Springsteen. I don't know him, but he joins people in spirit." In thinking of how few places people get to be "joined in spirit" it makes this all the more important. Societal-level losses in people's worlds still need to be filled with opportunities for caring for others, joining together in tasks, and a sense of solidarity or kinship.

Much of the sense of community comes from the shows themselves, and for this woman, proximity to the stage is important. "Honestly I think he might recognize me from being way down in front for over fifty shows. I have also become friends with some of his fans. It's amazing how bonding over a rockstar can create lasting ties." Family, friends, and the energizing idea of a sisterhood can figure into the experience. "Not only do I think I have a relationship with Springsteen as a fan, but so do my friends and family who aren't fans. Whenever they see something published about Bruce, they make sure to send it to me. (As if I didn't already know/hear it about it!) I also believe I have a relationship with the other members of the E Street Nation. I've made many friends at concerts and the online community. It's a sisterhood!" "It's like he's my one very dear family member who's always there when I need him. As a fan I think also Bruce and the fans together we are like one big family. Most of us respect him for what he is, and when you meet another fan, you don't have to explain why his music is so important in your everyday life and what you feel. Another fan just knows it. It's awesome feeling to feel that togetherness all over the world, for example, in Facebook with some nice fans and like to have some 'extra sister' for me;)" Another fan emphasizes the sustaining relationships.

> It's hard to explain because this is the rare band that you can get up close and personal. I've met Bruce a few times as well as members of the band, and it does feel like you know them on the same level of a friend from school or work. They really are just like you and me, and they never talk down to you. The bigger relationship is with the women I have met and bonded with over the years. We rarely see each other outside of a Bruce tour since we all live in various parts of the country, but they are like sisters to me and I wouldn't have these relationships if not for the community that is Bruce.

Images of sisterhood are notable given the critical commentary on Springsteen and women described in chapter 3. Gender, again, does not constrain women in their relationships with him or the community; rather, it can create bonds between women identifying with a sisterhood of fans.

Two fans describe how community can be helpful. "I felt old and in a funk. Went to a concert and felt a part of something huge." "Driving home after a bad day at work—put Bruce on—by the time I get home—I'm out of here to win! I have a huge crowd of Bruce mates—tramps—who meet up in the pit queues every tour, every gig, and they are like family. E Street nation. We support each other." Immersing in the community and in "something huge" feels strong and transcendent, even if all go their separate ways as the concert ends.

The complexity of responses is vivid and layered.

> That is a very interesting, very thought provoking question, and I recently had a conversation sort of about this topic with another Bruce fan. I do believe that the Springsteen/fan "relationship" is a bit different than most artists. I suppose some other artists have fan bases that are passionate about them, and there may even be some fans that are similar to Springsteen fans; I don't know, because Bruce is the only artist I really feel this way about. My relationship to Bruce is about his art and his music, which are great gifts that I am privileged to receive (although yes, I do pay for them), but it's also about this community, this group that surrounds him. While I don't expect ever to meet Bruce, I've met so many wonderful Bruce fans, and he is the lodestone that brings us all together. That's very important, and as I've said, it's a role that he doesn't seem to be aware of, even though I think he has to be. At the same time, I don't feel like Bruce "owes" me, or any other fan, anything. If we get something from him besides his art, it's a bonus. He doesn't have a responsibility to be a moral leader or a "great father."

Springsteen's words at Boston College again describe how the inner world, friends and partners, and community come together in a way articulated by fans here. "Express your emotions, share your inner life and be emotionally generous with your friends and your partner. All of these things will make you a stronger presence in your community and will allow you to give more of yourself freely and lovingly" (Springsteen Boston College, 2020).

Bruce as Family

As we saw with family involvement in women's introductions to Springsteen, family is often mentioned regarding the relationship fans feel with Springsteen. For some, their family is immersed in Springsteen, introducing them to his music or going to shows together, or may share certain attributes, such as working class or New Jersey roots, or Springsteen himself feels like a close family member. There is both an energy and a casualness to descriptions of familial relationship with Springsteen. "His fans are like family." "When you've grown up with someone for nearly 40 years, they're family and as crazy as that sounds when that someone is Bruce Springsteen, I'd say that's very true. Yes I'm a fan, a proud fan, he's an amazing artist and human who has loved his fans for all this time and has given us everything he has night after night after night! But he also just auctioned off a lasagna dinner at his home so as you can see he's family." "After 100 shows he and the band seem like family. When I was backstage with them once, I felt so comfortable, they are such a bunch of down to earth people, no one is jaded." "A fan will always have a relationship with the 'Rockstar' but I can't describe it, Bruce has always been in my life he is like a family member." "I have relationship when he's on tour, most definitely. We are treated as his family and guests during his concerts. Not sure that there is any kind of relationship outside of that." "He is like one of the family. I am proud of him."

For this woman, the family aspect spans years and hits life's highlights, the sacramental moments, as one might hope for in family.

> I definitely have a relationship with Springsteen as a fan. He is like a part of my family only he doesn't know it. He was at my wedding, at the birth of my two children in the delivery room, and as I have mentioned, he will be at my funeral in song. I have seen him in bars, small concert halls, and stadiums. I've been in nosebleed seats as well as the

> pit and have no regrets. I get a lot more from him than he gets from me, and I hope someday to get to tell him that in person.

Yet also the sorrow that families share, including losses from childhood, are described.

> As I touched on a couple of times, he is my family. I'm from Philly. I can put on his music and remember my childhood at the Jersey Shore (from the roads to the beach itself). Both of my parents have passed and his songs bring back the happy times we were together. I saw him reschedule for Halloween because of Sandy 2012. I just wanted to go up and hug them all. I saw the pictures on the TV and was glued for any type of information. I saw places I went as a child. I was feeling his and the band's sadness. It was that we were all were trying to grieve over it. I felt not just a fan that night, but more like family. He did "Jersey Girl" that night, which he dedicated to his Jersey Girl, the State of New Jersey. I cried through that song. He sang it straight from the heart. At the end of the song, he thanked each member (I was in the front pit and saw him do it).

That sounds like "family" for this fan, and many others, as family holds and contains the people within it, honoring history and losses. Springsteen is there for celebrations and mourning, just as families should be.

BRUCE THE FATHER

When asked about a relationship with Springsteen, these younger fans from Europe said it directly. "He is my teacher and my second father." "I see him as a father, as an example of the values I want to have in my own life." Some were hesitant about whether a relationship exists, but the father connection was strong. "Not really a personal one, but I associate him as a father figure through his music because I discovered his music through my dad." For this woman, he mirrors something significant about her relationship with her own father, who is there but not there, as can happen. "It's similar to my relationship with my father—there isn't one, but he is in the background of everything in my life." Others struggled to define the role, whether as father or uncle, but certainly a respected role in their life. "I think we have relationship. I've mentioned a few times now that I consider him to be a father figure. Or, maybe an uncle. It's definitely a familial feeling—he's someone I would go to for advice or to just listen to his stories."

One woman's response linked Springsteen to her father, now gone, hearkening to his ability to look beyond this world and life, as seen in certain songs and the Catholicism noted by Cullen (2005). "His lyrics are so powerful and meaningful to me and I have a connection with my dead father through Bruce. The relationship is on an emotional level, no matter what I am feeling Bruce has felt it too and wrote it into a song, I can play that song and feel understood and express my emotion. Even if he wrote the song 30 years ago, it still resonates with me now."

BRUCE THE BROTHER

The image of "brother" stood out in some responses. "Like an older brother you would enjoy hanging out with." "I've been going to see him from the very beginning. And I'm just so proud of him. In the beginning I was rooting for him to be successful like you would for your brother or your cousin." For this woman it is complicated by the relationship with her own brother and includes connecting around their Italian backgrounds. "Springsteen replaces the relationship I would like to have with my brother and I often dream that I am at Bruce's shows in intimate clubs or that he is in my mother's house making meatballs on Sunday morning (Italian heritage and all that). His guitar is always slung across his back in her home."

It can be hard to define exactly which role Springsteen inhabits at any given time. The relationship is multifaceted and fluctuating. "He is my parent, brother, teacher, mentor and lover depending on my needs LOL. His songs comfort me."

> Well, I did meet him once, briefly, after a concert. Kissed his cheek! He's talked about his career being a long conversation with his fans, and of all of us, rock musicians and listeners, and I think he

> especially meant those of us who are "baby boomers," being "brothers and sisters" having grown up listening to the same music, having the same relationship with the music and thus with each other in a sense. And he seems to really try to continue that sort of connection—we're not just faces who show up at concerts, or who plunk down our credit cards for the new albums. If he and I ever got to talking we could probably have long conversations about music and politics and books (there are some interesting overlaps between what I read and the things he mentioned in the *New York Times* Book Review Q and A). and growing up in the sixties and Catholicism and baseball. And I still want to marry him. Which is a different kind of relationship than you probably meant. And one that odds are very long against ever happening. (Especially since he and Patti seem to be very happy, and I am happy for them.)

While she probably won't get her wish fulfilled, she has plenty of other roles and niches for him on which she can rely.

WHAT FAMILY CAN MEAN

A few women elaborated further, expanding the family image and exploring the impact of Springsteen as a "family member."

> I have always felt a strong relationship with Bruce. I would describe it as a close family member who has been in my life as far back as I can remember but I have never met him. Without him and his music I don't think my life would be the same. But I know one thing for sure, I wouldn't want to live my life without him or his music. He has a way of bringing people together. You find yourself at his show with your arm around someone that you don't even know, he brings the biggest smile to everyone's face. All of your problems are gone for 3 1/2 hours. And no amount of money in the world or no drug in the world can make you feel that way but Bruce.

This fan summed up much of this discussion on Springsteen as a close companion. "I'm listening to his songs since I'm 12, his music was always there, I met my husband because he is a Springsteen fan, too. Some of my best friends are Springsteen fans. So, yes, he and his music have a big influence on my life. If I'm feeling sad I'm listening often to his songs. And being in concert, the lights go out and he comes on the stage—it feels like coming home, at this second I exactly know why I'm on earth and that this is my family: The E-Street Band and Bruce."

Family life is typically complicated and multifaceted. Springsteen as family member can be an extension of one's original family, often reflecting the best of the family experience, and can also stand in for more troubling relationships in real families. Friendships, too, have layers of meaning and exist in many forms, some of them atypical as described here with a rock star whom one has never met. Underlying both categorizations is the sense of an intensely relational foundation, one that is not perfect, not always consistent, not everything one would want, but real and human, which may feel strange to say about a relationship with a mostly unmet rock star. We know from the literature and from our own experiences that friends and family, especially supportive ones, are important for people's lives, health, and well-being, through good times and hard times. Sometimes, for fans, friend and family communities extend to a beloved musician.

On the Road Together

All those early songs about cars, taking to the road, and driving into the darkness echo a journey that many women have taken with Springsteen and his songs. Sometimes that journey feels like two friends, traveling down the road together, and sometimes it feels more like a family, off on a summer vacation with all the fun and squabbles that happen in families. There is a sense of comfort and familiarity with Springsteen, who even before his much-acclaimed autobiography told of his life, his struggles, the dumb things he did, the disappointments and hurts from others, his failures and broken dreams. He was speaking of his humanity each and every night on tour and on each and every album. In doing that, in opening up to fans, he was inviting the fan community to join him in exploring their own stories, lives, sorrows, and conflicts, their ways of creating meaning in their lives. The resonance was palpable. Fans felt it and told us about it. We are reminded of Springsteen's last words in his prepared remarks to Boston College students. "Love is all there is. Love your neighbors, love your friends, love your family, love your partner, and love yourself" (Springsteen Boston College, 2020).

Lorraine, a few nights before her wedding, includes Bruce in a celebration with friends. Courtesy Thea Litsios.

The original Bruce fan who opened up the world to Lorraine. Courtesy Thea Litsios.

A big night in Syracuse with friends, family, and, of course, Bruce, on our way to the concert. Courtesy Lorraine Mangione.

Donna and her oldest friend—who accompanied her to her first Bruce show back in 1981—reunite at *Springsteen on Broadway*. Courtesy Donna Luff.

Donna meeting Bruce at a book signing for the release of his memoir, *Born to Run*. Courtesy Donna Luff.

CHAPTER 5

Teacher of Life, Guide of the Spirit

His music has helped me out, and his shows have changed my life. As a fan, I feel him reaching out to me to inspire those changes, and I'm respectful of the craft he puts into doing that and grateful that I could be receptive. It's kind of like a teacher–disciple relationship, but a lot of the "teaching" comes from holding up different ways of being and letting me reflect on what all those might be like to live through.

WHAT IS A TEACHER, mentor, guide, or spiritual guide? Sometimes in life you need to branch out from family and friends and find a mentor or teacher to help you along, to get you unstuck, to show you possibilities, to connect you to yourself or to others who can help in your journey. We find mentors and teachers in assorted places, including school, public speakers and writers, neighborhoods and communities, work, religious settings, books, and works of art. People whom one does not know personally can be teachers. Some people can single out a person instrumental in helping them become who they are, who has walked the path as a companion or cleared the path ahead by exposing treacherous pitfalls or matchless opportunities. Such people are teachers or guides, even without an official title. For many Springsteen fans, their relationship with him is different from that with a friend or family member, because the teacher or guide is a few steps "ahead" on the path. Springsteen serves in this role, steps ahead on the journey of life, in many women fans' experiences.

Teachers or guides have different roles and are described in various ways. Mentorship can be considered a more specialized form of teaching or guiding, as has been discussed and studied in the business world and in academic professions (Johnson, 2014; Johnson &

Ridley, 2008). Brad Johnson (2014) offers a definition that suggests how rich such relationships can be. "In academic and clinical training settings, mentoring has generally been defined as a dynamic, reciprocal, personal relationship in which a more experienced trainer (mentor) acts as a guide, role model, teacher, and sponsor of a less experienced trainee (protégé) (Johnson, 2002; Johnson & Ridley, 2008)" (p. 4). Those roles weave through this chapter on Springsteen as teacher or guide.

Mentorship is felt to be critically important to becoming a psychologist, maybe because it helps someone enter a profession that is profoundly personal, so that "Human Touch" is paramount. In a research article, one of the authors and her colleagues (Mangione et al., 2018) explored mentors in graduate programs in psychology, looking to broaden the traditional definition and role of mentors. Several descriptors of mentors emerged that could be relevant to Springsteen's perceived role as a mentor, keeping in mind the obvious one-sidedness to the Springsteen as mentor concept. For example, in describing interpersonal relatedness in mentorship, an emotional component, sense of connection, and openness and communication were noted. The category of academics included the mentor being invested in the growth of the mentee, and professional development included guidance and support. While the content of academic psychology and rock and roll differs, the actions and qualities can feel similar. Within the category of general mentor traits are themes of imparting knowledge that include wisdom and role-modeling, acting as a connector to others, being experienced and knowledgeable in their fields, and acting respectfully and reliably. Although students in psychology and women fans of a rock star are two disparate worlds, similarities in interpersonal aspects, emotional connectedness, help with specifics, the expertise of the mentor, and respect and reliability can speak to both worlds when one is exploring the views of women fans. A relationship with a mentor, teacher, or guide is perceived as a relationship that includes sharing of knowledge, wisdom, and caring.

Most people need help in navigating the world of love, work, what to do in life, and where and how to find meaning. Teachers offer support and encouragement and can bolster one's courage. They are ahead of us, but not necessarily on a pedestal or idealized. The best ones show their "mistakes" and their challenges. There can be a sense of egalitarianism, because the best teachers don't pontificate. They can be especially helpful at "turning points" in one's life, decision points where the path can become foggy. Their wisdom, whether they are 2 steps or 200 steps ahead, can help illuminate through fog. Although teaching psychology and Springsteen as a teacher may seem worlds apart, comments from research on excellent teachers in psychology echo some of what fans experienced. When psychology professors who had received awards for teaching were asked what constitutes an excellent teacher, the following domains were among those endorsed (Keeley et al., 2016, p. 177): enthusiastic about teaching and the topic, strives to be a better teacher, creative and interesting, knowledgeable about the subject matter, approachable/personable, effective communicator, respectful, encourages and cares for students, prepared, rapport, promotes critical thinking/intellectually stimulating. Such relational dynamics and other attributes feel relevant when thinking about Springsteen as teacher.

In Joseph Campbell's (1949/1973) journey of the hero, typically the hero is helped along the way to avoid or to work through obstacles and challenges. It is both a physical journey and a journey of the inner world, the heart and soul, and helpers are critical to its success. Campbell's ideas are echoed in many women's responses relating their journey to find themselves and figure out their lives, meaning, and purpose, with Springsteen as a helper.

Identity and Identification: Who Is Bruce? Who Am I?

We live in a world in which roles and identities are increasingly not fixed, no longer handed down from generation to generation; rather, each must create a sense of who they are and what they might become in life. People evolve their own narratives of who they are, why they are here, and what is important in their lives, and they try to live by those narratives. Writers in psychology speak of the foundational importance of constructing or creating a sense of self, an identity. Prominent psychoanalytic practitioner and author Nancy McWilliams (1999) traced the history, starting in the mid-twentieth century, of a greater concern with identity development, and how it may have differed between more traditional societies and more contemporary ones. Now searching for identity may occur in cultures across the globe: "Developing a solid sense of identity has become an unavoidable aspect of contemporary psychological life. Even people growing up in the world's remaining tribal cultures are no longer shielded from technology and its mixed emotional blessings; the identity struggles of those in cutting-edge, cyberspace-savvy 'developed' cultures are now shared by adolescents and young adults in the farthest-flung outposts of 'civilization'" (p. 17).

Since McWilliams's work in the late 1990s, the need to construct an identity has likely increased. In the twenty-first century, developmental psychologist Jeffrey Arnett (2006) pioneered the concept of "emerging adulthood" to describe a critical part of human development, expanding a previous notion that identity was worked through solely in adolescence. The concept of emerging adulthood captures an understanding of identity formation as an ongoing task from the late teens into the later twenties, and as a developmental period that has emerged in the last few decades as our world and economic systems have changed.

People often look for role models when growing up or even later in life, though that overused phrase doesn't truly capture their significance in construction of our sense of self and what it means to see our own deepest yearnings and self mirrored in another person. For many women, one of the role models is Bruce Springsteen, although it might be more accurate to say that Springsteen's music captivated them, and the psychological processes, such as identification, followed from that. Women didn't necessarily know they were looking to create an identity on hearing the first strains of "Jungleland" or "Hungry Heart"! Many women fans shared a strong sense of identification with Springsteen, who has been important in constructing their story of themselves, identity development, and psychological/

spiritual expedition. Some women see Springsteen as mirroring their own struggles, including how they might grow through them.

The *autobiographical author* approach to meaning and identity development, conceptualized by narrative psychologist McAdams (2013), also helps in thinking about fan relationships. McAdams emphasizes the importance of the stories that people live by and of authoring one's own sense of meaning and identity throughout the life span. This approach to life goes further than what he calls the actor and the motivated agent approaches, in a way that constructs individualized meaning. His description of what happens in emerging adulthood, the span in which many fans get to know Springsteen well, speaks to the growth process.

> In emerging adulthood, the self becomes an autobiographical author who works to construct, refine, revise, and live according to an internalized and evolving life story, or what psychologists now often call a *narrative identity* (McAdams, 1985; McLean, Pasupathi, & Pals, 2007; Singer, 2004). Narrative identity adds a new layer of meaning to life. Through the life story the author is able to explain, for the self and for others, how he or she came to be and where life may be going in the future, integrating the reconstructed past, experienced present, and imagined future into a personal narrative that gives new meaning and purpose to life. (p. 180)

This developmental process may be occurring with some women fans, and it continues on in life, encompassing culture too.

> People become autobiographical authors at this time in life, as they move beyond social roles and personal goals to articulate a broad and integrative story of the self. Who am I? How did I come to be who I am? What am I meant to do and to be in life? It takes a story to answer big questions like these, a story that provides a full temporal orientation for the self—encompassing the reconstructed past, experienced present, and imagined future. The life stories that autobiographical authors construct to make meaning in life are contoured by culture. Indeed, culture provides the canonical set of images, themes, plots, and character from which people draw in fashioning their own unique

> stories—stories that say as much about cultural meanings as they do about the meaning of the author's life itself. (pp. 185–186)

This view of growth and meaning accords with the ongoing construction of self, helped by Springsteen and his work, described by some women fans. The development of "stories" has been a major part of Springsteen's work for decades, described as part of the American realist tradition (Santelli, 2012, p. 9). In fact, he can sometimes sound like a narrative psychologist, emphasizing the whole arc of his stories, from beginning to end, whether in a single song, thematic album, or live show. His stories weave into fans' creating and unfolding of who they are. Stories and identity both have an internal and an interpersonal orientation: facing inward and facing outward are essential to identity development. Springsteen has been critical in constructing that story of themselves and their lives, their sense of identity.

Springsteen as Teacher/Mentor/Guide

While one respondent answered our question about a relationship with Springsteen simply, with "Teacher and student," other answers were more complex. But the theme of teacher/mentor/guide carried through women's responses to several different survey questions and reminds us of Springsteen referring to the learning one could get from a 3-minute record rather than in school. One fan, a writer herself, had a lot to say about this relationship and the way it has played out for her:

> I think fans do have a relationship with any idol—just not a "typical" one. I won't use the word normal—hell what is normal even in a typical situation? If you are asking do I think I know him—not at all. But I know the part he presents to us—the part that offers me something in my life—I'm a writer and he inspired me to pursue that career so I see him a little like a teacher/mentor. His music and lyrics give me a lot of joy. A relationship implies a two-way street, so what does he get from it? He gets the thing he gets from all of us—he gets the pleasure of knowing his music is loved, he clearly loves performing and with-

out fans there is nobody to perform to. So yeah, it's a relationship—simply not a typical one.

Moral learning figures into descriptions of the help that Springsteen has given. "Not sure specifically. But it's a foundational work in my personal sense of ethics and morality, so one could say in all ways. Some people get a sense of right and wrong from their parents, or religious texts, or scholars, but for me the primary teacher was Mr. Springsteen." "Bruce's music brought me together with my husband, for which I am eternally grateful. Our two daughters are also devoted fans, and Bruce—in some ways—has provided the moral compass that binds us together as a family. Some of our most wonderful memories are seeing Bruce together." Growth and development, which seem natural to a teacher–student relationship, runs through several responses. "Everything, every emotion I ever needed to know/feel came from Bruce and his music. A profound teacher." "Because I am the same age as Bruce, I have liked seeing him grow into the conscious man I believe he is. He is a teacher in many ways and wants us to 'get' his lyrics. They are as important now as when he was younger. His evolution as a great songwriter is another great gift. He grows so we get to grow also." Growing together and growing up together builds a relationship. The sustained companionship that many fans feel might disintegrate if they were not progressing along a mutual path.

Although "teacher" is not always used in responses about Springsteen's music helping, many answers described his way of enlightening listeners. For some, he opened their eyes to more marginalized groups of people. "His music explores different walks of humanity in a nonjudgmental way that helps me relate to folks I know: 'Then I got Mary pregnant and that was all she wrote.'" "*Tom Joad* album made me realise the plight of some Americans re drugs, immigration." Certain songs seek to give voice to the voiceless, and these women heard.

The word "mentor" stood out in a few responses, reflecting views of a mentor as taking special interest in the mentee, helping to shape them and move them forward in life or career. For this woman, the relationship includes caretaking. "As a fan yes. He is my comfort, mentor." Another woman is grateful for what he gives her as a mentor: "I see Bruce as representing my voice in ways that I can't—through his songs he expresses what I think and feel. He gives me new eyes/vision to see myself, and that's pretty powerful, I think. I see him as a mentor since I admire the work he does for causes that he cares about, and that inspires me. I respect the loyalty he demonstrates to his fans. I am loyal right back at him." Perhaps we all need someone to express that which we can't, someone a bit more articulate or savvy.

A guide feels different than a teacher or mentor, conjuring up images of movement and geography—maybe even a road trip—venturing into new territory. This woman speaks directly to that guidance: "His music has guided me, accompanied me in my 'life journey,' spoken to me honestly about things that are important (life, work, family), comforted me, helped me to understand my life, and feel less alone. When I see him live, I feel there is sometimes a more personal connection, but I don't have a relationship with, or really know Bruce, the person, except through what he communicates in his music."

Guidance comes in different ways and addresses varied content. "Helped me develop my voice, shaped my integrity, guided me to live by my word, to share my wealth in teaching young minds, to keep on keepin' on!! Persevere!" "It has always helped me. Guided me through hard times, lifted me up so many times I cannot count. His music has always been by my side, a companion." Springsteen helps with developing an autobiographical author voice with meaning and a sense of self. To inspire seems to move even further. "I think that we all—men, women, Black, White, etc.—all have struggles & are in need of inspiration & guidance. His music always provides that." This fan is quite sure that Springsteen's music helped her and boosted her confidence. "Absolutely, it guides me as to who I have become. After being chosen to dance (by Springsteen), I questioned people if they organized it for me, silly I know but I could not believe that my luck gave me the dance. After being chosen now twice I believe I can achieve anything, and it has helped guide me into a new job."

Teacher, mentor, guide, such significant relationships create a force for growth in people's lives. In fans' responses, we hear change, even transformation of the sense of self and identity, supported by Springsteen's work. In summing up this section, this voice speaks clearly. "My life is more enriched because of his music. His music guides me and has opened my heart, my brain, and my soul." We now look further into the spirit and the soul.

A Guide to Where? For Some, It's a Spiritual Place

The words "spiritual," "spirituality," "religion," and "religious" conjure up variations on a theme. They are not exact, precise words, but rather point the way to something usually ineffable, often profound, sometimes with more structure and content, sometimes with less. While we don't know exactly how these words are used or understood by participants, they point to something meaningful and significant in their lives and themselves, even assuming a range of usages and subtleties. Spiritual and religious struggles, pilgrimages, and seeking have been a part of human history and the human condition for centuries, and the dominant Western traditions are filled with religious stories, images, symbols, and archetypes. The importance of a spiritual dimension has been noted by writers on Springsteen, both in terms of spirituality and religion within Springsteen's writing and life, and within the fan community. Nick Ripatrazone (2021) describes Springsteen's current and ongoing relationship with Catholicism in this way, hearkening back to a concert Springsteen did at his Catholic school in 1996: "The St. Rose of Lima concert perfectly captured Springsteen's brand of Catholicism: visceral, penitential, profane." Jeffrey Symynkywicz, a minister with a deep understanding of life and Springsteen, wrote about religion and spirituality in his book, *The Gospel According to Bruce Springsteen* (2008). He explored issues such as community, justice, evil, the fall, and redemption and rising, with Christianity applied to Springsteen's work. Linda Randall (2010) wrote of the spiritual dimensions of fan experience in concerts, of the

"Church of Bruce and the Ministry of Rock 'n' Roll," in *Finding Grace in the Concert Hall.* Susan Woge (2011) artfully argued for Springsteen as part of the evangelist preacher tradition, with "their messages of conversion, perseverance, and redemption, and their ability to foster a sense of community" (p. 142), and likens his concerts to "tent revivals" (p. 142) with social and religious aspects and messages emphasizing hope.

In *Born in the U.S.A.: Bruce Springsteen and the American Tradition* (2005), Jim Cullen devotes a chapter to Springsteen's relationship with religion, specifically Catholicism, and its evolution, including the often missed but significant differences between Irish and Italian Catholicism, through analyzing Springsteen's music and actions in the world. Cullen comments that in Springsteen's work "religion functions not so much as a set of doctrines or rituals, but as a way of thinking, feeling, and living in the world—even when we are unaware of (or specifically reject) church doctrine" (p. 161). This offers a pertinent framework for understanding women's religious/spiritual connection to Springsteen and his work. Discussion of Springsteen's incorporation of issues, concepts, and rituals from religion and spirituality in his work has flourished at academic symposia at Monmouth University (Beach, 2021; Contino, 2018). In *Long Walk Home,* Cohen and Sawyers (2019) describe Springsteen as "a religious leader without a formal institution" (p. 2) in the introduction, and references to preacher, gospel music, faith, and spirituality inhabit other chapters. Irwin Streight's (2019) interview of singer/songwriter Martyn Joseph, described as "The Welsh Springsteen," and his chapter on the connection between Springsteen and Flannery O'Connor, intersperse a sense of God, religion, and the spirit among all three artists discussed. Jim Cullen returns with musings on "Springsteen in Senescence" to the role of Catholicism in his life and work now that Springsteen is older and his faith and relationship to Catholicism continue to evolve toward a deeper engagement with a specifically Catholic spirituality, even as he continues to maintain distance from the formal institutions of the church (Cullen, 2019; Cullen, personal communication, 2021).

Psychology has a rich history around existential issues and their importance in people's lives (Frankl, 2006; Markman et al., 2013; Overholser, 2005; Yalom, 1980), stemming particularly from the mid-twentieth-century rise of existential philosophy following World War II. An emphasis on meaning, purpose in life, aloneness, mortality, freedom, and choice is applicable across different frameworks of psychotherapy (Overholser, 2005). However, psychology tended to ignore religion and spirituality for decades, although part of psychology's birth involved a religious foundation (Plante, 2009; Wampold, 2018). In the last few decades, with emphasis on diversity and multiculturalism, psychology has acknowledged the power and importance of spirituality and religion (Pargament, 2007; Pargament & Mahoney, 2009; Plante, 2009; Shafranske, 1996; Shultz & Sandage, 2006; Sperry & Shafranske, 2005), encouraging practitioners to become more aware of these facets of human existence (Pearce et al., 2019;Sperry, 2012).

In an early edited book, Shafranske (1996) invited psychologists from across the field to speak to the history and culture of religion and psychology and to ways in which religion could be included within clinical practice. Plante (2014) suggests ways for practitioners to be more open to religious and spiritual issues and describes the value of aspects of religion and spirituality across a spectrum of major faith traditions. Sandage et al. (2020) have woven together more relationally oriented psychology and psychotherapy with a focus on spiritual, existential, religious, and theological issues in what they call the relational spirituality model, commenting, "We understand relationality to be constitutive of human experience, spirituality, and therapeutic growth" (pp. 4–5). Psychology is clearly moving toward acknowledging the integral nature of religion and spirituality in people's lives. Some Springsteen fans have known this for years.

Pargament and Mahoney (2009) do not polarize or divide religion and spirituality, as some writers do. Rather they define them in the following way: "We prefer to use the term 'religion' in its classic sense as a broad individual and institutional domain that serves a variety of purposes, secular as well as sacred. 'Spirituality' represents the key and unique function of religion. In this paper, spirituality is defined as 'a search for the sacred' (Pargament, 1999, p. 12)" (p. 612). They tell of people's searches and struggles that can be prompted from both internal and external events. In the survey responses we also see spirituality and religion as related and overlapping, and we assume that the women use these terms in their own ways. Their responses contain references to organized religion and to what might be categorized as the search for the sacred, even if they did not necessarily know they were searching until later.

A definition of "soul" from clinical psychologist Dean Hammer (2018) frames women's experiences and musings well by bringing together existential, spiritual, and religious facets.

> The soul represents the core of one's being—the vital center of one's identity and source of vitality. The soul can be experienced in the deep, interior space in which the mind and heart unite to attend to the meaning and purpose of existence amid our finitude and mortality. The yearning for a place of belonging in the world and the need to feel hope for a fulfilling life are two deep-seated strivings of our souls. The soul is the reservoir for our core values based on what really matters and what gives meaning and purpose to our life. (p. 2)

THE EXPERIENCE ITSELF

It is Springsteen's live performances that, for many women, lift them in a particularly spiritual/religious way. One can hear it in their words, in how they express themselves. "Bruce is an amazing performer. You come out of his shows transformed. It is the closest thing to a spiritual experience I have ever gotten." "Most of my happiness moments of my life have been at Bruce's concerts. I feel so connected, so spiritual, so alive there—it's probably how I should feel in church, but instead I get it from Bruuuuuce!" "I don't know that I can describe that- As I said it's a religious experience for me. The man and his music mean so much to me. My life would have such a hole in it if it went away." "I find that all of these songs and albums make me feel something, especially when hearing them live. I've joked with friends before that going to a Springsteen concert can feel like a religious experience because you can get so into what's going on that you feel very connected to the experience. These songs really do that for me." "It lifts me up, that wall of sound, higher than gospel music." "My experience as a Springsteen fan has been nothing short of religious. His performances are existential; they remind us why we are here." Often religious experiences have a numinous quality, something that we don't quite comprehend and cannot quite explain to others or maybe even to ourselves: the excitement, the intensity, and connectedness. Something ineffable makes fans label the experience as spiritual rather than a more earthly concept.

The inspirational nature of spiritual encounter is reflected in many responses. "He makes me believe anything is possible. When I go to a concert, it's a completely physical, emotional, and spiritual experience." And spiritual doesn't mean he isn't attractive in other ways. "I would use the word 'spiritual' to describe how the music makes me feel. The facts that he is a fantastic physical performer and not bad looking are just added bonuses, I'd love him just as much if they didn't apply." "He's a good looking guy but it's not a physical attraction. It's spiritual and emotional. Going to a Springsteen show is a religious experience." "I cannot imagine my life without his music. His concerts have been almost religious experiences as well as meeting grounds for so many long-term friendships. My life is richer because of it." A religious experience can be very much of this world, not separated off, away from other feelings. This person (italics added), when asked what attributes attracted her to Springsteen, describes a religious/spiritual event. "His commitment to give his all, night after night after night. His concerts are religious experiences—*uplifting, transporting, exhilarating, draining*."

Even fans who are not oriented toward a spiritual/religious perspective can feel it. "I don't believe in spirituality. But at his concert I feel spirituality is attainable." "He is by far the best live performer I have seen in my life. I am not religious but attending his concerts is kind of a religious experience for me. It makes living worthwhile and gives you a sense that mankind is wonderful!" "They speak to me. I don't know how else to put it. They touch my soul. I am not a religious person in the traditional sense. But listening to Bruce and seeing him live is what I call a religious experience." Springsteen shows can open new vistas for people who consider themselves "not religious." Cavicchi's (1998) use of "conversion" to describe how some fans become fans seems pertinent here in the more traditional use of a spiritual conversion.

While it may seem glib to call something spiritual, these fans seem serious about their choice of the word, intended to convey the depth of impact in their lives in more detail.

> I always loved his music. When I was 11 years old I went to a Springsteen concert. I couldn't get over how much I was inspired by the experience. It was a spiritual experience. I loved seeing the crowd raise their arms at certain parts of the songs like "BADLANDS" or singing about hiding in "Backstreets." I became obsessed with his lyrics after that and listen to everything he ever did. My awkward teenage years soundtrack was Springsteen. He provided a protective armor around me with his music. It was always about fighting back, fighting sorrow, depression and when I listened to it I felt stronger.

> My brother insisted I go see him when he came through Wisconsin. I was 16. The show was billed as "An Evening with Bruce Springsteen," and the coliseum had been cut in half with a curtain. Bruce hadn't made his mark in the midwest yet. I was speechless from the first note on. There were two women in front of us who knew every song and I remember thinking, "That will be me next time he's here." I was filled with an overwhelming sense of joy that night and knew that he was going to be a huge part of my life from that point on. Not to go overboard but since then I've assumed the feeling I had that night was the same as what very religious people feel when they sense they're in the presence of god. Bruce is the only person, place, or thing that has ever made me feel that way.

We also heard from a fan who has, like the two authors here, combined her personal and professional selves around her feelings for Springsteen.

> Yes. I consume his music, attend shows (when possible) as both public space religious ritual or mass to share with other devotees (now once a tour if I can rather than feeling like I have to make it to as many shows as I can) as well as private prayer (listening to his music in car, household). I look forward to new music (and complain when he recycles material we already have). I have written a couple papers and have brought his music into my professional work that way. I am one of millions who appreciates his music and message.

These detailed responses touch on identity, meaning, and life journeys, showing how women have been moved and inspired. Their lives and psyches have been transformed, in an avowedly spiritual framework.

For readers wondering what happened to the physical amid the more otherworldly spiritual experiences, some women combine them. "It's really about the spirituality of the music. Faith. Hope. But as he always says, sometimes it's just about having fun. It stirs my head, my heart—and sometimes my sexuality." "I have listened to him for over half my life and it has always been spiritual, never sexual. But last year there was a picture of him on the beach in orange swim trunks. HOLY COW!"

When asked how attraction to Springsteen had changed over time, this fan put it decisively. "On Facebook, where it asks religion—I put Bruce. So I went from a fan to a full blown convert? Clearly I do see it in religious terms!"

ANOTHER LEVEL OF UNDERSTANDING AND LIVING

While concerts were central to some fans, for others a more extrapolated set of beliefs or behaviors, and musing on Springsteen himself, were significant. A clergy member describes how music has added to her spiritual understanding.

> I am a clergy person and I have often used song titles as sermon titles. The music/lyrics help me focus on what message I need to preach. I get a lot of inspiration from the music because even though he tries to hide it, Bruce has got some deep spirituality that shines through in positive ways. For me personally, his music still helps me with my

> Jersey identity, and many images and values in the songs evoke compassionate response and thinking. These are important to me as one who wants to practice what I preach and spread the message of love.

Springsteen hiding his spirituality raised questions: Does he do that? How hard is it to be a rock star and spiritual? Has that changed recently? The connection to what one does, how one behaves in the world, as influenced by Springsteen, feels important here. There can be real-life consequences and sequelae to being a Springsteen fan.

For some fans, the music intertwines with them spiritually and includes Springsteen in a formative role. "It's so hard to describe—my husband of 35 years still doesn't get it. It's as close as I get to being 'spiritual'—and that's from someone who went to 12 years of Catholic school. The music speaks to me. It moves me. It's my life, it's my hopes, my dreams, my failures. It's almost as if Bruce has been watching my life and writing it down in music." This fan's family is involved with Springsteen, and her Christian belief in music includes Springsteen's.

> Being a fan for many years, I feel like Bruce and his music have grown old together with my husband and I. We've seen a lot of things we never dreamed we would see and faced a lot of challenges we didn't know we signed on for. I saw my husband cry when Clarence passed away. My sons both love Bruce and it's something we share as a family. This is sounding sappy but I feel like Bruce has been there through my life's journey. He (we) hasn't always been right but he's been authentic. The only music deeper for me is spiritual music because I am a Christian. I believe that music is a gift from God and connects my soul to the heavenly realm. God uses music, including secular music like Bruce's, to reveal his common grace to all men.

God is present, the loss of Clarence Clemons evokes a strong response, and music is essential to spirituality. The life journey includes Springsteen.

Spirituality is part of a larger holistic experience for some, with guidance as essential.

> This box would have to be as long as a book to fully describe the effect he has had on my life. He and his music have made me a more caring, giving, loving, thoughtful, and happier person. His music has moved me into places that sometimes I didn't want to go but made me feel richer once I've been there. He's asked me to truly think about not only my life but the lives of those around me; to see and feel a world larger than my own. To judge less and tolerate more. And besides all of that, through his music I've learned to dance and sing and rejoice not only physically but also spiritually. The experience has been priceless.

For some women fans, the guidance focuses on Springsteen himself. "I love what Bruce stands for . . . he cares about people—the everyday things that matter to people (family, relationships, spiritual beliefs, making the world a better place, humor). His work ethic on tour is amazing; night after night he gives himself emotionally, physically, musically, and spiritually to the audience." As with others, this woman shares his Catholic background. "Him being a lapsed Catholic and the spirituality of his music that resulted is important to me because it's a shared influence that means I strongly connect to him and his music. I understand the language he speaks. It also helps me make sense of and reconcile with the parts of my personality affected by my former religion." The nightly support of food banks in concert has influenced this woman's own acts of giving. "He helps me by speaking out about things that I find important—politics, poverty. Thirty years ago he asked his audiences to support local food banks so I did. I continue to help out with my time and money. It showed me the importance of charitable giving. He has also helped me through the loss of a friend and my parents. I'm not a religious person but I have discovered my faith through his music." "I joke with people and tell them I live by the gospel according to Springsteen. I was considering suicide when I first discovered him, so I suppose he saved my Life. When I'm down, he's what I listen to. When I'm happy, he's what I listen to. He's the soundtrack of my life. And seeing him live, as any fan knows, is almost a religious experience."

Religious dimensions include for some women the possibility that Springsteen was sent by God. "Other than my children & family, he is the most important aspect of my life. Seems hardly a day goes by that I don't discuss him with someone. Not necessarily to convert someone, just to explain why I think he is so wonderful, an actual gift from God. Although my family in the clergy thought I took that comment a bit too far. Yet I really do feel this way." "My soul and my heart are connected to him and his music. God put him on earth to help me." When living life through a spiritual lens, the idea that God put Springsteen on earth can make sense.

While Catholicism seems likely to be mentioned, given Springsteen's background and its presence in his music and his very personhood, as in this next response, spirituality transcends background for the second respondent. "Growing up as a Catholic, I was attuned to the Catholic references in the songs—it's rare that a songwriter writes about religious faith as something that's just ordinary and there in the background of life. I also love that his songs tell a story—you meet real people, ordinary people, and characters in his songs." "Because from the first time you go to a show and you realize that that one little man 'down there' can unite the thousands under that roof into a single body. It is the only time, ever, that I feel any kind of religious experience—and I'm the daughter of a rabbi and grew up with a whole lot of 'religion.'" The variety of ways his music touched fans spiritually maybe resonates with mystical and universalist traditions that suggest there is much that unites all world religions, something soulful or existential.

Spiritually Evolving

A few women described the evolving and maturing spiritual nature of their relationship with Springsteen and his work. "At first, just his appearance and fun songs, later his spirituality and humanitarian efforts make him even more Appealing." "The spirituality has deepened." "Emotional and spiritual it stood the test of time unlike many artists I used to like and got stronger and stronger." Becoming a parent added to this connection. "I listen, I learn, I grow. I've always viewed his music spiritually and it continues to inspire me whether it's on an album or live (with any band or solo). As a parent, I feel an added connection." Springsteen's evolution toward religion is noted, or perhaps she is noticing it more. "As he's gotten older, he seems to be more forthright with things going on in his life. For example in 'Real World' his verse that he says he'll stand by your side with his arms open wide he's saying he will be truthful about his relationship and is not embarrassed about it at all. I never realized until he got older that he was very religious and sings about it. A lot of people will be afraid to do that and he isn't."

The complicated nature of the connection to Springsteen comes through in this fan's evolution.

> In the beginning, I was attracted to him because I felt he wrote about how I was feeling. Then with the *Born in the U.S.A.* album it was more of a physical attraction. I have to say I was truly disappointed when he broke up the band, but as I matured I realized that we all have to change and cannot hang on to something that needs to move in a different direction. The energy just dies. However, I wished Bruce would have said I am going in a different direction and hope that one day we all will connect again. In any event, I feel more of a spiritual connection with his music now.

Spiritual experience can be all encompassing, yet shades of gray and intricacy also inhabit this space, yielding responses that are thoughtful and discerning, not cultish.

IT'S IN THE SONGS

While a sense of spirituality, religion, or God may feel amorphous, for many women the connection was specifically related to certain songs, highlighted here, especially the album *The Rising.* This fan focuses on listening more generally. "Listening to these albums is like going to church. It's a spiritual experience. He captures the working class experience better than any artist I know, and I grew up in a working class family, so these albums feel like home." The word "home," often used with a sense of longing, such as a spiritual or emotional home, fits well here.

For one European fan, leaving organized religion has been somewhat mitigated by Springsteen's music.

> Favorite album is *Wrecking Ball* and *Darkness*. Favorite song depends on the mood I am in! Maybe "Thunder Road," "The Promised Land," "Land of Hope and Dreams." Oh, I never noticed this, but there's a theme!!:-) That's what is special about his music compared to other artists, almost all the work has a very strong spiritual meaning. You really get that if you manage to get near the stage at gigs, but it's the same listening to them at home. There is a semireligious quality to being a Springsteen fan, certainly for me, the music (and that of a few other artists) probably fills the void left by organized religion, which I have left behind a long time ago. The songs I mentioned above certainly make me feel very emotional. Obviously, songs like "41 Shots" and "The Rising" are extremely moving, but like I said, most of the songs allow me to reaffirm certain personal and political values, which is a very powerful thing.

"Land of Hope and Dreams," with its palpable religious/spiritual overtones, caught the attention of some fans. "'Land of Hope and Dreams' always gets me. Thematically it ties in everything Bruce's music has been saying for years. Despite all the obstacles, you keep living. We are all in this together 'saints and sinners' 'losers and winners.' It also touches me because of the faith I grew up with—everyone is valuable. Everyone is welcome in God's kingdom." When asked about songs with an emotional impact, this woman noted similar qualities. "'Land of Hope and Dreams' is a good example of one of these. It always lifts me up, makes problems feel minimized, conveys a positive message of hope and redemption. A Bruce live show is almost like a religious revival—there's a lot of release and joy, hope and brotherhood."

Some of the large, anthemic songs inspire connections to spirituality. "'Dream Baby Dream.' Bruce closed with this in Rochester, NY, on the Devils and Dust tour, just him and this huge organ. I will never forget how he performed that song . . . very spiritual, almost like I just attended church or something." Early songs spoke spiritually to some fans. "'Jungleland.' Just wraps my whole being in the music. It's like being in church because Bruce's concerts are sacred moments of holiness and spirituality." "'Thunder Road' makes me cry every single time. And 'Jungleland' is spiritual. The entire rest of the show inspires me—Bruce inspires me every time I see him to be my best." This woman mentioned numerous songs, then described her response. "It made me feel connected to Bruce and to other people around me. I felt understood and that I could let whatever I was feeling flow out naturally, without restraint or inhibition. It was very spiritual for me, like going to church except 1,000 times better because I could relate to the hopes, struggles, fears, joy, and dreams in the lyrics." "Wow. I love so many. There is a beautiful song called 'Lift Me Up' that I love. I love the spiritual component he has in many of his songs. It is subtle and if you are a believer, you note it." This woman created a timeline showing evolution. "'Dancing in the Dark' makes you want to dance. 'Tunnel of Love' was about love. 'Human Touch' was real. 'High Hopes' because Jesus was depicted and I felt that Bruce had come to spirituality." It almost sounds like a theory of adult development!

The specific songs that speak to a person may change as that person and life change.

> I have just come through a major depressive episode, I went for a dream, aimed high and had my world collapsed around my ears. The songs I listened changed during that period and I went for the ones that reflected, I guess in some ways how I was feeling. But the albums while dealing with difficult issues all have a spark of hope too, a sense that we as humans can get through anything. There is also on most of Springsteen's albums a strong sense of his faith in God and love and the ability of family and friends to help out and stick by those they are close to, there is also a great sense of community and pulling together. For instance on *Wrecking Ball*, Jack of all trades is going to get through whatever the government throws at him. Even though the songs deal with the bleakness of the economic situation the music is upbeat, it carries you along, you know you will get through.

Hope, a major factor in religion, is well represented here.

The Rising: A Religious Hymn

Songs and concerts related to *The Rising*, Springsteen's tribute to the September 11 attacks in the United States and ensuing reactions, hold a special place for some fans, and either introduced or amplified a sense of spirituality/religion. Woge's (2011) essay singles out *The Rising* album as connecting to the spiritual with its religious images and the invocation of strength, faith, hope, and love, as do these fans. "'My City of Ruins' makes me want to cry. The first time I saw it live I felt like I had a religious experience, it was so powerful." "'The Rising'—I get chills with this one. From the very first time I saw it live it felt like a religious hymn (post 9–11)." "'The Rising' is incredibly interesting. 'My City of Ruins' is a religious experience live." "'The Rising' for the swell . . . the closest feeling to a religious experience." "I always cry during 'My City of Ruins' when I hear it live. It is a very emotional song and very spiritual." "They are all better live! And that's because Bruce is always reinventing a song or reinterpreting it. This, in itself, is moving and thought provoking. I consider going to a Bruce concert to be a spiritual experience. *The Rising* shows were particularly moving, given their 9/11 inspiration."

The complexity of the juxtaposition of these two songs by an African American fan underscored what Springsteen brings to the table emotionally and spiritually about what it means to be an American. "'The Rising' and 'American Skin (41 Shots).' Springsteen was able to reach deep inside himself, and bring out The Eternal HOPE each of us have in ourselves with 'The Rising.' With the song, 'American Skin,' I am an Afrikkan Amerikkan female, and have experienced racial hatred because I was born with a permanent tan."

A song from *The Rising* intersected with feelings for Clarence Clemons and the death of a friend.

> "My City of Ruins" played live after Clarence passed away. My friend passed away a day after Clarence, and I had taken him to his first and only Bruce show. He was young and I didn't think he would "connect" to the music but he did. He left singing the songs while we walked to

> the car in the parking lot. When Bruce re-created "My City of Ruins" after Clarence's death, including the words "If we're here and you're here then they're here" I just broke down. I was in Madison Square Garden singing along and just broke down. It was truly a spiritual experience.

Bruce's invocation of presence despite death was a powerful moment of affirmation of a spiritual world. He announced something seemingly radical that wasn't part of the "closure and move on" culture around death and dying: a sense of connectedness with and manifestation of a beloved friend who was physically no longer on earth.

This participant brings in a panoply of songs and what they can do and mean.

> The feeling I get from Bruce Springsteen's music/magic is spiritual. I feel he is here to uplift humanity & the planet, remind us to live fully in each moment, & treat life as a gift. He brings hope, love, peace & freedom, & always puts his heart & soul into his music, which I feel is a vehicle for his gospel show. I love the stories, how they reach into the heart & tug at our experiences in a way that words cannot always touch. "The Rising," brings tears. He shows us compassion, not just for ourselves but for humanity as a whole. Bruce reflects our inner struggles with light & dark as in "Jungleland," and love for each other with all our shortcomings, as in "Spirit in the Night." A celebration of all that is human, and a reverence for all that is spiritual in nature, as in god. And the happiness he invokes in our hearts with songs like "Waitin' on a Sunny Day" literally saves lives & reminds us why we are here and what matters in this miracle called life.

Hearing these responses affirms the minister who uses Springsteen's music as it highlights multiple aspects of humanity through his gospel show.

Guide and Teacher, Going Down the Path

A guide, teacher, or mentor can encompass wide-ranging content areas of a person's life or sense of self, whether around career, everyday choices, who one is, or connecting to something sacred or transcendent. The sense of the spiritual, God, religion is multifaceted and truly transformational for some women, and Springsteen is a guide into and through this realm. We hear a sense of constructing an identity over time, and finding meaning in their lives, with Springsteen as a teacher. Whether it arises first from a song, a concert experience, memories of childhood religion, or a particular challenge in one's life, this meaning-making and Springsteen's role in it are palpable. Springsteen himself often talks of "transformation" and of performing a "rock and roll baptism" in concert and has written about his own complicated but continuing relationship to Catholicism (Springsteen, 2016) and of "the need to be transformed" that is essential to much great music (Costello, 2009/2010, p. 379). He has also spoken of the spiritual elements that infuse his work and life: "The adult life is dealing with an enormous amount of questions that don't have answers. So I let the mystery settle into my music. I don't deny anything. I don't advocate anything, I just live with it. We live in a tragic world, but there's grace all around you. That's tangible. So you try to attend to that grace" (Sutcliffe, 2006, p. 319). Cullen's (2005) comments on the protagonist's "deep loneliness in his despair" in "Streets of Philadelphia" (p. 185) or Springsteen's "almost overwhelming longing for transcendence" (p. 184) seem mirrored in many responses, similar to Hammer's (2018) three parts of a "soulful internal space" for the therapist to cultivate in attending to spirituality in therapy: "A space of hospitality and compassion. . . . A dwelling place for wisdom. . . . A wellspring of serenity" (p. 3). While this description may lack the vibrant excitement of a rock concert, it encompasses some of what Springsteen brings to his work and some women take from his work. It also hints at the third companionate role, that of therapist, explored in chapter 6.

CHAPTER 6

Walking the Path Together through Darkness

Springsteen as Therapist

> Music heals. Plain and simple. Springsteen has helped me deal with PTSD, depression, and anxiety disorder. Some songs just make you feel like there is at least one other person who knows what it's like to be you.

Companionship comes in many forms and can address different needs and desires in a person's life and psyche. A devoted family member or friend, or a trusted teacher or guide, can accompany the person through various phases of life's journey, traversing known and unknown territory. Whether the journey involves heading out to new lands or staying close to home to explore the inner world, the territory is both vast and intimate. Yet life at times can be daunting, even overwhelming. Sometimes a person needs help on a foundational level, more than what a friend or teacher can provide, either for a crisis or for something chronically wrong in their life or their sense of self. Sometimes a kind of help different from spiritual guidance feels more compelling, and the problems or distress feel more worldly, complicated, or debilitating on an everyday level. The hurt and pain may stem from events in the world, a major loss, trauma from childhood or the present, problems within relationships, or internal struggles that have long simmered or suddenly erupted. Fear of losing hope altogether, that one is stuck forever, can take over, along with paralyzing self-doubt, questioning everything. Becoming trapped on this journey through darkness, unable to retreat or move forward, losing direction or destination, can be frightening. There are countless situations in which one needs something more, sometimes labeled as depression, anxiety, loneliness, feeling blue, or just feeling "stuck." People look to religion for help, seek out an elder in their community, call a doctor for a physical explanation, turn to substances to relieve the pain, search the internet, sit alone in a room, read an inspirational or self-help book, or write in journals. Others go to therapy for professional help. And some turn to Bruce Springsteen as their "therapist."

We heard reflections from many women fans who found solace or companionship in Springsteen's work when they were lost, afraid, stuck, in despair, mourning, grieving, barely coping with the "regular" stress of life as well as tragedies, both personal and collective. The arts are seen as healing, with whole therapies or practices in therapy, and accompanying research, geared to healing through the arts (see reviews by Djikic & Oatley, 2014; Regev & Cohen-Yatziv, 2018; and Stuckey & Nobel, 2010, and creativity and grief in DiCello et al., 2018). Pennebaker and Smyth (2016) updated Pennebaker's pioneering clinical approach and research on healing aspects of writing. The symbolic and metaphoric nature of the arts can add to what people need to learn, experience, or work through to grow and move beyond difficult times. Springsteen's work offers such healing art for some.

In this chapter, we present stories from women who turned to Springsteen in times of distress. Most commentaries were in response to our question, "Has Springsteen's music ever helped you in your life?" We read many "No" or "Not really" responses. Others shared stories of Springsteen's work amplifying happy times and contributing to meaningful celebrations like weddings or birthdays. Some told how his work energized them to keep running, exercising, or doing household chores, or helped them connect with family members and friends or excel at a job interview. However, the focus here is on the multitude of women who responded with a need for a more intense kind of psychological help that delved into their feelings about themselves, relational issues, enormous life challenges, and losses. These issues often bring people to psychotherapy, yet, for these women, Springsteen's work served in that capacity or as an addition to therapy. Springsteen himself has spoken of the importance of psychotherapy and his work with his therapist, Doc Myers, over 25 years. He describes his therapy as an "odyssey" in which his therapist's knowledge and "compassionate heart" helped to guide him "to the strength and freedom I needed to love things and be loved" (Springsteen, 2016, p. 312). While listening to music is not the same as engaging in psychotherapy and should not be a substitute when therapy or crisis intervention is called for, the similarities, for some women under certain circumstances, are notable.

A Brief Visit to Psychotherapy

Although psychotherapy comes in many forms and frameworks, and psychologists and other therapists sometimes disagree on what is important or effective, here we focus on a few different but related strains of psychotherapy, some previously mentioned. Springsteen's work, and the women's responses to it in terms of how, when, where, and why it helped, connects to many different strains in clinical psychology, several of which are briefly described here.

From the existential/humanistic framework (Overholser, 2005; Yalom, 1980) comes attention to existential aspects of life, such as loss, meaning of life, isolation, purpose, freedom and responsibility, death, finitude, and what Yalom (Overholser, 2005, p. 191) calls "life-altering decisions."

Attachment theory contributes an emphasis on relationships within and outside therapy, described here by Wallin (2007).

> The patient's attachment relationship to the therapist is foundational and primary. It supplies the secure base that is the sine qua non for exploration, development, and change. This sense of a secure base arises from the attuned therapist's effectiveness in helping the patient to tolerate, modulate, and communicate difficult feelings. By virtue of the felt security generated through such affect-regulating interactions, the therapeutic relationship can provide a context for accessing disavowed or dissociated experiences with the patient that have not—and perhaps cannot—be put into words. (pp. 2–3)

Relational-cultural therapy (RCT) (Jordan, 2018; Jordan et al., 2004) focuses on the value of relationships in life and therapy, as well as cultural backgrounds shaping people. "Mainstream Western psychological theories tend to depict human development as a trajectory from dependence to independence.... In contrast, relational–cultural theory (RCT) is built on the premise that, throughout the lifespan, human beings grow through and toward connection. It holds that we need connections to flourish, even to stay alive, and isolation is a major source of suffering for people, at both a personal and cultural level" (Jordan, 2018, p. 3).

An integrated relational perspective that brings together research and clinical practice (Muran & Eubanks, 2020; Safran & Muran, 2000), and a relational psychodynamic approach (McWilliams, 1999), show the layers of meaning within individuals and relationships with others and the therapist. The therapy relationship and alliance is a major focus of therapy and a major healing factor. Safran and Muran (2000) offer a robust description of this perspective: "Relational thinking opposes the rigid demarcation between subject and object, between observer and observed, with its emphasis on reason and rationality. What is real or unreal, true or untrue, is replaced by the recognition that there are multiple truths and that these truths are socially constructed.... The classical psychoanalytic emphasis on neutrality, anonymity, and abstinence has given way to an emphasis on 'interaction, enactment, spontaneity, mutuality, and authenticity' (Mitchell, 1997, p. ix)" (p. 10).

This description of the therapist and the interaction dovetails with how some women have utilized Springsteen's work, with traits and actions in common with relational psychotherapy. McWilliams (1999) offers this vision of what clients may need from therapy: "This vision of the objectives of therapy includes the disappearance or mitigation of symptoms of psychopathology, the development of insight, an increase in one's sense of agency, the securing or solidifying of a sense of identity, an increase in realistically based self-esteem, an improvement in the ability to recognize and handle feelings, the enhancement of ego strength and self-cohesion, an expansion of the capacity to love, to work, and to depend appropriately on others, and an increase in the [*sic*] one's experience of pleasure and serenity" (p. 12). These objectives fit with outcomes women describe from Springsteen's work.

From group therapy, relationships are also fundamental for creating and making changes in who we are (Rutan et al., 2014): "Human beings are essentially herd animals. We begin in small groups—our families—and live, work, and play in various groups. The formation of our personalities is predicated upon our experiences with the different groups in which we interact, and the opportunities for modification and change of our personalities are very much affected by the groups in which we are involved" (p. 1).

Finally, from a common factors approach in psychology, certain elements are found to be helpful in most psychotherapies. While there is not one finalized list of common factors on which all researchers and clinicians agree, Wampold's (2018) description may relate to elements of the Springsteen/fan dynamic: "Common factors are those aspects of treatment, such as a relationship with an empathic therapist, a client seeking treatment for distress, a treatment structure, expectations, and work toward a goal, that are present in most or all psychotherapies" (p. 39). Wampold quotes Jerome Frank's work in this area, citing common factors important to psychotherapy: "(a) an emotionally charged and confiding relationship between the healer and the client, (b) a healer who is given special status and is perceived to have the powers to heal, (c) a powerful and cogent rationale for the healer's actions, and (d) a set of treatment actions that are consistent with the rationale" (p. 49).

Hearkening back to the therapeutic factor of instillation of hope from chapter 4, hope threads its way through clinical work and research, as described by C. Rick Snyder, a researcher in hope theory and positive psychology, who speaks of hope as something active, realistic, and even purposeful (Snyder 1994, 2000; Snyder & Lopez, 2009). We can feel hopeful, which can lead to positive actions, helping keep a person on track when so much feels lost.

From this brief tour through psychotherapy frameworks, hints emerge of the significant help from Springsteen's work. These processes are fundamental in psychotherapy and in fans' discussion of Springsteen "therapy": a (perceived) close and trusting relationship, emotions as critically important, attentiveness to meaning-making and understanding, reasons to be hopeful or a mechanism to nurture hope, identity formation, bolstering the self, the value of relationship, a way forward, and psychological growth and transformation.

Yet, before embarking on this journey into the intense issues many women expressed, we need to add a caveat. Bruce Springsteen's work is not psychotherapy, and we are not advocating for its use instead of psychotherapy. It is its own unique creation and cannot be reduced to another process or experience. It can sometimes be extremely helpful to women in despair or in crisis, or who are going through normal life transitions or events that are daunting. His music is a tool that some women fans have used for psychological growth. It is not designed to be psychotherapy and does not include the basics of psychotherapy in a literal sense. Psychotherapy is an analogy to understand the tremendous impact that his work can have on some women fans, and to see what contributes to that impact. We consider his work as another potential healing practice, in the tradition of art's healing elements, and within practices that are not modern Western psychology, but not as a substitute for psychotherapy.

How Does Springsteen's Music Help?

Springsteen as a companion through darkness illuminates other hills and valleys in the journey: general help; consistency over time; teenage years; a variety of relationships; death/loss/mourning; intimate relationships and their breakups; depression and suicidality; the big challenges of life; and, once again, September 11. These content areas of distress include chronic situations, acute crises, trauma, and more predictable kinds of human suffering. We briefly comment throughout on the process of that help, how and why it helps, including alleviating isolation, fostering emotions, gaining in self-worth and self-confidence, finding meaning or perspective, and instilling hope. In our article about *Darkness on the Edge of Town* (Mangione and Luff, 2019), the intricacies of both the darkness and the help are further illuminated by women fans.

EVERYDAY PRESENCE: HE'S THERE WHEN NEEDED

For some women, Springsteen, through his music, is there often, even every day, helping through issues and conflicts, whether by inspiring hope, creating a sense of connection, or allowing a release or catharsis. A few use "therapist" to describe this presence. "He's my therapist. I listen to his music every day to maintain peace of mind." "It helps me every day . . . listen to E Street Radio on my commute to and from work. Hard to give an example . . . suffice it to say that Bruce music is my therapy." "The fact that you can feel his enjoyment in what he does and makes each show feel like it's just for you. He feels like my therapist I always leave a show feeling amazing and needing more." "It gave me energy in a very hard moment, the last concert was like a therapy bringing me back to the joy of living!" While most women did not explicitly say therapist or therapy, the healing image reverberates throughout descriptions.

These straightforward statements describe the heart of the help. "When feeling down songs I go to when feeling angry songs I go to when feeling happy songs I want to sing along too." "His songs relate to all of us, he inspires and gives you hope." "I can't think of a single time in my life when Bruce wasn't a way to help me. He has a song for every thing your heart needs!!" "If I'm pissed off or sad about something, the best cure for me is ride in my car with Springsteen up loud." "Yes, just get past things. Make me realize I'm not alone feeling certain ways." "It has definitely helped me during difficult periods of my life, more often to boost my mood. Occasionally by listening to sad songs and having a good cry." "It has helped me understand my feelings, helped inspire me to keep pushing forward, and helped me feel Understood." "It's made me pick my ass back up and get on with living." "Made me relaxed and it's comforting to know you will never be let down." The abiding presence of Springsteen and his work feels basic to their help and support.

THROUGH THE YEARS

The longevity of Springsteen's career and fans' devotion contributes to fans feeling helped over decades and across developmental phases and milestones. Many women noted low points of their lives and high points of his help. Therapy can be similar when it is "intermittent" (Cummings, 1991; Drisko, 2005), such that one returns to therapy when in pain or crisis or at a turning point. These women described ongoing, intermittent kinds of help, sometimes from a specific song or concert that evocatively spoke to them.

Intimate and grand existential moments, the big questions of life, often unbidden, stand out. "Springsteen's music helped me through feeling lonely in high school, through a breakup in college, through feeling homesick away from my family, through feeling stressed out on a day to day basis. Springsteen is my go to when I need an emotional pick-me-up."

> When I was in my teens I was diagnosed with juvenile arthritis and every time I heard *Born to Run* it helped me to overcome the pain and try to live a normal teenage life. I always felt that Bruce was singing it for me. As stated earlier "We Are Alive" more recently helped to deal with the loss of my mom who I was very close with. The lyrics in that song have helped me know that she is always with me. Also when my husband lost his job during the recession songs like "Jack of all Trades" felt like it was written for us personally and helped us to get through possibly the most difficult time of our marriage.

The breadth of help for these women is startling. These aren't just love songs, or motivational songs, or songs about work, or illness—they are experiences of deep meaning amid turbulence, with Springsteen in a healing role.

Songs do not have to be exact replicas of a person's life. "Relationship struggles, death of my mother, raising kids, getting older. Even though his characters may not be MY story . . . they still resonate with me. I can start listening to a song and my entire mood can and will change. . . . again, I FEEL the music." "It helped me in my youth and later as I had some hard times in some jobs. And I met my husband, who is a Springsteen fan, too, and we are married now and are since 20 years together. If my life gets in trouble Springsteen and his music are always like the big rock on the shore." That rock on the shore, its solidity and security, could be something people are searching for in a world where it may be harder to rely on what used to give people strength and solidity. A rock is symbolic of that which stands with you or on which you can stand.

Teenage pain can be intense, and while family or individual therapy might have helped navigate the terrain, for this fan Springsteen's music stepped in. "On an emotional level his music was an escape when I was dealing with parents who couldn't stand to be in the same room as each other when I was a teenager. I have used Springsteen's music to help me get through hard physical times like 25 hours of labour with my firstborn and long powerwalks when I was trying to lose weight. When my Dad was ill with Cancer and after he died my iPod and Springsteen kept me from cracking up."

As economic hard times come and go, Springsteen's songs continue to be relevant.

> All the time in so many different ways. As I said before "I'm on Fire" really helped me when I was younger. "Jack of All Trades" helps me to realize that I will be all right no matter what happens, especially in these recessionary times. I think a lot more people would benefit so much more if they heard his music. It's from the heart and really tells the story of my life. Even though I was born and raised in Ireland, when I first heard his music in the States I identified with it and still do all these years later.

That sense of identification can contribute to the bond that allows for help, whether in therapy or with Springsteen. Clearly, individual facts of existence do not have to exactly match for resonance or identification to occur.

For some women, specific songs played over and over become a companion, or a song relates to a certain phase of life, including developmental milestones and life crises.

> "My Father's House" and "Independence Day" helped me thru the death of my father. For me the individual concert experience defines whether I cry or feel elated. I experience so many emotions during the concert but ultimately leave feeling elated and alive. I have cried many times at shows when I hear a holy shit song like the "Prove It All Night" with 78 intro at Fenway Park on night 2 in 2012. But again a lot of this has to do with where I am sitting, who I am with, how engaged Bruce is and the songs played that night.... My dad's death ("My Father's House" and "Independence Day"), birth of my children ("Leap of Faith" and "Living Proof"), and now later years ("Kingdom of Days" and "Land of Hopes and Dreams"). Also HS graduation with "Thunder Road" and "The Price You Pay."

> The songs feel like they are saying all of the thoughts going through my head. There is nothing I have seen or heard by Mr. Springsteen, that I don't like. He talks to me with his music. But "The Rising" helped tremendously with the emotions being felt after the 911 attacks. And "Tunnel of Love" literally, kept me alive while going through my divorce. Just Amazing! I still use his music to give me strength, to this day. There isn't a song of his that I don't care for.... He helped me survive a divorce, survive the attacks of 911, survive life. Still does. When life is getting me down, I blast his music and gain some strength. Can't really explain it, but it is very real.

"'Better Days' helped me to believe that things were really going to be all right after moving my sons out of a bad neighborhood into my hometown. 'Jack of All Trades' gave me hope again after losing my teaching position to budget cuts." Traversing crises and developmental stages with Springsteen's music can make a major difference.

Springsteen's streets are heady images and can take the listener to untold destinations.

> "Thunder Road" has been with me since I was a toddler. I always come back to that song. It's been with me thru heartaches, deaths, all the times I've fallen in love, basically it's the song that grounds me. Whatever I'm thinking of, and wherever I go, "Thunder Road" will always remind me of who I am and what matters to me. "Loose Ends"

> is a tune that I just fell in love with as a youth because it made my mind wander and filled me with hopes for my future. It just put me in a happy state of mind. "Racing in the Street" I have learned to love since I got closer to 30. I think it appeals to me because I contemplate on how you always end up with a bittersweet sorrow on what you do and don't accomplish in your lifetime. And the song reminds me to be in every moment as I live. The moment I am living now, may be the moment I wish I could go back to tomorrow. . . . "Thunder Road" grounds me whenever I am sad, angry, or struggling with something else. After going thru some major changes in my life in my early twenties (losing my mum to cancer, and ending a long-term relationship) I felt like a stranger in my own life and skin. "Thunder Road" helped me thru. Whatever else is happening in my life, I always know that "Thunder Road" will be the same. That's a good feeling.

We see the security in attaching to something and knowing it will be there. In functional families, parents play that role when we are young and finding our way, friends can help, and a therapist can be that secure base. Or a Springsteen song.

The idea of Springsteen's music as providing a refuge in times of trouble was also important for some fans.

> "Jack of All Trades" helped me get through a really tough time. In general though I would say it helps me everyday—I listen to him everyday—not in an obsessive way (though I know it sounds that way)—but I guess I listen to it the way some people watch a certain show or go for a run—it provides a stable point for me. A security blanket I guess. All Springsteen fans talk about how it feels as though he knows us—and when I'm struggling with something, hearing that in his music, hearing that story being told so completely from the character's point of view—I find that comforting. Often it just provides a refuge—a place I can hide. Life rarely gives you a chance to really hide and knowing I can put on my headphones and lose myself in one of his songs—that helps me put one foot in front of the other.

Hope is an ongoing theme both in Springsteen's work and in psychotherapy. "Many times his music has helped me through rough patches. Also, his generosity and general caring for humanity has awed me throughout my life. He has helped me keep going through hard times through his music about hopes and dreams." Like a refuge, and claiming elements of hope, finding that perfect place to thrive is a theme for this woman, and certain songs fit exquisitely into her struggles. "I remember being 15 or 16 and singing 'Born to Run' loudly almost everyday after school and wanting out of my town so bad. As soon as I graduated I moved (went to college) and then traveled the country and lived all over the USA. He got married so I thought it was a good idea for me too and so I did . . . but, alas, after all is said and done, I divorced and moved back to 'My Hometown.'" Seemingly she mirrored Springsteen's journey, from running to seeking a true home, with his help.

THOSE TEENAGE YEARS

Growing up is never easy, and teenage years can be stressful given physical and psychological changes as well as complex interpersonal situations. Hopefully those in need will seek help, whether with a trusted friend, family member, neighbor, teacher, guidance counselor, religious leader, coach, or therapist. This help can also come from Springsteen's work.

For some, the issues were normative ones common to many kids in high school and starting college. "In high school, listening to Springsteen got me through the stress of SATs and college applications. When I first got to college, listening to Bruce helped me when I was homesick." "I got so much out of his music in my teen years, when I was rebelling (against my comfortable and loving middle-class suburban family, of course). Each time I felt misunderstood, there was always a Bruce song about breaking free and busting out of class that made me feel less alone in the world." "When I was a teenager and had a lot of stress and 'drama' in my life (like any normal teenager) I used to drive around listening to his songs and enjoy my sense of freedom and my time 'alone with Bruce.' This was particularly helpful when I was in college and my parents were getting a divorce. I really found a lot of solace in his music." "As a teenager there was always a song that would match my emotions—fun, dark, romantic, political, despairing, euphoric—his music was an anchor in turbulent times and gave me optimism in the future when I needed it. That sense of optimism and the investigation of which choices we have in life (and what we do when we don't have a choice) has always been useful to me." "Bruce's music helped me as a young teenager, he put my feelings into words, the restlessness and uncertainty of life, the universality of wondering who you are. 'Born to Run' brought everything out in the open and made me realize that it was okay to question life, authority, parents." Validation, finding a kindred spirit, knowing you are not alone, hearing the normalcy of one's concerns, giving words to inchoate feelings, introducing hope are parts of healing practices and help a young person on her journey to find and believe in herself. What teenager does not want to "fit in" or be understood? How many young people have asked Who am I? as they tried to pull together a sense of self and identity, searching for answers?

Yet, for others, there were more disturbing events, or a darker tone overall to their teenage lives. "When I first started onto the Bruce bandwagon . . . I had had a life-threatening accident in my high school years. Kids and people were not very subtle on how I looked and I was not fitting in at all. Long story, no therapy for me . . . my therapy was someone who understood and was on the same wavelength. He helped me in more ways than I ever thought he could." "Yes as a young teen I was raised in a very toxic and traumatic home. When Springsteen hit me like a thunderbolt I escaped my life in the music, and it gave me so much hope for my future." There are always teenagers experiencing aloneness, isolation, hopelessness, rejection, and despair. Connecting with Springsteen's work certainly helped. This simple quotation makes one shudder to think of this girl without Springsteen. Would she have gotten help? Would anyone else have known? "It was basically all I had for a long time as a teenager."

For some fans, help from Springsteen started when they were teenagers and carried through to their adulthood.

> Bruce's music has helped me in so many ways. As a teenager, his music helped me thru many dark and trying times. It also helped me to bond with my friends and helped us to become individuals and create identities that still define us today. I STILL go to shows with those same high school friends from the '70s. . . . Throughout the years—I always managed to find solace in Bruce's songs—whether I was having a good day or a bad day or just needed quiet time. The songs always were able to offer me contentment. Bruce seemed to grow up with me as did his songwriting and music.

"Lots of times. Through hard times as a teenager, when I felt I didn't belong to anywhere nor felt comfortable with anyone, I felt like he could listen to my doubts. At university and work, having to deal with 'adult problems' and not knowing how to escape them, I found strength to continue fighting and trying my best. His songs have been helping me later, especially with my mental disorders (I have a diagnosis of depression). Listening to the albums nonstop makes me calm down." Believing in something, creating identities that carry into adulthood, and belonging set a foundation for these women.

Springsteen's own struggles, which he disclosed in many ways even before his memoir, were helpful to some fans. "I listened to 'Darkness' a lot as a teenager and it helped a lot. Knowing he went through some tough times too kind of got me thru those tough teenage times. Also, I was laid off around the time the *Wrecking Ball* album came out. The timing was perfect for me and helped me cope." Finding someone who has lived through what you are living through, who understands where you are, can change the experience of adolescence.

FRIENDS, FAMILY, SO MANY POSSIBLE DISCONNECTS

Close relationships are a distinct area where difficulties arise, even in the most caring environments. "His music got me through tough family issues." "'Blood Brothers' was a song which helped me when I have trouble with an old friend."

Yet his work has been helpful in forming bonds, not just in working through tough issues. It may not be surprising, given Springsteen's writings about his relationship with his father, that some of these bonds are with fathers. "Springsteen's work helped myself and my dad form a strong bond. Last year my dad was seriously ill and in hospital for 9 months—at the beginning we didn't think he was going to make it. Listening to Springsteen helped me to process my emotions and try to understand them. Listening to Bruce's songs made me feel close to my Dad." "*Darkness on the Edge of Town*. I had a very rough, turbulent relationship with my father growing up. Listened to that album ALL the time! It felt through the rough times that he'd gone thru the same things. That album always had hope just under the surface. I felt someone understood and was able to offer hope as well" (Mangione & Luff, 2019, p. 31). "'Independence Day' helping about my dad even on his death bed. I guess also 'Born to Run.' I was eager to shed Brooklyn, NY. Nothing good happened to me there. I played it the day I left. It has helped me have a stronger bond with my dad." Sometimes the troublesome parental relationship is with the mother, but words translate. "My relationship with my mother was difficult and parallels with that of his father, so much of the music he's written in regard to that particular relationship has been something I was able to relate to through the years. Knowing someone else had these troubles with their parent and managed to work through it was a great help to me."

Family bonds can be reactivated at challenging times of life.

> It helped me connect with my son. I have always been a Springsteen fan, but I was never that loud about it at home. A few years ago my son was home from college, he was having a very difficult time. He asked me if I had ever heard of Bruce Springsteen. I literally fell out of my chair (yes, literally, not figuratively) and went to get my albums, my books, my posters, my ticket stubs, etc. We talked long into the night about our shared passion for Springsteen, and I took him to his very first Springsteen concert.

Specific moments of help can stand out, and sometimes a song returns reinvigorated years later. "The music has been there throughout my life, every step of the way, helping me navigate both momentous occasions and day-to-day events. It's enhanced all the good times and offered solace during the not-so-good moments. All the experiences I've shared with friends and family at live shows are unforgettable. *Tunnel of Love* did not do much for me as a 20-year-old, but 8 years later, as a newlywed whose parents were going through a divorce, it became my favorite album." "Yes he helped me in difficult times to hold on. 'Better Days' as I described earlier about the difficult time dealing with the cancer of my young daughter. But he also gave strength during the many times of my physical and mental abuse by my parents and later my ex-partner. I really don't know if I would have survived without his music. I always felt him near as if I had a soulmate that could feel my pain and my loneliness." Knowing there are connections out there can help someone survive.

This last response chronicles interpersonal issues and ends with a major loss, the topic of the next section.

> The difficulties I was going through were compounded by the feeling of betrayal by someone I had considered a friend and a few family members. The songs "Streets of Fire" and "Code of Silence" really rang true at the time. Other times during that period, I would listen to "Janey Don't You Lose Heart" and "Ties That Bind" to feel better. While we went through a rough period following my husband's passing, I often quoted a line from "Tougher Than the Rest" to my sons: "The road is dark and it's a thin thin line. But I want you to know I'll walk it for you any time."

The pain and hope in that song, especially following loss, were present and alive.

DEATH IN THE FAMILY

Living in a culture with ambivalent frameworks and practices around death and loss, it makes sense that people look for something during their grieving, and that something can be Springsteen's work. Loss is often viewed as something we need to "get over," and many assume that we need to "achieve closure" through prescribed stages.

The grief and loss world of practitioners, researchers, and theoreticians has long acknowledged varying paths of grieving, rather than one undeviating path, as well as culture's influence on loss, and the need and desire to sometimes continue the bonds with the person who is gone (Klass & Steffen, 2018; Neimeyer et al., 2014). However, updated attitudes and frameworks are not always widely known among the general population. Grief can become a very personalized and private experience, sometimes enhanced by books, music, art, religion, or spiritual practices. One of us has worked with loss and grief, doing research, publishing, and giving workshops, emphasizing the continuing relationship with the deceased that can exist after death, and the contributions of culture, art, and spirituality to loss (DiCello & Mangione, 2015; Mangione et al., 2016). Springsteen understood that when Clarence Clemons died, stating in his eulogy (2011) and in concerts, "Clarence doesn't leave the E Street Band when he dies. He leaves when we die." Cullen (2019) notes Springsteen's songs that are "part of an ongoing dialogue between the living and the dead" (p. 191), a dialogue not usually encouraged in American society. For many women fans, enrichment and ongoing processing around loss happened with the help of Springsteen's work.

In both "up" and "down" times Springsteen's music worked for these women. "Used to play 'Born to Run' in college to get me pumped up for finals. Played 'Land of Hope and Dreams' in my car after I finished settling my late brother's estate to let out my emotions. I cried and cried."

> It's hard to explain. He makes you feel like you are a part of his life or something. Back in 1984 I took my mom and dad to a show in Syracuse, Born in the U.S.A. tour. My dad just loved it. So much so that I bought us tickets for an upcoming show. Somewhere between the two shows my dad was diagnosed with cancer. We had never known anyone that had cancer, yet. By the time the show was close Dad was too sick to go. He still wanted Mom to go though. My grandparents sat with him while we went. Our local radio station had two busloads of fans going. We didn't get home until the wee hours of the morning. Mom told Dad all about the show, he passed away the next

> day. It was like he hung on long enough for Mom to go. . . . Back then I wished I could have told Bruce that story. Many years have gone by since then but I can't hear "Born in the U.S.A." without choking up, I think of my dad when I listen to Bruce. . . . His music got me through my dad's death.

For some, the line of losses is long, with multiple deaths or sustained illnesses, and grief can be long also. "Of course, following my mum's sudden death 3 weeks after my first child is born; keeping faith while my dad was dying that he would be at peace; waiting to hear from my husband during the London, UK, July terrorist attack on the tube." "I discovered bruce at the age of 11 just after my father died. Losing myself in Bruce's music saved my life. Looking back I see how his music kept me from spiraling into the depression I was feeling growing up." "When my mum was ill, had a cancer, I listened to Bruce's music before I went to hospital. It helped me to face that reality there. My mum died 2 months ago and I listen again to bruce's music and I cry a lot." "I was depressed during my sister's illness and eventual death. 'Wrecking Ball' helped me to realize that life has its ups and downs, but that I am strong and will survive. Sometimes when I feel stressed or sad, if his song pops up on the radio, I feel comforted."

The love and the depth of the loss are palpable, and for these women, companionship with Springsteen was sustaining. "The first Springsteen concert I went to was with my mom and aunt, shortly after my maternal grandmother's death. It had been a hard time for all of us, and the concert definitely allowed bonding and time to put aside the mourning for a little while." "When my husband was killed I listened to his early music and found hope in it." "'We Are Alive' took away my crippling fear of death."

> I love "I'll Work for Your Love" since it always reminds me of my mother. Her name is part of one of his songs and I always think of her when I hear that song live. I love hearing "Working On the Highway" live just because it's a fun, upbeat song and I love the way Bruce performs it live. He usually takes a drink of water and sprays it up in the air (we got a Jersey baptism from him once during this song). I also

> love "My City of Ruins" . . . totally emotional for me—great song. . . . Magic helped me through my mother's death. Again, I love that he writes realistic relationship songs. Life is going to throw stuff at you as a couple, and his lyrics remind me that you need to be mindful of how/where your partner is at.

"Got me through the death of my beloved husband, who looked just like Bruce in the '70s. Gets me through the tough times by showing me there is always hope." "'Land of Hope and Dreams' helped me through my mom's passing: 'This train carries sweet souls departed.' . . . I would picture my sweet mom on that train headed for glory. That picture gave me peace."

A few responses offer wisdom about the unfolding process, showing what worked for them. "I think the Jazz Fest show in 2012 that I mentioned previously was very healing following my mom's passing. Bruce and E Street were mourning Clarence's passing, as well. The show reinforced how strongly I felt the loss of my mom, but it also helped me to move beyond it. There's no disputing the sense of loss, but there's also the acknowledgment that life goes on and we have to, too. And that it's okay to feel good and to celebrate, as well." Clarence Clemons's death and the shared personal and public mourning stand out.

Closeness with families and friends comes through another respondent's experience. "My Mom passed. I was lost for about 1 1/2 years. That's what happens when your best friend dies. One of my kid's friends told me to get an iPod or mp3 player and put his music on it. When I was down thinking she wasn't here, just put his music on as high as I could, sing on the top of my lungs, and dance like there's no tomorrow. I did that and still do when things get tough." For an only child, having Springsteen along as she cleaned out her parents' home helped enormously. "Bruce has always been there & most events in my life I can associate with a Bruce song. When my father passed away after a long battle with cancer, I had to clean out his house & sell it (I'm an only child & my mother had passed several years prior). Dad & I had always been very close, thru good & bad, & cast from the same mold. My final song in the house was 'Adam Raised a Cain.' So fitting."

Grieving can intersect with religious and spiritual beliefs and practices. "Brought me back into the stream of life after an intense grieving period after losing my father to ALS. I observed traditional Jewish mourning rituals, including attending no live performances of music for a year. My first concert after that period of time passed, and also the first time I'd seen him live since the River tour, was a concert during the Magic tour. I felt a distinct shift in my emotional life after that concert." "I discovered Bruce shortly after my husband passed away, who by the way, would have loved Bruce. His music kept me going and I'm still going." Springsteen shows up at key moments in life, when she's ready to listen, similarly for this woman. "When a friend (a fellow Jersey girl & Springsteen fan) was murdered, I happened to be in NJ. Shocked by the news I jumped into my car and started driving just to process the terrible event. Three Springsteen songs in a row came on the radio. That is mind-boggling but helped me to deal at that moment with my feelings. And I felt my friend and Bruce and God had sent me a message." In this harrowing moment, songs as messages carried her through.

ROMANTIC RELATIONSHIPS AND BREAKING UP

The Song That Says It All

Breakups were a key time when women turned to Springsteen for help. Some of them associated it with specific evocative songs. "After a breakup the song 'Bobby Jean' helped me. I don't know why but wallowing in misery listening to that song got me through my sadness." "When I was younger, I was going through hard personal experiences—the song 'Thunder Road' was so inspirational because he describes the Long Walk from the front door to the front seat and it was so true. Also the song 'The River' was important through a divorce because it reflects back on remembering when that person was so important to you and now they aren't." "*Wrecking Ball* came out shortly before my husband of 25 years left me for another woman. That album was my lifeline. As I sank to the depths of my own depression I felt Bruce perfectly understood in 'This Depression.' 'Rocky

Ground' buoyed my spirit and 'Wrecking Ball' became the thing I drew my most strength from. The line "hold tight to your anger but don't fall to your fears" was my mantra. That song helped me realize that to get through the divorce I had to use my anger to fuel my fight and not let my fear make me fold." "'Backstreets.' I have used those breakup lines in a real relationship. That song helps you deal with the emotions if a once powerful relationship that was broken by unfaithfulness." "In so many ways, constantly—gotten me through despair and helped me celebrate. I connected with almost everything he produced through the early 2000s, except *Tunnel of Love* and *Human Touch*. I didn't quite 'get it' but when I was going through my divorce, I played those albums constantly. The songs were exactly what I was experiencing, it was comforting to know I wasn't alone in that." "Many many times. 'Land of Hope and Dreams' is a recent example . . . gave me hope when my life was in a shambles after a recent divorce. Gives me strength to keep moving forward." "When I was going through a divorce, certain of his songs were there for me, partly just to let me know that I was not alone with what I was feeling. In particular, the song 'One Step Up' from the *Tunnel of Love* album, sad as it might be, gave me comfort." Obviously *Tunnel Of Love* feels meant for divorce and discord, but others speak to these women in hard times of betrayal where there had been trust, and schism where there had been connection.

Can Anything Good Come Out of This?

Learning something about life, the world, and oneself can happen in relationship breakups. "I was in a very physically abusive relationship and lost everything. I had to live in a shelter. During those years of abuse I totally stopped listening to music because it would upset me. At my lowest point I turned to Bruce's music & it got me through it. It was like reconnecting with an old friend." "After my divorce I realized I had spent my life trying to do what others wanted me to do. I hadn't been to any concert in over 20 years. In 2009 I went to my first Bruce concert by myself. I had the best time of my life. I have now seen him three times. Won't miss him again as long as I live!"

"I have E Street Radio in my car. At the present time, I am going through a divorce. Bruce's music helps me every time I turn it on. It helps me escape, it helps me to put things in perspective, and it can be a balm for the pain. If Bruce reads these, please let him know that I thank him for his music and how much it has impacted my life for the last 30 years." "At a very dark time in my marriage. I was separated with three little kids. I had lost myself and became this shell of a person who was supposed to be a perfect mother. I heard 'Jungleland' on the radio on New Year's Eve. I was overcome with sorrow. I started listening to massive hours of Bruce and started to reconnect with ME and everything I have always been about. I will never lose myself again and Bruce's music will always be in my life to remind me." Putting things in perspective and connecting to someone in times of despair come through the music. Perhaps this woman learned the ultimate lesson, that life was worth living. "His music helped me survive through my divorce, and helped me go on living when I really didn't want to."

For some women his music helped build an assertiveness and a more active kind of self-determination, a refusal to be cowed by events.

> Music helps me in life all the time. When I was sick and going through a lot of MRIs I'd play "Jungleland" over and over in my head and visualize Clarence on the sax. When I was going through a divorce, I became my own lawyer. I kept focused on a picture as Bruce looked on stage and remembered this is why I'm fighting—to bring joy back into my life. Kept me alive and focused on bringing myself back into a joyful life. At times all I could afford was to listen to the music, in the dark, on my single mattress on the floor.

Anger and assertiveness are not easy emotions or acts for many women, and society often criticizes women for them. It sounds like Springsteen helped inspire both here. Given how important "assertiveness" has been in psychology for decades (Alberti & Emmons, 2008), and the need for assertiveness training, especially for women, this is a welcomed area.

This woman notes that "helping" is hard to define and can lead to unintended consequences. "It has encouraged me to take risks & to hold out for what is important to me. I'm not sure about helping—if I end my marriage because I want to be with someone else it will be partly because of his music."

CHALLENGES AND COMPLEXITIES OF LIVING

Life throws unanswerable questions and unwanted situations our way: illness, job changes, natural disasters, world events. The complexity of the world and relationships, identity, values, choices, and purpose can be confusing. In this section, we first look at illness, and then challenges mentioned when fans were asked about help from Springsteen.

When I Was Sick

Physical pain and discomfort, uncertainty about the future, anxiety, isolation, and questions about death can happen when illness threatens oneself or one's family or friends. For some women, Springsteen's work came through for them at this time. "'Janey Don't You Lose Heart.' Over the years I have been fighting cancer. I listen to this song so it gives me the inspiration to keep fighting. I have been battling cancer since 2005, and he has been a major part in my therapy." "I'm physically disabled and I've gone through many treatments, operations, therapies that were all excruciatingly painful. If it wasn't for singing along to Bruce on my mp3 and painkillers I think I would have just given up by now." "Often when I am struggling with an issue, his music soothes or inspires me. For example, 'Wrecking Ball' made me feel empowered when my mother had a spot on her lung and we went through a few months thinking it was lung cancer." "It has helped me many times. I remember dancing joyfully and joyously with my daughters to 'Rendezvous' before going in for a mastectomy to treat breast cancer. I remember hearing and singing 'Born to Run' at concerts and feeling as though I could go anywhere and follow my dreams, even though I didn't know what they were yet." "I remember listening to 'Badlands' and singing very loudly to it—'let the broken hearts stand as the price you gotta pay,' when I was feeling broken-hearted. It was very cathartic. 'No Surrender' has become an anthem for me (actually, I needed to modify it to 'No F****ing Surrender' for my second round of cancer treatment!)" "Bruce and his music/lyrics are helping me right now as both my parents battle cancer and I need to be the one who takes care of everything. . . . Springsteen is helping me cope and giving me strength." When health and life are threatened, it helps to find an outlet for feelings, support and strength from someone, or even a diversion. These women, with broken hearts, found that in Springsteen.

Work, Life, Disasters, Life, Roadblocks, Life

Sometimes we don't know what we need to survive and thrive, but we know it when it isn't there. For these women, in various circumstances, Springsteen gave them something to hold onto and helped them move forward. This first woman says it succinctly and definitively. "Got me through my addiction." For others the challenges ranged from moving to hurricanes to growing up. "I moved to Greece when I was 16. I could hardly speak the language even though I was from a Greek background. But moving halfway across the world to a new country with a different mentality was devastating. I would put myself to sleep by listening to Bruce all through the night!" "He played a concert in 1997 in Vienna, and he said something like "there comes a time in your life where your answers don't match your questions" (or something similar)—and then he paused, smiled his typical smile and said "and that's normally at 30," and there I was sitting, 32 years old, in a bad relationship, being unhappy . . . so I changed it . . . and Bruce was the one who gave me the strength to do it. This was 17 years ago." "'Badlands' got me through Sandy. . . . I lost my business and every time I heard it . . . it pumped me up to take another step forward." This woman found answers to essential questions. "Many times. Lyrics often give me answers. For example coming out as gay. Cancer." Such huge questions of identity and one's very existence cry out for help. Companionship when alone, moving forward when stopped, learning where you are and how you got there, deciphering the questions and answers, are Springsteen's contributions.

Some fans referred to him as a "healer."

> Yes, I had a difficult youth & young adult period Bruce was with me thru high school & college. I listened to his music all the time, & he got me through. I would highly recommend anyone going through challenging times with health, family, finances, addiction, abuse, depression to listen to Bruce's music. He can open your heart & give hope to your every waking moment. He is a healer through music. We need him desperately on the planet. He is an invaluable resource for love and healing. Examples of how he helped me personally? Through difficult relationships (abuse), loneliness, feeling "different" from others, losing hope when being persecuted, I'm a sensitive person, Bruce gave me a voice, I will forever be grateful for this.

A psychotherapist speaks of healing, noting the complexities of life that therapy addresses.

> I first became aware of Springsteen in the mid-1980s with the *Born in the U.S.A.* album. I was a casual fan then—Springsteen was all over the radio, MTV, etc., . . . and I was a teenager so I was exposed to all that. Then, in 2002 with *The Rising* album I became a SERIOUS Springsteen fan. Attending multiple concerts on all his tours since *The Rising* and scouring his back catalog. I am one of those fans who believes that Springsteen's music truly is the soundtrack to my life. His music is also my therapy—and I am a psychotherapist—so I use his music all the time with clients to help them live more comfortably in the contradictions and complexities of their lives.

This woman describes a complex emotional process when life was caving in around her, and the song that rescued her.

> I know exactly why I love this song, "This Is Your Sword" . . . I attended the concert. For a variety of reasons, a good deal of which were my own fault, I entered the arena furious at the world. I was standing at the back of General Admission area in tears. I was on the verge of leaving, going outside to have a cigarette when the show started. Mind you I had traveled pretty far to go to this show, and

> I had quit smoking 11 months before. The first song was "Don't Change," a cover that Bruce had started playing in Australia, a song I really liked but I couldn't pay attention to because I was near hysterics. Then next he played "My Love Will Not Let You Down" and "No Surrender." These three songs all have lyrics that spoke to me and my feelings right that minute, but the message was coming in only subliminally. Finally "This Is Your Sword" got through. Bruce, in my mind was talking directly to me . . . "here take this shield, take this sword, take my love and take my (Bruce's) existence in this world and get up and live to fight another day." And I did. It was a great concert and I was walking 10 feet off the ground leaving the arena. I am an atheist but even though Bruce references religion in so many songs it does not offend me. He writes with so much respect for humanity and with such intelligence I feel he is my spokesman to the world. Even though Bruce writes mostly about men and situations that I don't really relate to personally he does express my worldview.

DEPRESSION CAN CRIPPLE ONE'S LIFE; SUICIDE CAN TAKE IT FOREVER

What does it mean to speak of clinical depression or not being able to get out of bed? What makes people think about suicide and even seriously consider it? The language women used in some responses went beyond feeling down or unhappy, which are normal and expected emotions for most people. While Springsteen's music is not the cure for serious depression, and we urge anyone with serious thoughts of suicide to reach out for professional help immediately, for some women fans his work eased their depression. "Sometimes when in a tough situation, I will wonder how Bruce would handle that same situation I am into. Also, when I was suffering from a clinical depression, I went to his concert and felt it was part of the cure process." "His lyrics have kept me from severe depression at times." "I suffer from depression. When I am struggling to find the energy just to get out of bed, the song 'Better Days' helps me remember that despite whatever sorrows we may be experiencing, if we try hard enough we can find the little things that give our life purpose and meaning.

I especially like the last lines of that song: 'This fool's halfway to heaven and just a mile out of hell, and I feel like I'm coming home!' Sometimes the distance between pain/suffering and hope is really not that wide."

Some women fans faced other mental health issues. "I suffered for many years from anxiety and panic attacks and I have used his song lyrics and mantras to get over my stumbling blocks. In 'Tunnel of Love' the lyrics are, 'You've got to learn to live with what you can't rise above.' I say that to myself and instead of living with something that may bring me down, I work hard and rise above it."

At times, despair can expand to encompass all of one's being, resulting in not wanting to live or contemplating suicide. "Lord yes!! There were a couple of times where I know that he's saved my life. His music can find me in the depths of depression and lift me up to back to where I need to be. Thank goodness those times are a rarity now." "It once made me decide that I wanted to live instead of committing suicide. And his music has given me support, faith, joy, and friends. It has carried me through my life."

> It has gotten me through many rough times. As a teenager I was suicidal many times due to my family life, and listening to "Thunder Road" kept me from following through with killing myself. It gave me hope that someday I might be able to escape and be able to breathe and be free and maybe even happy. When I got divorced with small children, I was poor . . . barely making it. I lived within a few miles of the stadium and when Bruce came to play there, I struggled with myself over whether or not I could spare the money. I never could because it meant taking something away from my children . . . like new shoes, or a needed winter coat, etc. So on nights when he was playing . . . I'd sit in my window after my kids were in bed, and I'd just stare at the night with tears running down my face, listening to his music wondering if things would ever get easier. But his music inspired me to keep going and to keep taking care of my precious babies. He helped me hang on and reach a point in my life where I am finally content and happy.

That sense of inertia and diminishment that often accompanies severe depression, being unable to function or even get out of bed, can feed on itself and hijack one's existence. Springsteen's music seems to have interrupted that downward spiral, or held it in check, for these women.

Beyond interrupting the spiral of depression, Springsteen's music can be a trigger for reconnecting with joy and love. "His music has saved my life! From day one, his music has helped me in every way. His music has given me hope when I've felt hopeless. After eight personal losses of every kind, a friend flew me to a show and it saved my life. His music has given me inspiration to pursue a life outside the norm and to believe. His music has connected me internally with joy and happiness. People travel all over the world for his shows because of the love fest that happens inside that arena." Many women experienced support, healing, and even love from Springsteen's music and performances in the face of devastating depression.

RISING . . . AGAIN

The act of rising invokes images resonating with strength, hope, love, and faith, whether they be the rising of the phoenix from the ashes, Christ from the dead, or a multitude of people gathering for a cause. Something forward looking is happening, something requiring but also giving energy and action. Yet what one is rising from is often death, despair, ashes, the grave. *The Rising* album and song emerged from ground strewn with dust and ashes, yet they convey hope and movement. The word "trauma" hardly seems adequate to describe the beginning point of this rising, and "collective trauma" adds only slightly more, as it was, for many Americans, a totally unprecedented and completely unexpected event. Women mentioned it throughout different survey questions. It was not unusual to have a personal relationship with September 11, given where they lived or knowing someone directly involved, so *The Rising* resonated on many levels. "His music on *The Rising* is very healing and uplifting and maybe never more so than after 9/11 when he wrote it. The country (US) really needed that, and when I saw him live for the first time, and he was performing those songs, it was cathartic and magical. It lifted me up and gave me hope." "Yes, his songs always make me feel better if I need a pick-me-up. Most important was his music in *The Rising* album when all of New York and New Jersey needed him very badly. He helped us heal." The idea of New York and New Jersey needing him feels weighty and true, given their ground zero location and the thousands of friends, neighbors, and family lost, although fans beyond those states needed him too.

"I think *The Rising* was a message to all fans that although the events of 9/11 were horrifying, we were going to be ok and together, we would be strong again." "There are probably a ton of ways. One instance I can think of is after 9/11 and *The Rising* came out. It was a great comfort listening to that album and having some outlet and connection through the lyrics." Although each experience is unique, common themes emerged in terms of what the music offered: giving words to feelings, healing, uplifting, togetherness, strength, connection, comfort.

This album had a special power for some. "After 9/11 listening to *The Rising* made me start to feel 'normal' again." One can ask what "normal" means, particularly in quotation marks, but it sounds positive. "Yes, for sure his music has helped me. One of the best examples goes back to *The Rising*, again. That album and those concerts helped me come to terms with the sheer horror and devastation of all of the lives lost, the impact to NYC and the rest of the country and world." "Horror" and "devastation" are not words used lightly, but they clearly expressed what she was feeling. "He articulated my feelings. He puts my vision into words. He continues to do this. For example, when I first took a ferry boat over to the World Trade Center after 9/11, my first reaction was to think about how empty the sky looked. Sure enough on *The Rising*, Springsteen wrote 'Empty Sky.' He helps me to understand my feelings." Deep and troubling feelings, inexplicable at times, may need some intervention. How many of us had lived through a massive terrorist act before in our lives? And if one had lived through such a horrific event, how does adding another event of this magnitude contribute to and intensify one's response? For some women, Springsteen helps with that level of understanding.

Losing people and grieving can be a long and complicated process. A traumatic loss can linger and become more complicated over time. The vividness of September 11, the very streets of New York City and Washington, DC, and the fields of Pennsylvania, are something that many Americans felt intensely and some still feel. The layers to this loss are multiple, from the personal/individual to the neighborhood, city, region, country, and world. "After 9/11, I did find comfort in 'The Rising.' I had lost many friends in the towers and I felt the song gave me (us) some hope and purpose." "Always, I can usually relate just about any song to my personal life. Easy answer is 'The Rising.' I live in DC and knew several people who were killed at the Pentagon and the plane that crashed in Pennsylvania. After living through that nightmare we needed hope." "I also listened to *The Rising* a lot after 9/11, which I had a very hard time with. I think *The Rising* made me feel comforted during that time when I was very scared and confused about what was happening to our country." Permission to grieve and companionship in the process are sometimes necessary, particularly in a culture that easily "moves on." "When *The Rising* came out, I think it allowed me to grieve 9/11 in a way I hadn't before. In the early '90s I worked in Lower Manhattan near the WTC, and remember watching TV and 'knowing' those streets, and almost being able to imagine myself there. His music on that album covered all the pain, and subsequent hope that people needed." "His music and lyrics have helped me articulate ideas and feelings that I couldn't articulate for myself. I lived in Brooklyn and worked in Lower Manhattan on 9/11. I got out, reasonably unscathed, but went home to an apartment covered in WTC dust. *The Rising* put words to the feelings that I couldn't manage." This New Yorker felt the catharsis after her immersion in the event and its aftermath. "After 9/11 his album helped in a cathartic way particularly as a New Yorker who spent months reading obituaries and hearing peoples' stories and seeing how it changed life in the New York metro area. When I feel sad or happy I can generally find a song to address my feelings (but not necessarily the same song for the same emotions)." New York became a small town filled with friends and family and, simultaneously, even more of an international symbol on the world stage after September 11.

Along with its power in memorializing and processing September 11, *The Rising* speaks to other losses and disasters. "I lost many friends on September 11 and his participation in the benefit concert was done with grace and respect. I needed to know that someone understood what I felt. His words and performance were spot on. I was a crisis counselor for Hurricane Sandy survivors, and his appearance at the benefit concert truly inspired my work with my survivors."

The Process: What Is Happening Here?

Springsteen's work offers a chance for some women to move beyond isolation; find hope for themselves; feel, express, and understand intense emotions; be who they are, more confidently; gain perspective and find meaning. He also offers one more positive support: himself as a role model for therapy.

SPRINGSTEEN IN THERAPY

While most psychotherapists have gone to therapy at some point in their lives and education, it is probably not as true for most rock stars. A few women commented on how important it was that Springsteen has, in fact, been in therapy, showing a path to greater personal understanding and working through painful times. These fans responded to the survey prior to Springsteen's 2016 memoir, so they understood this about him before much of the world did. His therapy and use of antidepressants was noted in Carlin's (2012) book, *Bruce*, and in Remnick's interview (2012), speaking of his depression for the first time publicly, with grace and candor.

These comments came when asked what attracts fans to Springsteen. "His connection to his family, and his relationship with his mom and siblings, children and wife. I can remember seeing his mother introduced on stage in the 1970s and despite his anger at parts of his upbringing, you could feel the importance of family to him. I also like that he has been open and honest about his struggles with depression/anger and using therapy when needed." "The fact that he has gone to therapy for decades. Great father and husband. The man reads voraciously, and I find that very attractive." This came in response to Springsteen's changes in physical image over his career. "He got caught up in the whole superstar thing for a while but was very honest with himself after finding that success wasn't holding any answers for him and he sought out therapy. Some of it may have been the foolishness of youth. As we age health becomes much more important than appearance. I believe he stays in shape now more to stay healthy." His use of therapy and his psychological mindedness were appreciated, and perhaps his openness inspired others. His journey through darkness says to fans that he continues searching, learning, flourishing. In recounting a dream related to his therapy, Springsteen writes of that journey: "*We're all honorary citizens of that primal forest, and our burdens and weaknesses always remain. They are an ineradicable part of ourselves, they are our humanity. But when we bring light, the day becomes ours and their power to determine our future is diminished*" (Springsteen, 2016, p. 311, italics in original).

As Mangione and Keady (2007) noted, "We argue that for Springsteen, healing and transformation lie within relationships, even complex and difficult ones" (p. 180). That still holds true, and for others the relationship is with Springsteen and his music.

CHAPTER 7

From New Jersey to the World

The Guy on the Boardwalk Becomes a Cultural Icon

I feel very fortunate to be alive on the planet at the same time he is performing and evolving as a musician.

SPRINGSTEEN'S CAREER OVER many decades can be described in terms of expansion—in terms of geography, his art forms, and his role in the nation and around the world. Springsteen has become a national and international phenomenon, even while remaining an iconic New Jersey rock star. The geographic and national origin range of fans contributed immensely to responses to our first survey. Further, beyond the geographic diversity and growth of his audience, Springsteen's work has expanded into other art forms, politics, and issues of conscience. The last few years have seen an acceleration of such ventures, and women fans' responses to this artistic expansion were captured by our second survey.

We explore those expansions by first focusing on geography's contribution to local and international women fans' experience from the first survey. What does it mean to be a fan from Jersey, or a fan from Australia? Did we hear much in the way of difference? We then move to fan responses to artistic expansion in his recent work from the second survey: his memoir, *Born to Run*; the Springsteen on Broadway show; the *Western Stars* album and movie; the *Letter To You* album; his pandemic activities, such as DJ and a New Jersey fundraising show; and the *Renegades* podcast with former president Barack Obama. Each of these is discussed, as are general comments about the last several years' expansion.

Location: The Geography of the Connection

While Springsteen may not be the only musician or performer for whom geographical location and references are an important factor in their work, his image has been indelibly tied to the state of New Jersey. Yet, his audience has expanded to include fans from all around the world. Here we explore the ongoing importance of his connection with New Jersey for fans and the ways in which fans across the world connect with him and his work.

JERSEY GIRLS: "A RITE OF PASSAGE INTO OUR TEENAGE YEARS"

Jersey . . . New Jersey . . . the Jersey Shore . . . Asbury Park . . . the boardwalk . . . the swamps of Jersey. Location strikes a huge chord for fans, whether they are from New Jersey or not. His writings about his life and the lives of those around him, in a designated time and place, particularly in his early years, resonated with many women fans who hail from similar backgrounds. Given the rootlessness and displacement in today's world, with many people living far from where they grew up, or in a hometown irrevocably changed, perhaps a sense of rootedness and connection to place becomes even more important in Springsteen's appeal.

For more than twenty years, ecopsychologists or environmental psychologists have been interested in what "home" means and have coined the term "place attachment." While there are many definitions of place attachment, a straightforward one that fits here is "a multifaceted concept that characterizes the bonding between people and their particular places" (Najafi & Kamal, 2012, p. 637). Given environmental concerns, and more mobile lifestyles, among other issues, some researchers fear that the relationship between people and place is threatened (Najafi & Kamal, 2012). Many people reflect on the meaning that places hold, particularly places where we grew up or spent important early time, such as vacations, college, or the military. Perhaps, especially, if we have left those places.

Numerous women from our first survey (105) live in New Jersey, and 121 originated there. Springsteen spoke of his "rootedness" in New Jersey on the *Spectacle* television show, telling Elvis Costello (2009/2010),

> I lived locally most of my life . . . part of the reason is it was sort of the most quiet local life I could find and we're still there, we've stayed there. I looked at my heroes, a lot of my heroes, the people that came before me seemed to lose something when they lost a little sense of, I hate to say roots because you can go any place and take it with you anywhere you go, it's not necessarily being in a physical place so that may help somewhat. But it's just that sense of your own history, what your initial motivations were, what the point was. (p. 366)

This has played out in Springsteen on Broadway in which his rootedness to home and taking that sense of place with him on the road are evoked. Springsteen has clearly maintained psychic and literal roots, and an ardent fan base, in New Jersey. His work resonated with women sharing the Jersey background, intensifying their connection.

While many variations of connecting to place exist, it does not get more fundamental than "I live in New Jersey—it's in the soil." Another fan articulates many facets associated with the word "home." "I went to Monmouth College (now Monmouth University) in W. Long Branch, NJ, in 1979. Bruce's music and he himself were everywhere around my college county. Instantaneous love of his music was easy. And, then to catch a glimpse of the master himself was very memory making. He was us. He was home. He is what my best memories are made of." Communal rites of passage speak powerfully, maybe especially for teenagers. "I grew up in NJ, in a township adjacent to Freehold. Knowing who he was and listening to his music BEFORE *Born to Run* was a rite of passage into our teenage years. BTR came out when I entered high school in 1975. It, and later *Darkness* were the soundtrack to my growing up."

Sometimes Springsteen was needed when home was missing. "I was born and raised in NJ, so I'd always heard his music around but I was never a fan. When I moved to Arizona at age 25, I was so homesick I started listening to him to make me feel better and it worked!" A sense of "home" can cross generations. Springsteen helped some women connect with home and childhood, as this woman expresses.

> My Dad introduced us to him, with of course every other classic rock and folk and R&B artist on all the time. He would always play "Sandy" on the guitar in the basement and of course "Thunder Road." We always knew the "fun" songs—we finally went to see Bruce on the Human Touch/Lucky Town tour at the Meadowlands—and I was hooked for life. Every album, every show my folks would take us to. It wasn't until a bit later, when I was in high school, that my dad finally went on a very descriptive, almost emotional monologue about Bruce and how in 1972, when he first saw him, he could not believe it—how much he captured the sights, sounds, tastes, thoughts, etc., of the Jersey Shore—where my dad's grandparents would come in the summer and host a boardwalk game booth. This was almost too much to handle, in a good way—and going to the Shore meant so much more to us—the rides, the ocean, the games, everything.

For some women, growing up in New Jersey and listening to Springsteen sing about their lives was powerful. "I grew up in Central Jersey. Heard his music in high school, and thought he was singing about my life." Most high school concerts don't feature the next Bruce Springsteen, but if you were in New Jersey at a certain time, and lucky, yours did. "I saw him play a concert at a local high school in April 1973. I went largely on the 'strength' of the opening band, Satan's Jury, who had played at a school dance some weeks prior. That this local boy Springsteen, who had an album out which spotlighted our area was the headliner was a bonus. He hit the stage, I fell in love and the rest is history."

Geography is compelling, even for a peripatetic nation such as the United States, where corporate culture has so homogenized once-distinct regions that the same over-priced coffee thrives throughout the country. Perhaps that makes the few markers of local culture even more vital to who we are, allowing fans not from New Jersey to appreciate the importance of place to him, finding universality in his particularity. *New York Times* columnist David Brooks (2012) tapped into this idea after attending Springsteen concerts in Europe. "It's a paradox that the artists who have the widest global purchase are also the ones who have created the most local and distinctive story landscapes."

Many examples exist of people forsaking their roots or being uprooted against their will and forced to leave their homes, cities, or country. The United States is a nation of immigrants, many of our ancestors having left homes by choice, necessity, or force. Yet roots remain an intractable part of the human experience and identity, contributing to who we are and how we move about our world. One uprooted fan from Italy expresses this. "I've been taking away from NEW YORK when I was 12, my parents took me to Italy to live for good, but I've always been homesick and his music always makes me feel at home!"

INTERNATIONAL EXPERIENCE: "THE WAY HE UNITES PEOPLE FROM ALL OVER THE WORLD . . . IS REMARKABLE!"

Springsteen is certainly not the first performer to have an international following, but the extent of his international audience—which according to Springsteen (Obama & Springsteen, 2021) is now much bigger overseas, with only around a third of his audience in the United States—may be surprising for someone whose work and commentary are passionate about his country. One could imagine these characteristics might not appeal internationally given the varying worldwide role of the United States over his career. Yet Springsteen notes an ongoing "deep fascination" in other countries with the positive aspects of the United States that the band represents, and an appreciation for the complexity of the band's message. "We celebrate what's best about the country and we criticize the country's failings, and I think that overseas people respect that" (Obama & Springsteen, April 5, 2021, No. 8). We found very few differences in the substance of international women fans' comments, with two exceptions: the worldwide Springsteen communities and travel involved, and the learning about, or commenting on, America.

Traveling for Live Shows

Extensive, international travel to see Springsteen, missing concerts because of expense or inability to get tickets, wishing they could see him more often, and missing events not easily accessed overseas, were parts of international fans' experiences. Still, nothing sounded as important as seeing Springsteen live and engaging with fans, as one from Finland captures.

> English it's not my mother tongue but I hope I could say what I really feel and mean. I think it is so so difficult to explain (usually I don't) someone what happens in live show when you are in a pit and experience everything with Bruce and the band. I'm not religious person at all but that experience is something I can't find the right words to describe it the way I really feel:) I love traveling abroad too so live shows are such a nice (best) reason to spend your holiday . . . and you get to know some other fans too and feel happy with your life! We have also here in my home city a fan forum and we meet every now and then . . . so it's not only fans abroad.

These fans describe similar events and feelings. "I have visited some interesting cities and been brave enough to travel abroad on my own (a big deal for me. I hate flying) just because of Bruce Springsteen. He has also cost me a lot of money I could have spent on other things but I don't begrudge a penny of it." "The bigger way that it has helped has been when I have traveled in order to go to shows (because he has never come to Nova Scotia where I live) traveling to see Bruce has usually involved trips with my sister. It gives us a connection with each other and a great excuse to spend time together."

> The thing that really stands out for me is actually Bruce's fans. I've had the pleasure of seeing him in Ireland, England, France, Italy, and Spain and to be honest it's truly amazing to witness how serious his fans actually feel about him. It's like being a member of this worldwide club that some people have absolutely no concept of. For example, at home in Belfast many of my friends actually think I'm quite "stalker" like in my pursuit to see him live when in actual fact it's all

> about the music for me not the man! I've tried to explain his live performances and his performances but until you have witnessed this phenomena then you can't really imagine it. For me, it's definitely about the music but in particular the live concerts. So come on Bruce, get touring again so that I can get my fix!

Internationalism runs deep, with travel to other places, Springsteen's connection to other countries, and connecting to fans. This fan from England perhaps identifies with Springsteen and appreciates the fan relationship. "He's half Italian so that appeals to me as a fellow Italian;) I love his passion for music, it's genuine and how he connects with people. It's great to see how happy he is performing. He recognises his fans and listens to them. He comes across as down to earth and approachable." Following Bruce led this fan to a desire to visit his places. "I'm from Austria and met many other people from the austrian springsteen community we are traveling together to concerts, we meet regularly, I found many new friends. Springsteen improves my life! For my birthday, I want to travel to america with some friends, attend concerts and do the 'sightseeing' tour in new jersey (asbury park, freehold, e-street, the stonepony, etc."

Yet there are obstacles to international fan involvement. "I feel like he is a rockstar that you can get near. Having been in the pit for 9 concerts and been able to touch him is so awesome. There's so many singers that you would not even get near. His 2013 Australian tour felt so personal private but when he came back in 2014 his groupies/followers from all over the world came and took over a bit and it didn't feel as personal or special." "I just wish I had seen him on his 1978 tour but he never came to Europe for the Darkness tour." "Curse not being an American, where the opportunity to see more live shows would have been greater. Also, wish Bruce had brought the TOL, Seeger Sessions, Magic, and BTR tours to Australia. We missed out on so many down here."

Relationship to the United States of America

Learning about, or commenting on, the United States seemed important for a few fans. One fan thought that sexism was the "American way."

This fan delved into that issue. "[Sexism] does not disturb me, because the vast majority of his songs are so good. It may be the reason why some intellectual people don't see the quality of his work as a musician and important thinker about America, because of video clips like I am on Fire." Springsteen's vision was welcomed. "It's an America that doesn't often make it into the news over here. I like what he stands for." From a history perspective, one fan "realised with each album it builds the history of the American people." An Australian fan commented "I guess with age you have greater understand of the subtle meanings or a great sense of world history that has inspired them. It also encourages to dig deeper and discover why and what he was singing about. Seeger Sessions and GOTJ both got me interested in US history and the depression, especially the Dust Bowl years." While this came from only a few women, understanding others' history feels relevant in our interconnected world.

A Last Plea!

From our second survey, we heard what many international fans feel: "Bruce please come back to Italy!!" Bruce's memoir should offer hope, as he notes, "Playing for our fans overseas was, and continues to be, one of the greatest experiences of my life" (Springsteen, 2016, p. 288).

That memoir offered much else too, including the straightforward and unprecedented insights into his life and career from Springsteen himself for the first time. We turn now to explore responses to the artistic expansion in the range and types of work and commentary that Springsteen has offered his audience, domestic and international, in recent years.

A Leap of Faith: Stepping Out and Into

Our second survey specifically asked about Springsteen's expansion into newer areas of work. Most of the respondents appreciated his endeavors, citing content and structure, such as changes in formats (movies/Broadway show), new and different genres, acknowledgment of aging, his pandemic presence, getting to know him more fully, and learning about themselves and their lives. We asked respondents to rate these newer works on a 5-point rating scale (with 1 as least important and 5 as most important) as well as to elaborate on their meaning. The responses were similar to the first survey in intensity, depth, and honesty, including admitting to negative or mixed feelings about particular works and branching out as a spokesperson. In the following sections, we explore responses to these newer works and the meaning they have for fans.

PERHAPS: "A VOICE FOR HIS GENERATION"

Many comments captured the most common spirit expressed about recent works, that is an appreciation of how he continues to evolve as an artist and engage with a changing world: "Bruce continues to keep me interested in his work through the varieties of outlets he has explored as an artist, as an American, and as a human being. He helps me keep exploring our world." "All of these (productions) have affected me profoundly because they all spoke to specific events going on in my life and the world—the death of my mom, cancer diagnosis, the pandemic, racial reckoning." "I loved the recent works that look different from his past work, because they showed another and deep part of Bruce."

Some responses added to the relational experience of Springsteen's roles of teacher, guide, and therapist/healer.

> With each of these releases, Bruce revealed increasingly intimate and vivid details about his early life, his evolution as an artist, his personal beliefs, and world view/political ideology. Somehow he keeps coming up with different ways to make essentially the same points! I've always said: "I don't want to meet him, I want to KNOW him." Having listened to all this relatively recent material (on top of everything else Bruce-related that I've consumed over the decades), I now feel like I do know him very well and I am certain my moral compass and ideology strongly align with his, which is important to me.

> Bruce's lyrics have always been relatable, the search for one's self and finding the ability to trust yourself for the unknown trek of life. The innocence of the ongoing search for sanity and self. Him relating his details, how the road he traveled with those warts led him to discoveries that he'd never realized, then being able to place them in context, to learn and repair when he needed to. He is relatable in the fight we all have growing up and then discovering and sustaining the person we want to be. How to cope with who he/we became and learning the solutions. He grew with us through the torment of childhood and adolescence into an inner person we all strive to become. Warts and all and realizing that is OK if the heart is where it should be.

Yet there were dissenting views. Sometimes these gathered around a certain artistic production, such as *Western Stars*, the accessibility of specific offerings, or political actions.

MEMOIR AND BROADWAY: "BRUCE LETS US IN, SCREEN DOOR WIDE OPEN"

Although Springsteen's memoir and Broadway show are two separate "products," it is hard to separate responses to them, including the ratings, which were the two highest (4.57 and 4.53 on a scale of 1 to 5). Fans, including from abroad, expressed gratitude about attending the Broadway show, and serious disappointment about missing it. Their discussion continued themes noted throughout this book of psychological challenges and growth, closeness and intimacy of the felt relationship, the ongoing conversation, his authenticity, and community. This fan very simply reminds us of the life journey. "His book and Broadway performance were life changing. Understanding the journey for him over the years was so special."

These longer replies unpack that journey.

> I bought two memoirs. One for the shelf and the other for marking and highlighting! I took my time reading that and it was everything a long-time fan was looking for. There are many moments in that book that stand out: the opening chapters about the influence of Catholicism, Clarence's death (hungry for anything at that point. *Letter to*

> *You* filled in the rest) his awakening to the power of Patti's love, his stories about his father and his mental health issues in his 60s. His frank honesty made for an even more intimate relationship with the man. The Broadway show was the best of the book and performance in one. Intimate, powerful, funny, and a once-in-a-lifetime chance to see him in such a setting performing those songs in that way. Tremendous.

> Memoir: a kind of a bible to me. Read it twice (German and English version). It's on my bedside table and sometimes before going to sleep I turn to any page—mostly I find a reference to my own life. Bruce always makes me think of my own life. When you talk to others you always try to protect yourself—but when I'm listening to Bruce (or reading his book or some interview)—I'm in a conversation with myself, I open up and can be honest to myself. He shows you what is important, what is at stake.

> The memoir is important because I have felt such a connection to Bruce, like he really knew my pain, when I listened to him. I didn't know very much about his back-story until the Peter Carlin book and then the lengthy *New Yorker* article. I don't like to google his every movement and didn't read the David Marsh book. And I don't have Sirius radio. When I read the memoir, it was the first time I saw how much our upbringing had in common. Alcoholic dads that yelled and hit and were underemployed. Also the shame of poor living conditions. That was what I thought the connection could be as well as my own depression. However, what makes the book important and the Broadway show important is how hard he worked and worked and worked to be a great rockstar but also to understand himself and his barriers to love and commitment, to express such empathy for the human condition in his songs, to own his luggage and learn to be an adult with the courage to be vulnerable and for me, a role model. Those four aces are a magic trick, and I don't know how he does it but he does.

Her description of his process echoes the psychology of resiliency and posttraumatic growth (Tedeschi & Calhoun, 2004), reminders that life-enhancing changes can come from adversity.

Springsteen's authenticity figures into this commentary. "Bruce's memoir and Broadway show were very important to me because until then, accounts of his life had only been compiled by other people. Those two vehicles felt like Bruce was finally giving his fans his version of his life and what he felt were the important parts of it, and we had been waiting for that. I think because Bruce's music can be interpreted so personally, it makes sense that most of his fans want to know him on a more intimate level, and those two projects helped to give us that opportunity." His openness gave mental health issues some favorable press. "His book and Broadway show together encourage us great ways to view our own lives; our roots, people involved, our relationships, our pains and joys. The book diminishes stigma concerning mental problems."

As seen before, connection to specific people, either for the fan or Springsteen, mattered. "I identified deeply with the Broadway Show. It still can bring me to tears just thinking about particular parts of it, specifically his tribute to Clarence and his stories about his mother." "I saw Springsteen on Broadway with my Dad, and I will remember each and every moment of the day for the rest of my life." "My Dad died 3 weeks before the event. It was just a surreal experience to sit in the audience for something I had wanted to attend so badly while I was still in the fog of grief. My experience was very different than what I had anticipated." "Broadway show came at a time when my father was very ill. My husband bought the tickets to cheer me. It really was a magical weekend. When Bruce speaks of his Catholic upbringing, it always makes me smile. I feel quite a kinship. It is the sincerity of his stories that touch my heart. One feels like he is having an experience with friends. . . . He always seems to be glad to see us and we have so much fun together. What a special man!" The relationship with fathers, which can certainly be mixed, continues to seep deeply into the Springsteen experience.

New fans also joined the audience because of his writing. "The Broadway show is what made me a fan." "About 4 years ago, I was looking for an audiobook to listen to while swimming laps. At that time, I knew very little about Bruce but the book got rave reviews & sounded interesting. One of the best decisions I ever made & one of the few books I've read twice. I have been a devoted E Street fan ever since."

Yet these works were not above criticism or skepticism. One fan's initial skepticism transformed.

> The Broadway show (streamed) turned me into a fan—I went in fairly sceptical because its premise makes it sound incredibly narcissistic, to be honest. But it turned out to be an absolute masterpiece of storytelling that resonated deeply with me. On a personal level, I connected the most with his recollections of his relationship with his father and reaching a truce with religion and spirituality, as well as being young and having a whole unknown ahead of you. I also found his approach to the authenticity of his own persona and attitude toward social issues interesting and refreshing. I love this show with all my heart and I'm grateful for its accessibility. Most theatre isn't so lucky. 2. Memoir—Good book (of course), but Broadway was a tighter, improved version of this in basically every aspect and I can't help but compare. Also, I knew he was very heterosexual but I really didn't need to know that much detail. I do appreciate that he does explicitly acknowledge and reflect on his own misogyny though.

Other fans remained more clearly critical. "Saw Broadway Show via DVD, very disappointed with Mr S, as this live show only accessible for Americans and the wealthy." "Broadway show felt 'stagey' to me, and if I think about it too long, makes me angry. EGOT [Emmy, Grammy, Oscar, and Tony Award] grab, very bougie, and that he basically confesses to his persona being a fraud. I honestly hate this show and am still so disappointed in him."

That possibility of narcissism threads through this discussion.

> The audiobook and live Broadway show are touchstones for a real fan of not just the art but the artist. Autobiography is a tricky genre and can be as much about creating or supporting a mythology as it is an opportunity to tell the truth. It's the former 99% of the time. Somehow, Bruce lets us in, screen door wide open, in a way that acknowledges the mythology while he shares his truth plainly in the light of day. As the receiver of the message, there is something special about the way Bruce bares his heart for us and in doing so helps us acknowledge our own heart—there is a glint of otherworldliness in the exchange and in

> that smile, an acknowledgment of joy at the exchange that comes from both sides. It's magic, love, and life hard won, all acknowledged in the exchange of two open hearts. He is a truly exceptional human being who has done the work to get there!! I feel the same way about other fans.

Yet that possibility of narcissism perhaps was tempered by the risk this woman sees.

> I thought the autobiography was very brave and demonstrated a high degree of vulnerability and trust. Would all of his fan base understand or support his story? Perhaps not but he told it anyway with integrity. I was very fortunate to attend the live Broadway show. It was a unique and intimate community experience. My emotional reaction to his performance on Broadway totally caught me off guard, but I was grateful for it. I respected the mental stamina required to perform the Broadway show with that level of intensity night after night. He calls it a magic trick, but it's so much more. He demonstrates respect and empathy for women, and he reflects upon the mistakes he has made in his relationships and how he wants to do better.

This fan echoes those who felt that Springsteen was talking directly to them. "There were times during the Broadway show that I felt like we were sitting together in his living room while he told me the pains and joys of his life."

LETTER TO YOU: "CAPTURED DEATH AND DYING"

This album with the E Street Band released during the pandemic, including some older songs, was mostly positively reviewed, and considered important by fans, with a 4.44 rating, one "meh," and a few other naysayers. It clearly brought to the forefront the pandemic, losses, need for connection, awareness of aging, and spirituality. A couple of replies were unequivocal. "LTY is a top 5 Springsteen album." "I think *Letter to You* is best album since *Darkness*." "The older the wiser he gets—with *Letter to You* it was a stunning return to his and the band's roots!" "*Letter to You* is one of his best works. I am bowled over by the fact that this far into his career he can still produce music that moves me as much as *Born to Run* did 40 years ago."

This fan describes the album's accomplishments.

> And then there's *Letter to You*. I feel that this is the band's best album. I know that's a pretty outrageous comment to make but I stand by it. Like *The Rising* that held the musical mirror up to the days of our lives, LTY did the same. Name another artist that could have captured death and dying and all that goes with it during a pandemic in which a half a million people died like he does on that album. And the movie is a gift beyond gifts. To see the band at work at this stage of their mastery and brotherhood is truly one of the best gifts given to a Bruce fan.

It provided help in coping and offered hope. "*Letter to You* was my daily escape during some of the hardest months of the pandemic. Admittedly, I gravitate toward the three songs written in the '70s for some reason . . . a sense of familiarity in the lyrics maybe." "Bruce Springsteen has kept me company through these hard pandemic months. He's always there, no matter with which work or if it is good or it could be better. I mean, *Letter to You* is not his best album, but it is his and it is enough for me." "The *Letter to You* album made me weep. It was exactly what I needed before the election." "*Letter to You* was a fresh blow of hope and life in the pandemic. Just to be able to hear new music was tremendous. and the hope to see a live show again at one point in the future is something to look forward to." "*Letter to You* and the accompanying Apple TV movie were extremely powerful to me. The return to some semblance of the original E Street came very full circle for me as a young fan who grew up on his old stuff."

A few fans recounted a specific loss that made *Letter to You* even more poignant. "Lyrics on *Letter to You* album poignant as I lost my dad to COVID." For this fan, the question of the future with Springsteen arose while grieving for her mother. "*Letter to You* came out a month after my mom died. I bawled my eyes out for about four months and was at the time also fearing Bruce might be telling us this is my last album. I was worried about never seeing him live again (40+ times), and then I was feeling like who was I going to call on in tough times." Sometimes a letter is exactly what is needed. "*Letter to You* is very haunting to me. I can barely listen without feeling like he wrote the songs about me and how my life has been. Losing family and friends has been life changing for me, and the songs on that album are beautifully written and sung. His voice, emotion, passion, sorrow, and joy are comforting."

This concern with and wish for what happens next was reflected. "*Letter to You* is like a promise of great concerts to come. Love the mature sound of his voice. Contains all his life experience." "*Letter to You* bridges the past and the finality of the future." That future is discussed further in chapter 8.

WESTERN STARS: "OUR DIALOGUE JIGSAW"

Responses to the *Western Stars* movie or album were quite mixed, ranging from "genius" to "neither here nor there" (with ratings of 3.93 for the album and 3.79 for the movie). Relational themes seem significant in considering works that captivate fans versus those that feel more remote. Given that, *Western Stars* may not have fit with what many women fans see as foundational to their fandom.

Several responses encompassed *Western Stars* and *Letter to You,* and the life cycle stage for Springsteen infused some thinking. "*Western Stars* and *Letter to You* are works of genius very rarely seen in an artist as they age. The lyrical content matures and he sings my life. He's not still pretending to be young. His work reflects his—and my—age while still being rock music." "It's exciting and inspiring to me to see that Bruce is still creating vital, relevant, high-quality music all these years later. *Western Stars* and *Letter to You* are among the best albums he's put out since the 1980s in my opinion. I love how throughout his career the theme in his work has both stayed consistent in terms of expressing his values and also changed to reflect his (and my) advancing age." "*Western Stars* was all right but nothing too memorable, the film was a beautiful piece of artistry. *Letter to You* packed more of the E Street punch."

These replies convey the range of feelings around *Western Stars* and how it fits with other work and fans' lives. "*Western Stars* was good but didn't 'Wow' me. I was in the West taking care of my mom and listening to it nonstop so now I'm glad that it reminds me of that time." "*Western Stars* showed different facets of creativity and insights into the human condition which have become a trademark for Bruce." "I didn't like *Western Stars* at all; it was too orchestrated." "*Western Stars* movie was great! Unique and it was a nice glimpse into his barn." "I thought of *Western Stars* as a one-off, sort of like the Seeger album that many fans (including me) didn't care for but appreciate that he is an artist and can do what he pleases." "The *Western Stars* movie was a great experience to introduce my friends and family to Bruce as we all went to see the film together in theaters." "I'm an old head and a long time fan of rock and roll Bruce and the Band. Not a fan of cowboy Bruce; seems phony and stagey." "I really enjoyed his recent movie *Western Stars,* as a lifelong Californian, I relate to his view of the West." "I really tried to like/enjoy *Western Stars*—his twang, gotta be honest—I HATE THAT TWANG."

This fan adds context and where and how this work fits.

> *Western Stars*. My Bruce friend LOVES that album and loved it time and time again when it came out. At the time, I was dealing with grief and loss and I had great difficulty listening to those songs. First time ever I couldn't listen to a Springsteen album in its entirety as soon as it came out! I could handle "Hello Sunshine," and "There Goes My Miracle" is one of the most heart-wrenching songs ever! The movie was a different story altogether. Saw that three times and wanted the transcript of Bruce's narration! That was and remains some of the most insightful and poignant prose he's ever written. That he composed all the strings on that album is indicative of his genius.

Perhaps this remark places it eloquently within the interpersonal context. "Was unable to see the Broadway show but that and the autobiography was an important missing link in his career-long dialogue with us fans. *Western Stars* was a departure from the rocking Bruce I first knew in 1978 but still part of our dialogue jigsaw."

PANDEMIC ACTIVITIES: "THE ARCH OF EMOTIONALITY RISE OVER TIME"

Themes of comfort, companionship, presence, realness, connection, and caring pervaded responses about pandemic activities of Sirius DJ shows and the New Jersey fundraiser, along with frustration from fans, typically outside the United States, who couldn't access these, giving it a 4.06 rating. Some fans noted the introduction to a new song or musician as adding to the radio shows.

The relief and joy are palpable in some responses. "The Sirius Bruce DJ shows have been one of the most encouraging and inspiring parts of quarantine life for me. I miss radio and theme mixes so it was a perfect combo. Much of the music was familiar, but I also learned some new songs so that is always a blessing." "Loved the Sirius DJ show, but here in England I think what was broadcast was cropped. Would have loved to hear in realtime . . . and we only hear first batch." "Bruce's activities during the pandemic have helped immensely during this difficult time of the pandemic AND domestic terrorism in the U.S." "The DJ sessions, especially early on in the pandemic, were everything! He gave us hope, a reminder that we are all in this together and truly got me through this mess." "Of all of them, it was probably the DJ sets on Sirius that meant the most to me. Especially in the beginning when day-to-day life was so strange and depressing just hearing his voice was such a comfort." "As far as the DJ appearances on SXM, I loved them! They were insightful, and his intros with the ambient noise in the background felt like meditation sessions on the feelings of a Jersey summer or somber feelings. Truly loved those." Unfortunately, this international response stands out. "It's not possible to listen to Sirius XM radio DJ in Norway. It's sad. It would have been nice to hear his voice during this lonely year."

This response weaves together the how and why of radio.

> Radio shows: unbelievable! I love them so much. For me Bruce was always that friend that introduced you to his favourite music. I wouldn't know anything about the history of "rock 'n' roll" (starting

with folk and Woody Guthrie) without him. So the radio shows are a dream came true! The radio is so streamlined these days, but Bruce played all the music he loves, all the music that speaks to the events of the day, introduces you to all different kinds of music (from the Consolers, Paul Robeson, to Lee Jung Hwa and J. S. Ondara . . .). I learn so much from him! And his stories—I love them so much. It makes these shows so personal. In these hard times he gives you something to look forward to.

If one still wonders why Springsteen became a DJ, this fan explains. "And lastly, the DJ! Here we are waiting for Bruce to play live from the barn and what does the Jersey guy who grew up on radio do? Of course! Play DJ. As a radio jock myself, I knew exactly what he was doing because I do that too! That's the art of radio. Meaningful conversation accentuated by the music. When you listen to that first show which was reflective of the difficulty of the time to the most recent one, you can really see the arch of emotionality rise over time."

THE MORE POLITICAL EVENTS: "TRYING FOR THE AMERICAN IDEAL . . ."

This quotation continues with "Bruce captures a lot of emotion within the journey." And there were certainly emotions expressed about the Super Bowl half-time ad, the *Renegades* podcast with Barack Obama, and Springsteen's political moves, with *Renegades* garnering a 3.92 rating and the Super Bowl ad with the lowest rating at 3.12. While not the first time Springsteen has been publicly political, these were very visible stages. Becoming an obvious spokesperson for a position, person, or values opens one up to reactions, perhaps more so in this politically divided time. Following are positive comments about *Renegades* and the Super Bowl ad, and then critiques of them and Springsteen's political stance.

Renegades and Meet in the Middle

Many fans were delighted that Springsteen and Obama held public conversations, using words such as "amazing" and "awesome." What particularly brought out their admiration varied. "His exchanges with Barack Obama are a must listen to. Wow. Two high-consciousness men of different generations speaking about those subjects like that was tremendous. Bruce speaking about the riots in Asbury was very intense. Whatever may have been missing about the importance of his relationship with Clarence was sealed in those discussions." "Two of my favorite humans on the planet just chilling and hanging together."

Specific admiration for both Springsteen and Obama's perspectives on America was important for some fans. "Bruce remains quintessentially for me an American icon. I have grown up with his music and admire him personally and professionally. I admire both Bruce and President Obama so that is a gimme." The bond between them and their openness to discussing fraught issues such as race mattered. "*Renegades* podcast: actually a dream came true. Remember when Bruce played for Obama during the first election campaign? Bruce joked, "He calls me once every week"—and I thought: well, he should! And when they went on vacation together—who wouldn't have liked to play a little mouse and listen in secret?" "In this time of America's history and social reckoning, it was very helpful to listen to them both talk about the past and present regarding racial issues." "The back and forth and clear friendship between two of the people I respect most was remarkable. They were both so open and real! Holy shamoley. I appreciated their thinking around race, masculinity, family, music, fathers . . . and the parallels in their very different lives illuminated each of them more clearly." "I specifically resonated with the podcast because it was so interesting to hear two successful individuals of completely different careers share common ground on the things that make us all human."

Some women saw great value in the Super Bowl ad, naming long-standing themes, such as relationship to America, hope, and authenticity. "The Super Bowl ad was a promotion for America, and it made sense that he did it. Bruce loves this country, and he found a way to speak from his heart, sow seeds of hope with heart-filled imagery that left me feeling filled up. The last image of his hand surfing the invisible wind was everything." "JEEP AD SAID SOMETHING VERY IMPORTANT." "I flipping loved the Super Bowl ad, I loved that he took his moment to get across to a billion people a message he's been trying to get across everywhere he goes. The haters are going to hate but I say BRAVO."

Those who did not appreciate or were mixed about the podcast or ad were also quite expressive. "*Renegades* I was looking forward to but it sometimes felt a bit too buddy and not deep enough." "Seems a bit pointless." "I enjoyed the podcast, particularly the first two episodes, but the conversation mostly wasn't all that deep or hardhitting, and I think the topics probably demanded slightly more of that. And as a non-American I did have to roll my eyes occasionally, though more so at things Obama said than Bruce did. I also thought it was a bit far to call a podcast by two very established people *Renegades*. But I suspect I'm not at all in the target demographic, and can still see its appeal." "I don't know how to even assess the *Renegades* thing. Two of my heroes who could be doing literally anything else to save democracy and make the country better and they chose to be podcast bros."

The fact that Springsteen did a Super Bowl ad at all rankled some women. "I was NOT happy about the Super Bowl ad—Bruce has always stood for not selling out. Ugh." These women offer detailed analyses.

> Like a lot of other fans I was not at all happy to see him do any kind of ad, though I recognise it as more of a Jeep-sponsored Bruce PSA rather than an actual real product promotion. I have no problem with the core message of the ad, but I feel it was executed poorly, probably due to rushed production and a lot of yes men—it used language that is often used in bad faith in political arguments, which someone should really have advised him about. I also question how effective his particular presence is for a message like this, especially when projected far outside his fanbase—his long-term status and wealth doesn't appeal to the left, his core political stances don't appeal to the right, and moderates of all persuasions don't need to be told. It unfortunately did feel very out of touch, and I was not surprised by the negative reactions it got.

"The only time I was disappointed in a professional choice of Springsteen camp was that ad. To not participate in an ad campaign all this time and to have it finally happen and not be something that really mattered like the food bank really confused me. It won't change my financial support of his future projects but it felt like a bit of a betrayal to all of sudden do a commercial for such a oil/gas guzzling giant."

The Politics of It All

Several fans commented on Springsteen's politics that either brought them closer to him or invited alienation. While this theme appeared in the earlier survey, it seemed to blossom here given that Springsteen's political acts have grown, as has divisiveness in general. Some fans rejected his political statements unequivocally. "His Superbowl ad was a shitshow. His interview with Obama was horrific." "Superbowl ad and podcast mostly for American audiences. Interested solely for Springsteen." "I thought the Superbowl ad and podcast were lame, just cause neo-liberalism isn't my cup of tea." "I love Bruce but do not appreciate when his politics becomes the focus of his work. Would never listen to a podcast that he participates in with any politician, Democrat or Republican." "While I am a long-time fan of his music and writings, I do not hold any regard into his political views or opinions. That is why I did not go out of my way to listen to the at-home recordings or the Barack Obama interviews." "Bruce is veering away from the musical style that always appealed to me. He is becoming more political, and leaning to the left (which I disagree with)."

Others emphasized what they would rather hear. "I'm more interested in Bruce talking about Bruce rather than politics." "Bruce is certainly THE VOICE for Americans. Yet, I think he should keep quiet on actual policy/political movements and for whom he sides. I'm interested in the man, his music, the band, and how they create their magic . . . not the politics to which they subscribe." "The music wasn't bad, however, the Politics have turned me off. Many Republicans are disgusted." "I love his work. Not in line with his politics. Love his live shows. Missing them the past 4 years." Given the political divisiveness rife in this country, it was almost refreshing to hear from people who can hold the ambivalence and not let politics turn them away completely, as can happen, even in families and among friends.

Some respondents straddled the middle or relished the political tone, sometimes identifying with him. "I share his politics and also grew up in the Catholic faith." "I feel in these times it is very important for me to feel there is someone who can be heard able to expound my views on social and political issues. Bruce's work enables this." "His lyrics and music are always relevant to the current country/world situation." This woman hopes to hear more about the country's situation. "Personally, I am drawn to and relate more to artists who have been vocal about opposition to the Trump administration and racial and societal inequities. The Superbowl ad didn't do it for me. Springsteen has a platform and voice, and I'd rather see it used to further justice. His voice was missing when it was most needed, so that left a sour taste in my mouth and probably impacted my receptiveness to new projects."

Finally, the shared journey is both political and personal for some. "New works have become markers in my life. Definitely on a journey with Bruce and, especially in recent years, both the political and person references in songs resonate increasingly strongly. The chatter I enjoy, but the music, writing, and theatre stick in my brain."

Expansion to New Territories

Any voyage into uncharted territories promises both unexpected joys and disappointments, and while we see some of each in women fans' responses to expansion into new geographic, genre, and content areas, for the most part there has been a growing together, even with differences, and new fans have joined. The heart and soul of Springsteen's early roots, attachment to place, and foundational relationships do not feel diminished by his movement onto the international stage that opens new doors for experiencing his work. Springsteen reached a pinnacle with the memoir and the Broadway show, meaningfully sharing himself and his struggles. Yet while other voyages did not always sail so smoothly, the thoughtful and heartfelt comments speak to continuing the journey. Of course, we do not know who has dropped out along the way, who has felt that these excursions no longer resonated or held them close, especially the political moves.

Two themes appearing sporadically included hope for the future (live concerts!) and some sense of aging. Springsteen is in his 70s, as are many fans, giving pause to consider time of life, where they are in the developmental arc from birth to death. This takes center stage in chapter 8.

CHAPTER 8

Twenty-First-Century Legacy

What Does the Gypsy See Now?

In the beginning I saw him as a star, now I feel him closer.

LEGACY AND ITS POSSIBILITIES ultimately confront everyone as they age and start to accept that they won't be alive forever, that the world will continue without them, that friends, family, work buddies, and neighbors may continue to hold them in their hearts, but they themselves will no longer be here. Questions often arise, such as how will I be remembered? What will be my footprint from my time here on Earth? What will others think of when or if they think of me? While we may think about legacy mainly in terms of people with public personas, such as celebrities, politicians, athletes, intellectuals, or artists, wondering what one is leaving behind and how one will be remembered strikes a chord for many people, as it seems to do for Springsteen. His undiminished level of productivity suggests he continues building his legacy as he moves into new areas while reaffirming long-standing themes. This chapter focuses on women fans' commentary about Springsteen's legacy in two ways. First, we look at responses from younger fans from the first survey who may carry some of that legacy into the future, exploring which areas may have staying power and speak to forthcoming generations. Second, we draw from our second survey, in which we specifically asked for thoughts about Springsteen's legacy.

Legacy has become an area of study for scholars in gerontology and aging, psychology, and sociology, and purposeful approaches to leaving a legacy have been created to help people in this process. It makes sense that legacy is being researched and discussed more, given the aging of the massive cohort of baby boomers—and Springsteen and many of his fans are part of that generational process. Erik Erikson's (1993; Erikson & Erikson, 1997) classic work on later-life developmental stages discussed the importance of generativity, giving to the next generation and the world, versus stagnation, and ego integrity versus despair, a time for reflecting on one's life. While leaving a legacy may be exponentially more complicated for a rockstar than for most of us, concepts around legacy seem relevant to many people. Gerontology researchers Hunter and Rowles (2005) describe legacy in this way:

> We propose that legacy creation and transmission is a multifaceted and complex phenomenon. Enmeshed in an individual's culture, legacy offers the potential for a highly personal contribution to the future. One's belongings, one's memories, one's values and even one's body may each be transmitted to the next generation. The process of leaving something behind, a legacy, is intimately tied up with our life story and with shaping the manner in which we are to be remembered: it is a mechanism for transmitting a resilient and enduring image of what we stood for. This drive to make life meaningful and to continue existence on some level after death can manifest itself in diverse forms and behaviors. (p. 327)

Hunter and Rowles ask a pertinent question when considering fans' views of Springsteen's legacy. "How does one create a satisfactory end to one's life story?" (p. 329). They offer a typology of legacies, including biological, material, and values, and they cite values as very important. More research and interventions are fleshing out legacy, including this pertinent question, "*What about 'me' will be remembered and have an impact after I die?*" (Meuser et al., 2019, p. 169, italics in original). Newton and Jones (2016) noted that there can be both selflessness and selfishness associated with legacy. Looking at generativity, narcissism, and community involvement in legacy showed the complexities of what one leaves behind and why. One of their conclusions, "The kind of legacy adults hope to leave behind is predicted by the sociocultural environment in which they live" (p. 351), suggests that the motivation for and content of Springsteen's legacy will be influenced by his many intersecting environments. Hunter's (2008) research with women supports a broader notion of legacy, connecting it to Yalom's existentialism and meaning-making cited in earlier chapters. She notes his view that life purpose is enhanced by "altruism, leaving the world a better place, serving others and participating in charity; dedication to a cause; creativity; and self-actualization (Yalom, 1980)" (p. 315). Her view of legacy is that "legacy emerges as a means of passing on the essence of one's self, in particular one's values and beliefs. Legacy is a method of leaving something behind after death and making meaning of the end of life" (p. 313).

Legacy can remain unspoken for some people, but that seems unlikely for popular performers. Here we turn the question around to ask fans rather than Springsteen about his legacy. Springsteen himself contributed to this conversation about legacy and death a decade ago with the loss of Clarence Clemons, cited previously, stating that Clarence remains in the band as long as the band is alive. Clarence would be there, his legacy living on. In what ways will Springsteen's legacy also live on? What might be the essence of Springsteen that will survive?

Younger Fans: What Resonates? What Might Continue?

The first survey asked fans to rate several areas in terms of attracting them to Springsteen. The areas included the meaning of his songs, the political/humanitarian stance he takes, his role as a working-class hero, the way he dances, his physical appearance, his connection to the E Street Band, and connection to his audience. Responses from younger Springsteen fans (ages 18–34) did not vary much from those from other age groups. Fans of all ages chose the meaning of his songs, connection to the E Street Band, and connection to his audience as most important (although among 65-to-74-year-olds political/humanitarian stance barely edged out connection to the E Street Band). However, fans elaborated their ratings in their comments. Here we look specifically at younger fan comments, including those addressing changes over the years, and reflect on what this might bode for his legacy.

IT'S THE MEANING: "A GUY NAMED BILLY WORKING AT A CAR WASH COULD BE ANYONE"

The depth and meaning in his work are clearly major contributors and might carry on the Springsteen legacy. "The themes that are written into his music will be able to carry on for years. It is going to last so much longer than anything else that is being produced." "I think he's excellent at illustrating life as it really is. He's good at explaining tragedy and darkness—like how it feels. At first glance some of his lyrics may seem literal and precise, but I feel like a guy named Billy working at a car wash could be anyone, really. That's how I can relate. It's the overall feelings/issues he writes about that really appeal to me. He's more abstract than he may seem to some." "His language, whether in songwriting or conversationally, is a huge part of what attracts me. The depth of his ideology is incredibly important, especially in a world that doesn't allow for deep thinking in pop culture." "What's important for me is Bruce's ability to continue to capture the depth of human emotions in his songs. He draws us into his stories about everyday people and which make us feel sad, happy, inspired, etc. This is key. The honesty of his performances is also important. He never fails to give 100%, which means that no matter what show you go to, no matter what songs make the setlist, you know he is going to take you on an emotional roller coaster for 3+ hours—which is exactly why we go again and again and again!!" This response encompasses meaning, caring, compassion, connections, values, and the band.

> His song meanings are the most important to me. I love literature and I listen to his songs like a piece of audible literature. I like that he's very connected to the E Street Band. In interviews I've read, it seems like he has a very realistic friendship with them. They've gone through very public ups and downs, and I like that Springsteen talks about that and doesn't gloss over the significance of friendships and how

> LIFE LONG friendships must be maintained and there are hard times along with good times. I agree with his politics and I feel connected to Springsteen so that's important.

One hears a universality here, a going beyond the particular to a greater meaning, that these younger women are capturing—a legacy of values perhaps.

WHAT HAS CHANGED? "I LIKED THE CATCHY LITTLE SONGS"

Some changes over time for younger fans might be expected, such as taking Springsteen's work more seriously as they grew older. "As I grow older I understand the hidden meanings and interpretations of his songs." "I think it grows as I grow. He's my father's age and I never really had a father so he's been almost a surrogate figure for me. In some ways, I learned more about men through my relationship with Springsteen as a fan than any other force in my life." "When I was first introduced to him, I liked the catchy little songs. As I listened to more and learned more about Springsteen and the E Street Band I started liking the deeper music. Then I went to his concerts and that was it. I was a fan."

> When I was a kid, my admiration for Springsteen was purely instinctual; I liked the sound of the songs—they were catchy. And, my dad loved Springsteen, and I loved my dad, so I almost didn't have a choice. We listened to the albums *BORN IN THE USA* and *THE RIVER* on repeat. It wasn't until I was in my late teens/early 20s that I started really thinking about the words of his songs. The first song to really resonate with me as a piece of social criticism was "Streets of Philadelphia." I wrote a term paper about that song my first year of college.

The Rising, again, seems to have a power of its own. "When *The Rising* was released after the 9/11 attacks, the music changed from my parents' to my own. I understood and 'felt' what he was writing about." Younger fans pondered growing up and growing into Springsteen's depths, perhaps a clue to his enduring legacy, to what lasts.

PASSION AND CARING: "FULL OF LOVE AND ENERGY, FOR PEOPLE"

Springsteen's dedication to his fans and the connectedness of the E Street Band drive the attachment for many younger fans, offering hints about future remembrances.

> He is so passionate! I feel like he means everything he says, he cares about the issues, and he cares about the E Street Band—he is full of love and energy, for people, and for his music, and it's infectious. I can't get into musicians who just stand around and play, so the passion that Springsteen has, though I have not seen him live, even is evident in his albums. It is because of his strong and passionate love that he fights against the injustices in the world, and has the energy and power to do so, thus inspiring me and my family to love more and fight more for what we love.

"The way he cares about his fans and always tries to make them feel great in his concert, etc. It's great that you can see that he really pays attention to his fans and plays every show like his last. It is amazing that he shows in many ways how important his fans are to him." "I started playing the saxophone because of Clarence Clemens and Bruce. Their music and connection was amazing to me." Passion underlies many responses, and this one says it succinctly. "He is so passionate that it is captivating." Can passion underlie a legacy?

His caring goes further into action. "The fact that he's a millionaire (billionaire?) and doesn't seem to care; the relationship he has with the band, especially with Clarence; the fact that he uses his influence to make a difference in the world (e.g., supporting Obama)." "His 'good guy posture,' he was never about that 'sex, drugs n rock n roll' lifestyle. Bruce's involvement with charities, such as helping people who suffered with September 11th. His talent and uniqueness and ability to develop a new sound every album he releases. His strength in life and belief in his own success." This fan prophesizes. "Today, I would like to say that Springsteen is the best musician ever. First, because he's very close to his public, he loves his fans, his fans love him. That is really important. Then, when I try to introduce friends to him, it's always successful. Not a lot, but they always love at least one of his songs. For example, my best friend loves a lot 'Fire' and 'Prove It All Night.' To bring a conclusion, Springsteen is listened by a lot of generations. And it will continue."

Many facets of caring and passion weave together.

> Springsteen is both humble and a demigod all at the same time.... He has an electricity that I've seen in no other artist (and I listen to a lot of music and see a lot of shows). Somehow he makes everyone feel important, like he's singing to them or about them. Even though he's kind of an enigma, he still comes across as being everyone's best friend or father figure (in my case). You believe him . . . you believe in him. You come out thinking that things are messed up but ultimately we'll all be ok if we just stick together. It blows my mind that a complete stranger can have such an impact on people.

Clearly, for many younger women fans, the personal connection remains important, and it might carry Springsteen's music and life legacy forward to newer generations, or perhaps it will be lost when there is no possibility for such personal connection.

CONNECTION TO PEOPLE AND PLACES: "SO THERE'S NOSTALGIA THERE"

Connection to people and places emerged throughout younger fan comments and often sounded like this one.

> I have associations with certain things. *Born in the U.S.A.* will always remind me of my father. He played it constantly. In my house growing up, we never had a treadmill, and my dad was a runner. When it rained outside he would literally run laps inside the house and I would sit on the stairs and wait for him to come by and tease me. He was always playing *Born in the U.S.A.* For some reason "Cover Me" and "Bobby Jean" especially make me think of that. So there's nostalgia there. In fact a lot of what Springsteen conveys is nostalgia.

Of course, the Jersey Shore fits in, perhaps as part of legacy. "Just more memorable. Brings back emotions of being on the Jersey Shore, the community, the family and overall good old times." Another connected it to his caring about community. "He stands for the everyday man. When the Stone Pony in Asbury Park was about to get shut down. He believed in community and took it upon himself to make it a historical center, where live music can still be heard until this day."

EVEN TO YOUNGER FANS: "SEXY ANIMAL MAGNETISM"

Attraction can include physical attraction and, although, as for older fans, this was not the basis of fandom for many, a few younger fans expressed it transparently. "I think he's gotten better looking as he's gotten older!" "I grew up liking his music because Mum likes him. Always loved the music. It changed when I saw him live for the first time last year, he has this sexy animal magnetism stage presence. It was so hot! So now I'm in love with him and his music! Haha!" "He was really hot in the 1979 live concerts. Now he looks great sometimes hot." Sometimes physical attraction grows as the psychological connection deepens. "My attraction to him has changed a bit. He has become more important in my life over the years with knowing more and more songs and understanding the meaning behind them. Moreover, when I first saw him in concert, I didn't think of him as a very attractive man. That has changed a lot;) I would now say, that he's very hot."

SO WHERE MIGHT THE LEGACY THRIVE?

If a major part of a performer's attraction to fans is the bond they feel to the performer, and especially the live shows, and encompasses the band, what does that mean for a musician who may no longer be so present, alive, and relational? Will just listening to his music, or watching videos, be enough to "convert" new fans, expand his reach, and strengthen his legacy? These fans, many of whom should outlive Springsteen, may continue to connect to him, but for others, will he become one-dimensional, a legend, not an experience?

Yet meaning that is so strong and deep, as was true for fans of all ages throughout this research, will not quickly vanish from the human landscape. The need for accessible answers to life's existential and relational questions and for a companion through art will not become obsolete. Passing on strong values can be the bedrock of a legacy. Music can and has continued to resonate with audiences for decades, even centuries, after its creation. Further, if we think of Springsteen in the storyteller tradition, of his songs as "audible literature," that too can thrive for epochs. Therein may lie his legacy for future fans willing to dive in and learn the oeuvre, to ask their elders or seek out his music and writings about Springsteen. For, as one youngish fan reminded us, the past can live into the future. "He is the embodiment of rock and roll. He is Chuck Berry, Bo Diddley, Little Richard, and Elvis Presley!!!"

Remembrance, Influence, Speaking to the Future?

When asked specifically about legacy in 2021, women fans had a lot to say, either briefly or more elaborately. His songwriting and lyrics, often described as poetry, and Springsteen as an outstanding musician, were named many times and deserve first mention. Of course, these are the foundation upon which everything else rests. Yet legacy could be fueled by something more, beyond excellence, and in this section the focus is on live performances, portrayals of America and its working class, connectedness to people, personal qualities, activism and politics, meaning and storytelling, and his role in the music industry.

LIVE PERFORMANCES: "NO ONE /NO BAND COMES CLOSE"

As to why the live shows are central to his legacy, fans described them as legendary, phenomenal, amazing, fantastic, unmatched, and best, and they mentioned the shows' length and energy. He was described as a "kick ass performer," "one of the greatest Live Rock and Rollers that ever lived," and "A great live performer who gave you everything he had every night." "A prisoner of Rock-n-roll!" After many compliments, this fan noted, "Plus he can Rock the House!" The E Street Band showed up. "Leading one of the best rock bands in the world." "His live shows and fronting one of the most versatile bands on the planet."

Details were added by comparing him to other artists and by reflecting on his performance and his impact on other performers. "His ability to adapt and change to all manners of performance." "A songwriter as good as Dylan and a live performer who no one can touch." "His music, his performances They are at the core of his *ministry.*" "Someone who changed a generation of future performers & fans." A few women elaborated in a way that infuses doubt into the staying power of live performances. "The live performances. The people in the future will never understand. They just missed out." "Us old timers will always remember the scrappy kid who busted out of NJ confines and those legendary 3- and 4-hour live shows." "Songwriting more than performing. There will be an endless number of artists covering his songs decades from now."

Some fans have plans for him—the next live concerts intensifying his legacy. "Playing with the E Street Band again." "The greatest live performance after Covid!!" "I'm hoping for at least one more tour." "Keeping in mind his age, as well as the ages of E Street Band, 'cause without them, and he goes solo, I'm done. But hopefully 1 maybe 2 new albums and tours."

CONNECTING WITH PEOPLE: "ALWAYS KEEPING THE CONVERSATION GOING"

Springsteen's ability to connect to people through his artistry has been thematic throughout this book, including his interest in and understanding about people, his welcoming stance to fans, and the "relationship" felt by fans. These recurrent themes are seen again in comments about legacy. His understanding of others was described by several fans. "His lyrics . . . the way he can put thoughts/opinions into words . . . his ability to somehow make an individual feel that he is your best mate and hears all the thoughts/fears/hopes that go on in your head." "An amazing songwriter who relates to the world we live in and understands what we all go through. Also he is very philanthropic. How much he cares about his fans and the special things he does for us." "His ability to talk to his fans through his music." "His songs about real life and real people—relatability." "His honesty and ability to relate to his fans on an emotional and empathetic level."

His global connectedness came through. "I know he will be known for his ability to reach millions of people all over the globe. He 'feels' people's joys, sorrows, hardships, etc., as only someone who has experienced life with depths of above mentioned. This is why he is relatable. He's like the 8th wonder of the world. Our national treasure!" "A songwriter who expressed in his songs the feeling of so many different people all over the world." "An artist that was able to bridge gaps across cultures and generations."

He has also done this for decades. "His ability to continue to write and perform relevant material that connects with many people worldwide." "I think Bruce is a poet who explores and expresses so much of what we all feel and experience. Well, the most important thing is that we will be known. For what? For being part of our family without having met him. For putting on words what we cannot say. For being there when there was no one else. For his commitment with what he does." He brings in those with no other voice or who feel hopeless. "Expressing the stories of those that feel like misfits, or the only one that something has happened to and you find through his songs and community that so many share these things. Putting that on paper and to song is amazing." "He gave us hope to survive this pandemic."

Connecting with fans, and their coming together, figured in. "Rock and Roll icon who inspired and soothed millions trough his music." "How well he relates to and inspires his fans. We can tell you our life stories with his songs." "To the way how it unites people and makes us feel, the lyrics give us universal messages." "A lover of people." The value of community asserts itself. "He will be known as a musician and songwriter that constantly extended himself to grow his craft and let us come along for the ride." "Beyond his work, I believe it will be the community he has led in building among his fans." "He will also be known to have the most loyal fans who would travel far and wide to see him. I have enjoyed his concerts in the U.S., Spain, and Paris." "Being incredibly intergenerational. My entire family back to my grandfather has been lifelong fans and even his oldest songs speak to me in a relatable way." This woman connects the journey metaphor to the whole group. "His unique style of bringing his audience into the fold so we are all a part of his journey and he is a part of ours too." His legacy speaks to mutuality in relationship.

Springsteen's impact is described as strictly generational, as in "impact on my generation," or as more generalized, as in "Music is loved by all ages." This fan describes the effects on younger fans. "The future for me is my son. He will look back and remember how Bruce brought me many years of joy. When he's older, and has his own family, and hears a Bruce song, he will think: here's a man who truly earned everything he has through dedication, perseverance, and love of craft. My son will know Bruce for being charitable, funny, crude, on the correct side of the political spectrum, musically gifted, insightful, and forever youthful."

Many themes come together in this description of legacy. "Being one of the most prolific, relatable, talented, honest musicians that made a huge impact on millions of fans' lives for his entire career, spanning decades. His fans are all over the world, of all ages and races. He continued to gain new fans throughout his career, young and old. And one of the best song writers ever, if not the best. And an all around incredible man who made a lot of people very, very happy. As many of us fans have said, Bruce's music has been the soundtrack to my life."

AMERICA/WORKING MAN: "A POET BALLADEER WHO SANG AMERICAN LIVES"

How does one describe America, and how does one both love and criticize it at the same time, holding the tensions inherent in America? How can a person be a working-class spokesperson long after that person's income far exceeds that of the working class? Somehow, for many fans, Springsteen manages to do both, as commentator on

America and as voice for the working class, two intrinsically complicated roles that can inspire a multitude of feelings and thoughts. Very positive and moving words, almost snapshots, about America and its working class wove throughout responses to Springsteen's legacy, and are included here at some length, almost as a mosaic, as they paint a multifaceted picture of those concepts. Descriptions included "love of country and the common man." "A voice of Americans." "The American experience." "As a world-class songwriter and poet." "Songwriter of the Common Man/Woman." "His commentary on the state of his country." "Standing up for the best of America." "A great American writer." "An iconic American songwriter and voice of the common man." "A genuine love for his country and his fellow travelers." "America's poet, truth teller." "Everyman poet." "A champion for the people." "His activism and voice for the working class." "A body of wonderful music that catalogs the human experience and America." "Social awareness in a completely capitalist USA." "Stories of our generation." "Equal rights for all people." "A patriot." "Music, representing the hardworking class." "A long career producing quintessentially American rock n roll music." "His ability to speak to the times and events. Heartfelt lyrics." "Erudite commentator of American mores." "To tell the stories of working class American white males." "An artist who understands the complexities of life, especially in the U.S." "American legend." "Perhaps the fact that's he's one of the last 'rags to riches' kind of celebrities might become more mythologized."

We hear images of what it means to speak to or about America, reminiscent of geography and location's importance, and a certain time in American history. He is seen as a voice for the voiceless, especially working-class people, aligning with folk traditions, yet also conveying universality. As an honest voice, telling the truth of lives.

Some respondents offered more detail, highlighting Springsteen's ability to incisively see and show complexity. "I believe he'll be known for being able to capture both the mundane and the significant moments in the American story with a love for his topic but also with a clear-eyed reflection of our weaknesses. ('Tom Joad,' '41 Shots,' 'Philadelphia,' 'The Rising,' etc.)." "For his love of America but also his honest discussion about its failures and shortcomings that he expresses in his songs." "Springsteen is an American poet for lack of a better word. His lyrics and ability to see the grandeur in everyday life really captures the East Coast mentality/experience." "As he is today the man Who speaks for the common regular person. Their hopes their dreams their woes their pain." "The most nuanced exploration of the space between the American Dream and reality that has ever existed in the art form. Revealing the beauty in the reality that exists in that space." "Relatable stories about the American Dream—the fantasy of it, and the reality of it." That space, holding the tension, fantasy, or reality, defines something critical. This person puts it into context. "His integrity, his legendary live performances, his prolific songwriting, his belief in this country's promise even when it's not fulfilled, and his enduring relevance."

History plays a role. "Like Seger and Dylan, he'll be known for being an American historian, a consummate entertainer, a lover of people, and the best there is." "A vast collection of excellent songs casting light on the times they were written in, the history of the U.S. & the human condition. Equally good at fun & serious songs." "His music in the context of his times, both sociological and political." "His revitalization of American folk music." American folk music, of course, has roots in history and telling the story of those whose stories would not otherwise be told. Conscience, moral vision, and striving to do better were mentioned. "I am inspired by his continuing call to celebrate, claim, and strive to be our best selves—individually and collectively. I do not know how some fans/people can misinterpret his vision and point of view. 'American Skin/41 Shots' is one of the most powerful critiques of our country." "Telling the American story in an authentic way from different points of view. Expressing the conscience of our time and shining a bright light in areas that need change or improvement." "The conscience and storyteller of American life, away from the glam of let's say Hollywood." "His efforts at keeping America as an open-minded and fair society."

For those fans, both in the United States and abroad, with perhaps a more pessimistic view of America, his vision was still important.

"For his views and depictions of (real) America, for showing the American dream is just a dream." "As an antidote to the myth of American exceptionalism." "As an American artist, who tried and failed to help change wrongs in his country." This fan situated several aspects together. "A long career with dedicated fans. An ability to speak to the common person and give us a voice. Songs full of memorable characters. A good man who loved his country even as it falls apart, and who believes in the promise of America."

PERSONAL QUALITIES: "HE'S A STRAIGHT SHOOTER. IF YOU LISTEN CLOSELY TO HIM THRU THE YEARS. HE HASN'T STRAYED FROM WHO HE IS"

Kindness, caring, honesty, genuineness, humility, authenticity, decent, principled, compassionate, dedication, earnest, energy, passion, sincerity, empathy, personal integrity, hopeful, candor, professionalism, and generosity—these are some of the ways that fans describe Springsteen's character and emphasize that who he is as a person will be a part of how he will be remembered and what will continue as his legacy. These personal qualities make him who he is, underlie his work, and connect to his fans. One woman said it simply with the word "heart" and another with "all around good guy."

For some women, honesty and being true to himself resonated. "His honest depiction of aging" and "his honesty about his mental health." "He will be known for his poetic voice of honesty, humility." "A class act who never gave up on his principles." "A songwriter who is not afraid of telling his truth. A gifted man who can say in a few verses the pain and the contentment life offers. He tells all our stories." "His honesty in telling his stories that resonate with so many and also to tell others' stories and his immense body of work." "As one moral conscience." "As someone whose career and personal life have set incredibly high standards." "Being true to himself and his fans." "For being a true entertainer for over 4 decades without changing who he was to sell a record." "Live performances with the E Street Band, his compassion for humanity, and his ability to speak honestly about things he is passionate about (without fear of losing his fan base)." "His willingness to bare his soul late in his career and talk about his human frailties, his faith, etc." "I think he will continue to create music until he can't anymore. He will continue to speak his mind through song. I feel as though he is humble and grateful for the good fortune he's found through a lifetime of pursuing his dream and using his talent." "As an authentic, reliable working-class Rock musician, but also a not always perfect human being." Even his relationship to New Jersey shows his transparency and his roots. "New Jersey love/hate/love, a lot of his albums talk about getting out, but he never really left. He still lives in NJ. His roots and his conflicted feelings (in his music) are really obvious and definitely tell his story." In an age in which authenticity and sense of moral compass feel rare and are often contested, it is not surprising that fans' belief in these traits has such bearing on their views of Springsteen's contributions to the world and his gifts to the future.

Caring for others, including acts of generosity and giving, along with hope, were mentioned. "His continued philanthropy. Always remaining an average, genuine guy when it comes to interacting with fans around the Jersey Shore." "His huge body of work, his social insights, his empathy and compassion for the plight of the disadvantaged and those left behind." "Hopefully also remembered for his work on hunger, somewhat similar to Harry Chapin." "A voice for the disheartened who always offers hope and redemption. A beautiful human being who cares deeply about society, history, responsibility, family, and connecting." Hope and optimism shine through. "Amazing music that really connects with people and gives them hope. For being a wonderful character who makes you believe in the good in life." "Story songs with a glimpse of a divine optimism."

Some fans connected facets of the Springsteen appeal, a reminder that these fit together and interact holistically, as his legacy. "Great songwriting. Enormous energy. A huge heart. The best live shows. His ability to connect with his fans. Character warmth and humor." "I feel Bruce will continue to be known for his ability to write such compassionate songs through the eyes of others, his unbelievable live performances & his remarkable stamina, the dedication to his craft & his fans, his decency, integrity, & vulnerability. Bruce has cultivated a community whereby his fans feel connected to him & one another. His willingness to expose his vulnerability can make a room full of 20,000 people feel intimate. Bruce's music, his values & his energy will continue to define him."

ACTIVISM/POLITICS: "BEING AN OLD ROCK STAR WITH A STRONG SOCIAL CONSCIENCE!"

Where is the line between humanitarianism, philanthropy, activism, and politics? Are all such acts ultimately political, or are some more blatantly so than others? Is one person's politics another person's humanitarianism? While the dividing line is indistinct, Springsteen's more obviously political acts drew the most divided reactions about legacy from fans. Many included words such as "politics" or "activism"; more decisive phrases, such as "political engagement," "peaceful activism," "Liberal voice"; or ambiguous phrases, such as "social influencer" or "culture-shaping." Others elaborated on how he will be remembered, such as, "First as a performer, Second as a songwriter, Third as a social justice activist."

So, what activism might Springsteen be remembered for? "Taking on and fighting inequality from the start and throughout his career." "He cares about equality and human rights and defends those who cannot get their voices heard." "A persistent supporter/voice for vulnerable people, most notably persons who are homeless and children and families who endure food insecurity." "As a political activist when he felt he had to speak up." "His legacy will be more than music—it will be about his stances on issues that matter to his fans (transgender bathrooms, voting rights, democracy). He is a true patriot and will be remembered that way." "Innovative, able to incorporate current events into song, his politics." "Springsteen will be known as a rock-and-roll legend, but will likely be boxed into the 'old white dad' category of music, which I personally don't agree with. I think his activism and voice in certain issues such as immigration and his public denouncing of Donald Trump will also be a part of his legacy."

A vocal group of fans was unabashed in their disapproval of his politics and concerned that this would negatively affect how he would be remembered. "I hope for his music and NOT his political stance!!" "Unfortunately I feel his political involvement in 2000s will colour his legacy for the average person." "In America? Being a commie (partly joking)." "Great Music and bad politics." After positive comments, this fan added, "But also a huge sellout of we the working classes, the hoi polloi that he abandoned for virtue-signaling with the Democrats." The disappointment and disapproval are sharp, and the questions for legacy speak loudly, but the connection to his work continues.

These two comments capture the intertwining of his work and political actions. "One of the greatest American songwriters of all time. One of the greatest writers about America of all time, particularly working-class and workaday America. The greatest rock-and-roll show person of all time. And he stood up consistently for his values. When he canceled that North Carolina show because of their bathroom bill I wept, and it cemented my fandom even further." "I think he'll have somewhat of a complicated legacy, as a critic of policies in the United States, but also a supporter of the nation as a whole with his particular brand of patriotism. Debates over what he really stood for or who gets to claim him will probably become more and more contrasting from each other." Perhaps just enough layering and ambiguity reside here for opening the door to people of diverse political approaches to maintain, or craft, his legacy in different ways.

STORIES/STORYTELLING: "PHILOSOPHICAL STORYTELLER WITH SOUNDS THAT PENETRATE AND RESONATE WITH ONE'S SOUL"

"Stories," "storytelling," and "storytellers," these words are used multiple times in fans' responses abut legacy. From his earliest days Springsteen created and told stories, and their relevance for fans came through when asked about legacy. Springsteen will be known for writing "Songs full of memorable characters," "Beautiful stories told thru song," and "Songs that paint a picture, tell a story no matter where you live," and for being "The storyteller of my generation and beyond." Both universality and particularity, critical for stories, come through.

Fans described different but related angles of what will matter. "Passion for truth in storytelling thru music . . . he has something to say and we love to listen then sing along." "He will be known for telling stories to which people can relate and addressing universal themes in his work." "His humanity as expressed through his words and music. Philosophical storyteller with sounds that penetrate and resonate with one's soul." "His empathic ability to tell stories that resonate. He makes the personal universal." "His ability to relate stories and emotions that cross all racial, economic, and social lines." "He'll probably be known as a Songteller (to borrow a title from Dolly Parton). Also as one of the best live performers ever (both with and without the E-Street Band)." His powerful storytelling connects to who he is and the capacity to hone huge themes in particularities.

Reverberating with a theme of helping, a mainstay throughout this book, this fan connects the help to stories. "His great and honest storytelling in his songs. They have gotten me through some hard times." Turning the experience around, this fan notes, "We can tell you our life stories with his songs." Clearly the relevance of his work for people's lives connects to stories and may constitute part of future remembrances.

THE SEARCH FOR MEANING: "NO ARTIST CAN SPARK OUR HUMAN IDENTITY, SPIRIT, LUST, SORROW, AND EMOTION LIKE BRUCE CAN"

While the concept of meaning has threaded through most categories of how Springsteen will be remembered, its singular importance for women fans calls for elaboration. As seen throughout this book, Springsteen's work overflows with meaning for many women fans, for their lives, their challenges, and their sense of who they are. He helps to create meaning by his works and helps others to find meaning. The way these fans see his legacy fits with existential psychology discussed earlier, especially Frankl's classic text on the search for meaning.

Fans' comments continue to exude meaning and consequence. "He will be known for his growth as an artist and always being relevant and true to his vision of what music should do for the listener." "His way of living that is about searching and learning and understanding." "A rock-and-roll legendary songwriter whose work is an abstract observation of human love and social injustices." "His songwriting is what he is and will be known for. No artist can spark our human identity, spirit, lust, sorrow, and emotion like Bruce can." "In these last interviews, Bruce has used the phrase 'spiritual songwriter' quite a bit, which I found to be really spot on. Bruce is a bodhisattva!"

These are fans looking for a deeper understanding of themselves, their lives, the world around them. "Providing a religion of sorts (direction) to those that might be lost otherwise." "His music which is so much more than notes and lyrics. It is a worldview and love of humanity that knits together his writing (in all modes) and performances." "For his music that goes from rock to popular music until funk and soul: a complete artist. For his lyrics so full of meaning and of human compassion. His message of equality and peace." "Extremely talented songwriter that can put into words the basic and complex feelings all humans experience." "A voice of social and emotional intelligence who understands and expresses the struggles of the human condition." "For saving many lives with his music."

This capacity for meaning-making and relevance late in his career remains robust to fans. "Someone who can still be vital at any age. He is simply ageless in his ability to write and create meaning for his fans." "Relevance. For always having the right message at the right time whatever the situation." "His ability to give us what we needed to hear at any given time—*The Rising* post 911, 'American Skin (41 Shots),' *Letter to You*." The emphasis on meaning calls to mind great literature, as this fan expresses. "The fact that he means so many things to so many different people, kind of like Shakespeare. People assume their own meaning and identity to his work because of his themes of inclusivity and interdependence." Yet the future is a mystery, and the selectivity of legacy, the "greatest hits" approach, may lose the meaning that is so present now to fans.

PARADOX: "A LOT OF PEOPLE THINK OF HIM AS A HAS-BEEN"

Several fans saw an important role for him within rock music, such as "Elder statesman," "icon of Rock and Roll." "I think he'll be known as an elder statesmen for Rock n Roll and for his contribution to American folk music." "He seems to be a legacy artist for Rock and Roll and Americana type music. He is someone who has had a lot of influence in younger artists." "His songwriting—his songs are being covered often (e.g.) Wild Pink covering 'When You're Alone.'"

Yet with that status comes concern about different ways he may be remembered. "People who are not fans—White guy singing about being poor while being rich. People who are fans—relatable music that describes hardship but offers hope." "The lack of airplay for the breadth of his body of work (just the few hits played) means most, even in the rock/pop arena, will not have appreciated why he is so loved around the world." "'Born in the U.S.A.' to the general public. To his fans he will be known for spotlighting the human condition and his philanthropy." "Alas, most people still will remember him for 'Born in the U.S.A.' I'm sure a lot of people think of him as a has-been, even though he hasn't stopped working or gaining fans since then." The public persona doesn't necessarily resonate with fans' deeper knowledge of Springsteen.

The future is not so clear, given all that goes into making Springsteen what he is today, and given the natural course of time and familiarity. This fan pulls several threads together to voice her hopes and concerns.

> Great question! Considering his fans are mostly older people and his albums are at #1 when they come out but don't stay there, it's going to take a new generation to keep him in any way popular. If you mean the future after he dies, he could represent the 70-20s Woody Guthrie. Which means that people are going to know his name and that he was a popular musician and patriot but maybe have to look up more to know why he was popular. I look at K-pop and the way TikTok and other media are changing how music becomes popular. I don't think

acts will have the staying power of the early bands that came up and were together for a while. So much is moving so quickly and as media change, so will what happens to historical music. I would not have felt like I knew Bruce's music if I only knew his greatest hits. For me, the depth of his collection is what has been my entertainment, literature, and religion. I heal when I listen to some songs and meditate on phrases that I think differently about like a flash of insight even though I have heard them many many times. I hope his genius is well cataloged for the future, but I don't think he will have a following like he does now. I would love to be wrong!!!!

Which Is the Road to the Future?

As with many legacies perhaps, it feels hard to home in on one or two aspects that stand out as the definitive ways that Springsteen may be remembered. Will his songwriting, person skills, concerts, politics, voice, values, or stories define the Springsteen legacy? Or will his legacy continue to be as multifaceted as his career has been? Given his role as commentator on America and representation of the working class, will he stand as the next Woody Guthrie? Among these possibilities, fans' emphasis on his values being handed down—also an area noted in current theory on legacy—feels paramount. Women fans respect Springsteen's personal and professional values of honesty and genuineness, caring for others, humanitarian actions, commitment to his craft, and giving his all. The primacy of meaning and purpose in life was vital to fans and connects to concepts oflegacy as tied to one's life story. Springsteen creates meaning for his life as he addresses meaning in the lives of those who hear his music.

It is harder to predict how these attributes and actions will translate to future generations. It can be argued that one must be present to fully appreciate these in the context of Springsteen's times and his performances. How well his work will stand the test of time remains to be considered by journalists and by future writers and researchers in American studies, music, or cultural studies. Yet musicians themselves also have a voice here. As this book was going to press, one of the authors was stopped in her tracks while driving one morning by a cover of "The Rising" by a Western Massachusetts band called The Whiskey Treaty Roadshow. She sat, stunned, as though she was hearing the song for the first time, as it was so compelling. A legacy continues, and even grows, when other vibrant performers take on Springsteen's music.

It is clear that after decades of music-making and public fame, his legacy continues to evolve just as his work continues to evolve. Fans who climbed in early on the journey and fans who joined recently share similar perspectives on his work as they continue the ride to see where it will take them next and what, in the end, it will leave behind, what will resonate into the future. In our final chapter, we reflect on where the journey of this book with women fans has taken us, what understandings we leave with to carry us forward. We do so by returning to that invitation from "Thunder Road" to "climb in."

CHAPTER 9

"Further on up the Road"

We have immersed ourselves in women fans' lives, feelings, connections, conflicts, identities, thoughts, hopes, and dreams. We heard women's pains and sorrows, alienation, and isolation, and drove with them down some dark roadways. We also traveled through exhilaration and celebrations, growth, and learning, and shared in the joys of companionship and community on the road trip. We explored decades of impact and reactions to being a Springsteen fan. Creating meaning, and creating the self, were major features of the journey, and in fact infused it with necessity and purpose. Joining in "relationship" has defined the journey and provided a foundation for the travels. Our exploration revealed much that is shared by women fans from across the globe, commonalities in how Springsteen's work has touched their lives, yet there was also always a different take, a unique focus, a personal way of making Springsteen fandom one's own.

What else is there to say? The voices of women fans—quiet and tentative, and strong and resolute—have been heard. They spoke with fervor, reflection, and eloquence. Each was an individual voice, yet together they expanded our understanding of the perspectives of women fans as a whole.

For our concluding chapter, the end of this particular journey, we capture our learning from these two cadres of women fans of Bruce Springsteen. This is not the final word, and it does not include every female fan of Springsteen, but our concluding points illuminate what we have gathered through listening to the voices of women fans, our objective from the beginning. We end with our own reflections on this project, on being Springsteen fans ourselves, and on "Thunder Road," an important song for many fans and the song that, for both of us, has stayed with us on our own journeys through life and as Springsteen fans.

How to Summarize Many Lifetimes of Fandom?

We designed a survey and wrote this book because we felt there was more to be understood about Springsteen's women fans, that their experiences as women had been underexplored and often misinterpreted, that depth was missing. In delving into women fans' experiences, we have learned much that closes that gap. Having traced some overarching themes throughout this book, here we summarize what we see as key dimensions of the collective experience of Springsteen's women fans.

- Identification is central.
  More than any romantic or sexual attraction, what is essential for women fans is the way that Springsteen speaks to and for their feelings, experiences, hopes, and dreams. Our work has expanded the primacy of identification as the root of fandom (Cavicchi, 1998) and emphasized that this is paramount for women fans as it is for men. Women identify with the characters in Springsteen's songs and with Springsteen himself, recognizing their own feelings and struggles reflected in his work and his life. Women fans identify across gender, hearing universal human experiences in his work. Tapping into a sense of the universal, beyond the confines of gender, was important for many and seems to speak to the multiple ways in which our lived experiences so often transcend simple binary gender distinctions

- It's about growth, and growing together.
  Being a fan is a significant part of women's developmental life journeys. It helps them to grow, to address fundamental

questions of meaning in their lives and questions of identity: Who am I? What is important in my life? Springsteen's role as a companion on this journey has an important dimension of complementarity in addition to identification. As a trusted guide and friend, Springsteen shows them new ways to be or takes them to new places emotionally or spiritually. Fans also noted ways that Springsteen and his music have grown over his own journey too, especially in relation to his writing about women. This evolution mirrors their own, further enhancing his reliability and authenticity as a companion. The challenges and opportunities that we associate with any meaningful journey animate the lifelong drive with Springsteen.

- It's relational.
  Relationship, connection, and community are drivers to becoming and staying a fan. Most women fans feel they have a relationship of some kind with Springsteen, and we see them as active co-creators, not passive recipients, in the relationship. Though not a comparative study with male fans, the repeated emphasis that women placed on connection and being in community with other fans and the E Street Band suggests that these dimensions may be especially salient for women.

- It's a source of guidance and support.
  It provides guidance for women on how to live their lives, offers support in the darkest times, provides a spiritual home, and restores hope. This support comes from fans viewing Springsteen as a friend or family member, teacher or guide, or therapist in their lives. Springsteen's music and sharing of his own life struggles are healing and comforting in challenging times, as well as providing joy and uplift that enrich life. His empathy and ability to communicate that empathy, and the resilience that many women see in his work and in his life, are foundational to this support. The psychological depth of women's comments belies any simple notion of fandom.

- It's diverse and shared.
  Fans were diverse in many respects—age, background, geographical location throughout the world, sexual orientation—and they do not all share the same perspectives. Springsteen's politics were perhaps the biggest source of divergent opinion among fans. However, across their differences, key aspects of being a fan—meaning, support, connection—remained. As Springsteen's reach has expanded over the decades, both geographically and in terms of his role in society, the differences among fans continue to stand next to universal and shared responses.

- It will continue.
  The similarities in response between older and newer/younger fans suggest that what women fans value about Springsteen, enunciated in this list, may be part of his legacy. Fandom seems a lifelong journey for women fans, it has an enduring impact and they see it as continuing in their own lives and, hopefully, in the lives of others. Fans described many facets of his potential legacy, from live shows to American icon to storyteller to caring and connecting, but we must leave it up to the future to decide what will most endure.

The Long Road with Springsteen

Writing this book made us reflect often on our perspectives as Springsteen fans. To end, we share a slice of our own journeys—our responses to the invitation from "Thunder Road" to "climb in" that inspired the title for our book—to add our voices to those of other women fans.

DONNA: SEARCHING FOR THE WIN

I wanted to understand other women fans in part to understand my own fan journey, as well as more about female fandom in general. Growing up in Britain, I was surrounded by punk music and friends with mixed views of America, and my love of Springsteen was often a source of jokes or puzzlement. In the early 1980s, when I became a fan during The River Tour, Springsteen was acclaimed by many British music critics but largely unknown among my new wave and indie-loving friends, perceived as old (he was in his early thirties, but we were teenagers) and out of touch with our lives. It got worse when, a few years later, *Born in the U.S.A* exploded, as did Springsteen's muscles. My defense of this American megastar was decidedly uncool, and my friends assumed that sexual attraction was the source of my devotion—that, like those black and white films of women screaming at Elvis or The Beatles, my fandom was built on a giddy, infatuated longing. To me, nothing felt further from the truth. I was less infatuated by the physical Bruce (though I would have been lying if I had said I was completely oblivious) than by the sense of someone singing for and to me, articulating what I felt within my own heart. I identified with the feelings in Springsteen's music, and nowhere did I feel that identification more than when listening to "Thunder Road."

Years later, a male Springsteen fan—the British writer Nick Hornby—expressed a similar identification, writing that, despite all the ways in which his world was different from Springsteen's, "'Thunder Road' somehow manages to speak for me" (Hornby, 2003, p. 10). As a British woman, sharing this sensation was even more improbable but true. At key moments in my life, the song I return to is "Thunder Road." I listened to it on the drive to my wedding; my friends and family know that I want it played at my funeral. Why do I love this song so much? It is an invitation, a challenge, and a reassurance. It is poetic and cinematic too. I love the romantic recorded version of "Thunder Road" on *Born to Run* but, almost more, I love the haunting acoustic versions that Springsteen has played live over the years and which to me reveal the complexity of the song and the depth of its ongoing resonance.

I identified with both the male protagonist and with Mary. I wanted to drive the car, and to sit beside a kindred spirit. As a studious teenage girl who found her pathway to a bigger life in books, what I loved about the line "you ain't a beauty but hey you're alright" was it seemed to say that, in the end, judgment of beauty was irrelevant—what mattered was spirit, connection, meaning. In a world where beauty was and still is high currency for girls and women, this acknowledgment felt liberating. As did knowing that the singer understood he was "no hero." Nobody was saving anybody, but maybe together they could "make it good somehow." As a woman listening to "Thunder Road" it always seemed to me that the promise of the song was about leaving behind the trappings and restrictions of others' expectations, but I could take my smarts with me. What was required on this journey was a willingness to make your own path, to find and claim that journey of your own. And, if you were lucky, you would find a companion to ride alongside you.

As I got older, the youthful journey I embarked on with "Thunder Road" took many turns. "Thunder Road" is less an invitation to me now, more of a challenge to keep going—to continue to live and explore, to take all the chances life offers as long as you have life to do so. When I was young and leaving home—the first in my family to attend college, the first to move long distances from home, "pulling out of here to win" seemed a literal journey. I needed to move away from my hometown to find a place where I really wanted to go and, in dreary, grey Britain, to leave if I ever wanted to "walk in the sun." I did both, for better and for worse.

The triumphant, defiant hope of the song has taken on a different meaning as I age, not least because what I understand it means to "win" has changed. If it was once about leaving and searching for a bigger life—emotionally, intellectually, literally—now it is about balancing the things that have been gained on that journey against what was lost along the way. It is about the knowledge that, despite the complexity and some regrets, I would do most of it again. It is also about recognizing and cherishing the small, simple, daily blessings of life, along with grand dreams and visions. It is knowing that I have indeed found companions on the journey to meaning-making, including other Springsteen fans, and through this study and writing this book, I have gained a fuller sense of belonging to a wide and wonderful community of like-minded women.

"Thunder Road," has always been with me on my personal ride, as have so many other Springsteen songs and performances. His music has supported my growth and my feminism, provided a source of guidance and, especially in concert, uplifted me when I needed it most. I still hear "Thunder Road" as a commitment to view life as an adventure, and to trust that I can find my own version of the win if I can "show a little faith"—in myself above all else. Finding art that helps support and enrich your vision and voice is precious, and being a Springsteen fan has, sometimes surprisingly, served me well.

LORRAINE: ON THE ROAD WITH MARY, THE WOMEN, AND BRUCE

When I open the top drawer of my dresser every day, I see a two-inch, ivory-colored statue of Mary, the mother of Jesus, who has traveled with me since childhood from, most likely, First Holy Communion. If someone had ever suggested years ago that I was a devotee of Mary, I would not have seen myself in that way. Yet Springsteen has illuminated that path for me, as someone devoted to Mary in all her embodiments, from the porches to the streets to the parties, in the multitude of ways that women can be Mary. . . . And "Thunder Road" navigates the route most eloquently.

For four decades I have been obsessed, mildly or extremely, in good times and in bad, during sacramental moments and everyday life, with Springsteen's work, through tours, with friends and family, and then through new vistas opening through academic conferences. The work lived within me like a self-object or internalized relationship, something real to which I can relate. All my graduate students at Antioch University New England know of this obsession, and many continue to send me articles, leads on tickets, and sightings many years later. In the last several years, however, my obsession has shifted to the fan responses from our surveys. In qualitative research, one reads and rereads responses repeatedly. Their words come back to me, I enter into conversation with them, I learn from them, and they become part of that cognitive schema in my thinking that said, "Why is Bruce important" now expanded to "Why are Bruce and female fans important." Every day that I work on this project I feel a deep appreciation for the fans who responded and for what they have given me and the academics, journalists, fans, and fans' families and friends trying to understand Springsteen's appeal and consequence.

"Thunder Road" stands like a lighthouse beacon in my life. It evokes my growing up years, with the screen door, dancing, Roy Orbison (one of my favorites and first 45s) setting the stage. The painfully self-conscious alienation, so plentiful while growing up, is challenged by the faith, the magic, the hope, love, and unconditional positive regard. There is redemption, but it is not much and still so uncertain! And it is a *joining* in the journey for the two characters, not an all-powerful hand swooping down from the heavens. What rock song used the word redemption? It brought that concept to life. The naming of the promised land hit hard. We can reach it, at least the one here on Earth. But it takes grit, effort, paying a price of some sort. His guitar is his salvation. What is mine? Or Mary's? Not all the old boyfriends, certainly.

Immersed in the images while never taking it completely literally, with enough universal truth in the struggle between staying on the porch and blowing out of town to find a better way, such that I was there, with them. I live with both Mary and the guy inside me, feeling their complementarity, both needing each other. A dreamer and a realist, in some liminal space between heaven and earth. Strong, vibrant women, such as my mother, my two grandmothers, many teachers and friends, dwelt with me since early in life, and Mary fit that archetype, with a quieter kind of strength. The specificity makes me love the song and empathize but moving it to the universal helps to make it my own, reminiscent of Carl Jung's personal and collective unconscious (Jung & Campbell, 1976). The psychologist (both clinician and researcher) in me sees so many people's stories in his songs, and in an early, foundational way in "Thunder Road."

It was big, holy, together, and real, and stays that way over the years.

Now I feel joined with the women fans here, who saw the love, honesty, and hope.

But back to Mary, who reappears over the years, her presence transforming the music to occupy a genre gathering in hymns, rock, the blues, and folk, with the musicality of the heavens. Her weeping struck at the heart of destruction in Moses' day. She hosted the party we all needed after September 11th. And she dances, so often. My family and I visited her house in Loreto, Italy, and I embarked on a thwarted pilgrimage to see her with my friend Lisa almost 30 years ago in Georgia. A life imbued with the iconography of Mary.

So many things resonating throughout the years. Fans said it: We grow as he grows; evolution; identification; struggles; companions; celebration; meaning. "Working On a Dream" plays over and over when I drive. The whole of *Wrecking Ball* speaks to me. I am ready to dance at a moment's notice at "Sleepy Joe's Café" and that song, for some reason, brings Cathy, one of the original Springsteen fans in my life, back to me. Attending a concert in New York, canceled by snow and gratefully rescheduled, with my daughter was the best. Springsteen on Broadway: sacred. "One Minute You're Here" shocks me in its baldness as I am a few quick steps behind Springsteen in phase of life. I will include *Letter to You* in conversations with friends and my workshops on loss and grief and discussing developmental concerns in later life. The journey continues, vibrant and vital, and "Thunder Road" always speaks to it, as new challenges and new possibilities for connection arise, even if the ride ain't free. Now I know there are so many other women on their own path down "Thunder Road."

The Boss Has the Final Word

In his memoir, discussing the E Street Band's work on *The Rising*, Bruce Springsteen (2016) shares reflections that we think resonate well with women fans' views and experiences. We'll let him have the last word:

> When people wanted a dialogue, a conversation about events, internal and external, we developed a language that suited those moments. We were there. . . . I've always believed that it was this dialogue, this language, that was the heart of our resiliency with our audience. (p. 443)

ACKNOWLEDGMENTS

FOREMOST, OUR HEARTFELT thanks to the women fans from all over the world who responded to both our surveys and shared such intimate and important parts of themselves with us. They are the bedrock of this book, and without them there would be nothing to say.

Our surveys would not have been possible or gained such attention without the support of Christopher Phillips at Backstreets.com, to whom we give our deepest thanks. Sincere thanks also to fellow women fans who helped in our original thinking about the survey content: Herpreet Grewal, Susan Nathan, Susan Keady, Cheryl Newburg, Rebecca DiBrienza, and Katherine Chapin.

Many Springsteen scholars assisted us on the journey of this book. Special thanks to Jonathan Cohen for sharing his own experience and for all the guidance along the way; William Wolff for his support of our work and publishing our chapter from the first survey of women fans; the organizers of the Springsteen Symposia at Monmouth University, at which we presented our work and which were such inspiring and enriching events, in particular to Mark Bernhard for his early guidance, and to Ken Womack for all his advice and support, and to Jim Cullen for reading and commenting insightfully on our work, which was a tremendous help to us in shaping our book. We are indebted to Daniel Cavicchi for his original work on fans that inspired our own. Thanks also to the editors of *Boss: The Biannual Online Journal of Springsteen Studies*, Irwin Streight and Roxanne Harde, who introduced Lorraine and Donna to each other.

We are deeply indebted to the following colleagues at Antioch University New England for their assistance: Kate Evarts, whose diligence and creativity spanned a few years and many parts of this project; Larissa Grundmanis, without whose knowledge and skills we never could have done the second survey; and Dr. Theodore Ellenhorn, psychoanalyst, for his clarity in thinking through some tough questions. At Rutgers University Press, Peter Mickulas, our wonderful editor, helped us every step of the way with his good humor and steadfast belief in our work, and offered valued guidance while allowing us to maintain our vision for the book. Thanks to all in publication and marketing at Rutgers too for steering ably throughout. We are also grateful to Mona Okada for walking us through the lyric permissions process with grace and humanity.

Special thanks to Bruce Springsteen for all he has meant in our lives, and on behalf of all the women fans from our surveys who wanted to thank him.

The authors would like to add the following personal acknowledgments.

Lorraine Mangione: My first acknowledgments must go to my family, as they showed me from a very early age that to admire and care about a known figure who is giving so much to society and to each of us can add enormously to one's life and to one's personhood. My Mother's great love for Harry Belafonte, danced to often in our living room, and her recitations of Mark Antony's speech from Julius Caesar, a la Marlon Brando, echo inside me, as does her awe for remarkable literary storytellers and science fiction writers. My Dad's remembrances of Babe Ruth and his admiration and affection for Joe DiMaggio, as well as the ever-present Mickey Mantle, permeated our household and contributed to my idea that I would grow up and marry Mickey Mantle. Over decades my Dad would fill the house and his soul with Enrico Caruso, Mario Lanza, Luciano Pavarotti, and Andrea Bocelli, alternating with the big bands and Frank Sinatra and friends like Steve Lippia. Sophia Loren and the panoply of celebrated actresses of midcentury held court in our house. My sister JoAnn and her best friend Cathy McKay screamed with the radio and television in the 1960s to "I Want To Hold Your Hand" just as millions of other teenagers screamed. My older brother Ciro began the rock concert tradition with certain minor obsessions, showing me the excitement of such events but also the pragmatics of getting tickets and getting to shows. My favorite cousin and role model for so much in life, Trina Battaglia, loved Elvis and filled her house with him in ways that I can never approximate.

Of course the academic influences always whispering in my ear include Irwin Kremen at Duke, whose passion for art, meaning, philosophy of science, and self-exploration pushed me forward; Norm Guttman, also at Duke, whose belief in me and discussions about eminent thinkers such as William James inspired me; C. Rick Snyder from the University of Kansas whose emphasis on hope, groups, and relationships as fundamental to clinical psychology resonated deeply with me; and Franklin Shontz, my dissertation chair whose belief in the necessity of researching the most meaningful and influential parts of our humanity has energized me for decades.

That is the backstory, then comes Bruce. Most of all I need to acknowledge Martha Cook, who started all this and had to endure the taunts ("Bruce who? Bruce . . . Stringbean?") from my younger brothers Joseph and Bharvi, Cathy McKay, and me, about her newfound love, but she was right. . . . for all of us. The Bruce group joins in, so many, but I will stick to those with whom I have gone to shows and whose fandom is exuberant: Susan Keady, JoAnn Basgall, Sara Weinberger, Cheryl Newburg, Lisa McCann, Rob Weitz, John O'Reilly, Maureen O'Reilly, Joe and Cathy Rubsam, Eddie and Lynn Aberger, Joe Mangione and now his wife Angie Testa, Ciro Mangione and Jacque Waters, and Bharvi Parikh. It is not just the concerts but the conversations, and the Bruce books, given to me by my niece Krista Gloden for holidays.

It is tough to be the husband of someone immersed in Springsteen, but my husband Jim Schumacher has held that role with grace and support for years, even relishing some concerts and his own favorite songs, including these last few years as I worked incessantly on this project. And finally my daughter, Alessandria, for whom early in life the Seeger Sessions played nonstop on family and neighborhood hikes and hut trips, and whose millennial skills and awareness captured tickets for Broadway, an uncanny feat that will never be equaled. At one of the lowest moments in this process, she and her friend Sophie Vaughan, a young writer extraordinaire, helped me problem solve over outdoor dinner in Washington, D.C., and recommit.

So why wouldn't fandom be a normal and compelling part of life, one worthy of study?

Donna Luff: In a book about women, I want to first thank important women in my life. Lifelong gratitude to Rehana Doobay, my oldest friend, companion at my first Springsteen show in Birmingham and my last (to date) on Broadway. Jacki Henderson doesn't get the appeal of Springsteen, but she gets everything else about me and has saved me more times than Bruce. Hazel May's unwavering friendship has sustained me on two continents, and she tolerates my fandom generously, even accompanying me on my first trip to Asbury Park. Natalie McClain, first Boston friend, for all the heart-to-hearts and her many acts of kindness. Tracey Nathan, music queen, has brought notes of joy into my life for decades. Bethan Roberts, my enduring life guide, has shared many Springsteen shows and her profound friendship with me. Parisa Zamiri, for making Boston home and reminding me what it is to see Springsteen with new eyes.

I am grateful for the support and encouragement of many other friends over the course of writing this book and in my life. The friendship of Tara and Todd Washburn has grounded my family's life in so many ways; we are forever thankful. My regular dinner companions, Eve Rittenberg, Jennie Roffman, and Lori Beaumler, have offered support together and in their unique ways: Jennie's humor and insight are unparalleled, Eve's generosity is unmatched (not least in tolerating Bruce talk at Thanksgiving dinners), and Lori, though not a

Springsteen fan, understands fandom like no other. Jeff Liebman has been a great companion on road trips to Springsteen shows (and shares responsibility for that Thanksgiving talk). Special thanks to Lisa Horowitz and Deb Siegel for nominating me an honorary Jersey girl, and for the precious years down the Shore with our families. Sincere thanks also to my spiritual sisters—Siobhan Cunningham, Lynda Banzi-Sponholtz, Lisa Domigan, and Suzanna Schell. Many others have encouraged my writing or shared their love of music, including Sowyma Sundarajan, Gill Simkiss, Jean Sandler, Craig McClain, Loren Fox, Rosie Carnall, and Nick Stevenson. I have also made welcome connections with Springsteen fans at the Monmouth University Springsteen Symposia and at concerts: I am particularly grateful for striking up conversations, and friendship, with Herpreet Grewal and Steve Stecklow.

I have been truly fortunate to find the best companions on my writing journey. Thanks to all members of my writing groups, past and present, in particular Linda Dittmar, Jan Jacobson and Mike Sinert (fellow Bruce fan), stalwart advisers and cheerleaders. Special thanks to Molly Howes for always being my trusted first reader, and to Joe Fox for insights, humor, and cocktails when I needed them most. Thanks to Alysia Abbott, stellar writing mentor, and to Grub Street Writers, Boston, for offering the classes that connected us all and developed me as a writer.

Heartfelt gratitude, as always, to my family. My dear sister, Kate Luff, teased me for decades about Bruce, then finally caved and bought the *Greatest Hits* album. This book is also in loving memory of my father, Don Luff, who always called Springsteen "Springbean" (it must be a transatlantic nickname) but turned up the radio on "Hungry Heart" when I asked, and my mother, Joy Luff, who preferred Sinatra but stood on a stadium chair at Aston Villa football ground and danced with me during Springsteen's Tunnel of Love tour. I miss them both every day.

Finally, none of this would have been possible without the support of Gareth Parry, who accompanied me to a couple of Springsteen shows and was never converted but has nevertheless cheered me on through all the hours I have spent writing this book; and to my two hearts, Ellen and Nathaniel Parry Luff, who have grown up surrounded by Springsteen's music and with a tradition of us blasting "Born to Run" whenever we drive across the New Jersey state line. I hope they will remember it fondly.

REFERENCES

Adler, N. (2019). Our butch mother: Bruce Springsteen. In J. D. Cohen & J. S. Sawyers (Eds.), *Long walk home: Reflections on Bruce Springsteen* (pp. 155–162). Rutgers University Press.

Alberti, R. E., & Emmons, M. L. (2008). *Your perfect right: Assertiveness and equality in your life and relationships* (9th ed.). Impact Publishing.

Alterman, E. (1999). *It ain't no sin to be glad you're alive: The promise of Bruce Springsteen.* Back Bay Books/Little, Brown and Company.

Anderson, T. (2012). "Still kissing their posters goodnight": Female fandom and the politics of popular music. *Participations, 9*(2), 239–264. http://www.participations.org/Volume%209/Issue%202/15%20Tonya%20Anderson.pdf

Arnett, J. J. (2006). The psychology of emerging adulthood: What is known, and what remains to be known? In J. J. Arnett & J. L. Tanner (Eds.), *Emerging adults in America: Coming of age in the 21st century* (pp. 303–330). American Psychological Association. https://doi.org/10.1037/11381-013

Ashkanasy, N. M., & Tse, B. (2000). Transformational leadership as management of emotion: A conceptual review. In N. M. Ashkanasy, C. E. Hartel,, & W. J. Zerbe, W. (Eds.), *Emotions in the workplace: Research, theory, and practice* (pp. 221–235). Quorum Books/Greenwood Publishing Group.

Barreca, G. (2019). Springsteen's women: Tougher than the rest. In J. D. Cohen & J. S. Sawyers (Eds.), *Long walk home: Reflections on Bruce Springsteen* (pp. 1163–169). Rutgers University Press.

Beach, L. (2023, forthcoming). The artist as pastor: Bruce Springsteen and Darkness on the Edge of Town. In Wendy J. Porter & Stanley E. Porter (Eds.), *The McMaster New Testament Studies Series 18.* Pickwick.

Bengston, V. L. (2001). Beyond the nuclear family: The increasing importance of multigenerational bonds. *Journal of Marriage and Family, 63*(1), 1–16. https://doi.org/10.1111/j.1741-3737.2001.00001.x

Bigner, J. J., & Wetchler, J. L. (2012). *Handbook of LGBT-affirmative couple and family therapy.* Routledge.

Bishop, N. S. (2019). How Bruce Springsteen made a middle-aged woman believe in the magic of rock and roll. In J. D. Cohen & J. S. Sawyers (Eds.), *Long walk home: Reflections on Bruce Springsteen* (pp. 30–35). Rutgers University Press.

Blieszner, R., & Adams, R. G. (1992). *Adult friendship.* Sage.

Bowker, J. C., Rubin, K. H., Burgess, K. B., Booth-LaForce, C., & Rose-Krasnor, L. (2006). Behavioral characteristics associated with stable and fluid best friendship patterns in middle childhood. *Merrill-Palmer Quarterly, 52*(4), 671–693. https://doi.org/10.1353/mpq.2006.0000

Bowlby, J. (1980). *Attachment and loss: Vol. III. Loss.* Basic Books.

Brabender, V. M., Smolar, A. I., & Fallon, A. E. (2004). *Essentials of group therapy.* John Wiley & Sons.

Brooks, D. (2012) The power of the particular, *New York Times,* June 25. https://www.nytimes.com/2012/06/26/opinion/brooks-the-power-of-the-particular.html

Bruner, J. (1993). *Acts of meaning.* Harvard University Press.

Buchele, B. J., & Rutan, J. S. (2017) An object relations theory perspective. *International Journal of Group Psychotherapy,* 67:sup1, S36–S43, https://doi.org/10.1080/00207284.2016.1238748

Campbell, J. (1949/1973). *The hero with a thousand faces.* Princeton University Press.

Campbell, J. (1988). *The power of myth.* Doubleday.

Cantrell, O. (2018). "To stand shoulder to shoulder and heart to heart": Authenticity, community and folk music in the recent work of Bruce Springsteen. In W. I. Wolff (Ed.), *Bruce Springsteen and popular music: Rhetoric, social consciousness and contemporary culture* (pp. 147–160). Routledge.

Carlin, P. A. (2012). *Bruce.* Touchstone.

Casio, H. (2018). Is there anybody alive out there? Growing up queer with Bruce. In W. I. Wolff (Ed.), *Bruce Springsteen and popular music: Rhetoric, social consciousness and contemporary culture* (pp. 105–113). Routledge.

Cassidy, J., & Shaver, P. R. (Eds.). (2016). *Handbook of attachment: Theory, research, and clinical applications* (3rd ed.). Guilford Press.

Cavicchi, D. (1998). *Tramps like us: Music and meaning among Springsteen fans.* Oxford University Press.

Challis, H. (2015). *Women in pop music.* Crescent Moon Publishing.

Cline, C. (1992). *Bitch*: The women's rock newsletter with bite. In L.A. Lewis (Ed.), *The adoring audience: Fan culture and popular media* (pp. 69–83). Routledge.

Cohen, J. D., & Sawyers, J. S. (Eds.), (2019). *Long walk home: Reflections on Bruce Springsteen*. Rutgers University Press.

Coles, R. (2003). *Bruce Springsteen's America: The people listening, a poet singing.* Random House.

Contino, P. J. (2018). "The cross of his calling": Bruce Springsteen's Catholic imagination [Unpublished manuscript]. Humanities Division, Seaver College, Pepperdine University.

Costello, E. (2009/2010) *Spectacle*—September 25, 2009 and January 27, 2010. In C. Phillips and L. P. Masur (Eds.), *Talk about a dream: The essential interviews of Bruce Springsteen* (2013, pp. 365–384). Bloomsbury.

Cullen, J. (2005). *Born in the U.S.A.: Bruce Springsteen and the American tradition.* Wesleyan University Press.

Cullen, J. (2019). Summer's fall: Springsteen in senescence. In J. D. Cohen & J. S. Sawyers (Eds.), *Long walk home: Reflections on Bruce Springsteen* (pp. 189–199). Rutgers University Press.

Cummings, N. A. (1991). Brief intermittent therapy throughout the life cycle. In C. S. Austad & W. H. Berman (Eds.), *Psychotherapy in managed health care: The optimal use of time and resources* (pp. 35–45). American Psychological Association.

Delmonico, L. (2011). Queen of the supermarket: Representations of working class women. In D. G. Izzo, (Ed.), *Bruce Springsteen and the American soul: Essays on the songs and influence of a cultural icon* (pp. 45–55). McFarland.

Demir, M., Özen, A., Doğan, A., Bilyk, N. A., & Tyrell, F. A. (2011). I matter to my friend, therefore I am happy: Friendship, mattering, and happiness. *Journal of Happiness Studies, 12*(6), 983–1005. https://doi.org/10.1007/s10902-010-9240–8

Demir, M., Tyra, A., & Özen-Çıplak, A. (2019). Be there for me and I will be there for you: Friendship maintenance mediates the relationship between capitalization and happiness. *Journal of Happiness Studies, 20*(2), 449–469. https://doi.org/10.1007/s10902-017-9957–8

Dicello, D., & Mangione, L. (2015). *Daughters, dads, and the path through grief: Tales from Italian America.* Impact Publishers/New Harbinger.

DiCello, D., Pidano, A., & Mangione, L. (2018). An Italian American view of grief: Connection, transformation and resilience. *Mortality, 23*(3), 261–278.

Djikic, M., & Oatley, K. (2014). The art in fiction: From indirect communication to changes of the self. *Psychology of Aesthetics, Creativity, and the Arts, 8*(4), 498–505. https://doi.org/10.1037/a0037999

Drisko, J. (2005). Intermittent psychotherapy. *Smith College Studies in Social Work, 75*(2), 7–25. https://doi.org/10.1300/J497v75n02_02

Duffett, M. (2013). *Understanding fandom: An introduction to the study of media fan culture.* Bloomsbury Academic.

Edelman, H. (1996). Bruce Springsteen and the story of us. *Iowa Review*, January.

Erikson, E. H. (1993). *Childhood and society.* W. W. Norton & Company.

Erikson, E. H., & Erikson, J. M. (1997). *The life cycle completed.* W. W. Norton.

Frankl, V. E. (2006). *Man's search for meaning.* Beacon Press.

Galupo, M. P., & Gonzalez, K. A. (2013). Friendship values and cross-category friendships: Understanding adult friendship patterns across gender, sexual orientation and race. *Sex Roles, 68*(11–12), 779–790. https://doi.org/10.1007/s11199-012-0211-x

Gray, J., Sandvoss, C., & Harrington, C. L. (Eds.). (2007). *Fandom: Identities and communities in a mediated world.* New York University Press.

Hammer, D. (2018). Cultivating soulfulness in psychotherapy. *Spirituality in Clinical Practice.* Advance online publication. http://dx.doi.org/10.1037/scp0000173

Harley, E. W.-Y., Boardman, J., & Craig, T. (2012). Friendship in people with schizophrenia: A survey. *Social Psychiatry and Psychiatric Epidemiology, 47*(8), 1291–1299. https://doi.org/10.1007/s00127-011-0437-x

Hartup, W. W., & Stevens, N. (1997). Friendships and adaptation in the life course. *Psychological Bulletin, 121*(3), 355–370. https://doi.org/10.1037/0033-2909.121.3.355

Hill, RL. (2016). *Gender, metal and the media: Women fans and the gendered experience of music.* Springer.

Hornby, N (2003) *Songbook.* Riverhead Books.

Hubbs, N. (2018). The Promised Land: Springsteen's epic heterosexuality, late capitalism, and prospects for queer life. In W. I. Wolff (Ed.), *Bruce Springsteen and popular music: Essays on rhetoric, social consciousness, and contemporary culture* (pp. 90–104). Routledge.

Hunter, E. G. (2008). Beyond death: Inheriting the past and giving to the future, transmitting the legacy of one's self. *Omega: Journal of Death and Dying, 56*(4), 313–329. https://doi.org/10.2190/om.56.4.a

Hunter, E. G., & Rowles, G. D. (2005). Leaving a legacy: Toward a typology. *Journal of Aging Studies, 19*(3), 327–347. https://doi.org/10.1016/j.jaging.2004.08.002

Ignelzi, M. (2000). Meaning-making in the learning and teaching process. *New Directions for Teaching and Learning, 82*, 5–14.

Iver, D. (2019). From the Backstreets to the Badlands: My Springsteen journey. In J. D. Cohen & J. S. Sawyers (Eds.), *Long walk home: Reflections on Bruce Springsteen* (pp. 36–43). Rutgers University Press.

Johnson, W. B. (2014). Mentoring in psychology education and training: A mentoring relationship continuum model. In *The Oxford handbook of education and training in clinical psychology* (pp. 272–290). Oxford University Press.

Johnson, W. B., & Ridley, C. R. (2008). *The elements of mentoring*. St. Martin's Press.

Jones, H. B. (2001). Magic, meaning, and leadership: Weber's model and the empirical literature. *Human Relations, 54*, 753–771.

Jordan, J. V. (1986). The meaning of mutuality. *Works in Progress* (series). Wellesley Centers for Women, Wellesley College.

Jordan, J. V. (2018). *Relational-cultural therapy*. American Psychological Association.

Jordan, J. V., Walker, M., & Hartling, L. M. (Eds.). (2004). *The complexity of connection: Writings from the stone center's Jean Baker Miller training institute*. Guilford Press.

Jung, C., & Campbell, J. (1976). *The portable Jung*. Penguin Classics.

Keeley, J. W., Ismail, E., & Buskist, W. (2016). Excellent teachers' perspectives on excellent teaching. *Teaching of Psychology, 43*(3), 175–179.

Kegan, R. (1982). *The evolving self: Problems and process in human development*. Harvard University Press.

Klass, D., & Steffen, E. M. (Eds.). (2018). *Continuing bonds in bereavement: New directions for research and practice*. Routledge.

Knight, B. G., & Pachana, N. A. (2015). *Psychological assessment & therapy with older adults*. Oxford University Press.

Knight, R. (2004). *Psychotherapy with older adults*. SAGE Publications.

Larsen, G. (2017). "It's a man's man's man's world": Music groupies and the othering of women in the world of rock. *Organization*, 24(3). https://doi.org/10.1177/1350508416689095

Late to school? Bruce Springsteen's got you covered. (2016, March 18). *Times Union*. https://www.timesunion.com/local/article/Late-to-school-Bruce-Springsteen-s-got-you-6921775.php

Lee, H. J., & Szinovacz, M. E. (2016). Positive, negative, and ambivalent interactions with family and friends: Associations with well-being. *Journal of Marriage and Family, 78*(3), 660–679. https://doi.org/10.1111/jomf.12302

Mangione, L. (2012). Passion, containment, and commitment—essential elements of groups across the lifespan in Bruce Springsteen's work. *International Journal of Group Psychotherapy, 62*(4), 558–584. https://doi.org/10.1521/ijgp.2012.62.4.558

Mangione, L., & Keady, S. (2007). "Spirit in the night" to "Mary's place": Loss, death and the transformative power of relationships. *Psychology of Aesthetics, Creativity, and the Arts, 1*(4). https://doi.org/10.1037/1931-3896.1.4.179

Mangione, L., Borden, K. A., Nadkarni, L., Evarts, K., & Hyde, K. (2018). Mentoring in clinical psychology programs: Broadening and deepening. *Training and Education in Professional Psychology, 12*(1), 4–13.

Mangione L., & Luff, D. (2018). Who is Bruce Springsteen to his women fans? In W. I. Wolff (Ed.), *Bruce Springsteen and popular music: Essays on rhetoric, social consciousness. and contemporary culture* (pp. 114–130). Routledge.

Mangione, L., & Luff, D. (2019). Women fans' journeys through darkness. *Interdisciplinary Literary Studies, 21*(1), 26–41.

Mangione, L., Lyons, M., & DiCello, D. (2016). Spirituality and religion in the experiences of Italian American daughters grieving for their fathers. *Psychology of Religion and Spirituality, 8*(3), 253–262.

Markman, K. D., Proulx, T., & Lindberg, M. J. (2013). *The psychology of meaning.* American Psychological Association.

Mason, B. A. (1985). *In country.* Harper & Row.

McAdams, D. P. (2013). How actors, agents, and authors find meaning in life. In K. D. Markman, T. Proulx, & M. J. Lindberg (Eds.), *The psychology of meaning* (pp. 171–190). American Psychological Association.

McGoldrick, M., Giodarno, J., & Garcia-Preto, N. (Eds.). (2005). *Ethnicity and family therapy* (3rd ed.). Guilford Press.

McWilliams, N. (1999). *Psychoanalytic case formulation.* Guilford Press.

Meuser, T. M., Mthembu, T. G., Overton, B. L., Roman, N. V., Miller, R. D., Lyons, K. P., & Carpenter, B. D. (2019). Legacy beliefs across generations: Comparing views of older parents and their adult children. *International Journal of Aging and Human Development, 88*(2), 168–186. https://doi.org/10.1177/0091415018757212

Mikulincer, M., & Shaver, P. R. (2016). *Attachment in adulthood: Structure, dynamics, and change* (2nd ed.). Guilford Press.

Miller, A. (2014). Friends wanted. *Monitor on psychology, 45*(1), 54.

Mitchell, S. A., & Black, M. J. (2016). *Freud and beyond: A history of modern psychoanalytic thought.* Basic Books.

Moss, P. (2018). American Beauty nomads?: Ontological security and masculinized knowledge in uncertain times. In W. I. Wolff (Ed.), *Bruce Springsteen and popular music: Rhetoric, social consciousness and contemporary culture* (pp. 73–88). Routledge.

Muran, J. C., & Eubanks, C. F. (2020). *Therapist performance under pressure: Negotiating emotion, difference, and rupture.* APA Books.

Najafi, M., & Kamal, M. (2012). The concept of place attachment in environmental psychology. *Sustainable Architecture, 45,* 7637–7641. https://www.elixirpublishers.com/articles/1350368123_45%20(2012)%207637–7641.pdf

Neimeyer, R., Klass, D., & Dennis, M. (2014). A social constructionist account of grief: Loss and the narration of meaning. *Death Studies, 38*(8), 485–498.

Newton, N. J., & Jones, B. K. (2016). Passing on: Personal attributes associated with midlife expressions of intended legacies. *Developmental Psychology, 52*(2), 341–353. https://doi.org/10.1037/a0039905

Obama, B., & Springsteen, B. (hosts) (2021, March 22). Relationships with our fathers and masculinity (No. 6) [Audio podcast episode]. In *Renegades: Born in the USA*. Spotify: Higher Ground Productions.

Obama, B., & Springsteen, B. (hosts) (2021, March 29). Fatherhood (No. 7) [Audio podcast episode]. In *Renegades: Born in the USA*. Spotify: Higher Ground Productions.

Obama, B. & Springsteen, B. (hosts). (2021, April 5). Looking towards American renewal (No. 8) [Audio podcast episode]. In *Renegades: Born in the USA*. Spotify: Higher Ground Productions.

O'Donnell, K. (2018). Our Lady of E Street: The boss's virgin, 2002–2014. In W. I. Wolff (Ed.), *Bruce Springsteen and popular music: Rhetoric, social consciousness and contemporary culture* (pp. 45–57). Routledge.

Overholser, J. C. (2005). Group psychotherapy and existential concerns: An interview with Irvin Yalom. *Journal of Contemporary Psychotherapy, 35*(2), 185–197. https://doi.org/10.1007/s10879-005-2699-7

Palmer, G. (1997). Bruce Springsteen and masculinity. In S. Whitely (Ed.), *Sexing the groove: Popular music and gender* (pp. 100–117). Routledge.

Pardini, S. F. S. (2012). Bruce Zirilli: The Italian sides of Bruce Springsteen. In K. Womack, J. Zolten, & M. Bernhard (Eds.), *Bruce Springsteen, Cultural Studies, and the Runaway American Dream* (pp. 97–110). Ashgate Publishing.

Pargament, K. (2007). *Spiritually integrated psychotherapy: Understanding and addressing the sacred*. Guilford Press.

Pargament, K. I., & Mahoney, A. (2009). Spirituality: The search for the sacred. In *The Oxford handbook of positive psychology* (2nd ed.). Oxford University Press.

Parks, C. D., & Tasca, G. A. (Eds.). (2020). *The psychology of groups: The intersection of social psychology and psychotherapy research*. American Psychological Association.

Pearce, M. J., Pargament, K. I., Oxhandler, H. K., Vieten, C., & Wong, S. (2019). A novel training program for mental health providers in religious and spiritual competencies. *Spirituality in Clinical Practice, 6*(2), 73–82.

Pennebaker, J. W., & Smyth, J. M. (2016). *Opening up by writing it down, third edition: How expressive writing improves health and eases emotional pain*. Guilford Press.

Percy, W. (1998). Interview with Bruce Springsteen: *DoubleTake*, Spring. In C. Phillips and L. P. Masur (Eds.), *Talk about a dream: The essential interviews of Bruce Springsteen* (2013, pp. 218–232). Bloomsbury.

Plante, T. (2009). *Spiritual practices in psychotherapy: Thirteen tools for enhancing psychological health*. American Psychological Association.

Powers, A (2016, October 4). The limits of loving the Boss. *The Record*. https://www.npr.org/sections/therecord/2016/10/04/496544688/the-limits-of-loving-the-boss

Putnam, R. (2001). *Bowling alone: The collapse and revival of American community.* Touchstone Books by Simon & Schuster.

Putnam, R. (2020). *Bowling alone: Revised and updated: The collapse and revival of American community.* Touchstone Books by Simon & Schuster.

Randall, L. K. (2010). *Finding grace in the concert hall: Community and meaning among Springsteen fans.* Waveland.

Regev, D., and Cohen-Yatziv, L. (2018). Effectiveness of art therapy with adult clients in 2018—what progress has been made? *Frontiers in Psychology,* 9:1531. https://doi.org/10.3389/fpsyg.2018.01531

Remnick, D. (2012, July 30). We are alive: Bruce Springsteen at sixty-two. *New Yorker.* https://www.newyorker.com/magazine/2012/07/30/we-are-alive

Rhodes, L. L. (2005). *Electric ladyland: Women and rock culture.* University of Pennsylvania Press.

Riggio, R. E., & Riggio, H. R. (2008). Social psychology and charismatic leadership. In D. R. Forsyth, C. Hoyt, and G. Goethals (Eds.), *Leadership at the crossroads: Social psychology and leadership* (pp. 30–44). Praeger.

Ripatrazone, N. (2021, April 27). Bruce Springsteen's glory days. *Catholic Herald.* https://catholicherald.co.uk/bruce-springsteens-glory-days/?fbclid=IwAR1hhIqr8Ol2kOGNIyIkhSziYvo4Akp8LeQ2ooAhwEeYLVZzeFCdcBJXEKY

Rubin, L. B. (1990). *Just friends: The role of friendship in our lives.* Harper Perennial.

Rutan, J. S., & Rice, C. A. (1981). The charismatic leader: Asset or liability? *Psychotherapy: Theory, Research, and Practice, 18*(4), 487–492.

Rutan, J. S., Stone, W. N., & Shay, J. J. (2014). *Psychodynamic group psychotherapy* (5th ed.). Guilford Press.

Safran, J. D., Kriss, A., & Foley, V. K. (2018). Psychodynamic psychotherapies. In D. Wedding & R. J. Corsini (Eds.), *Current psychotherapies* (pp. 21–58). Cengage Learning.

Safran, J. D., & Muran, J. C. (2000). *Negotiating the therapeutic alliance: A relational treatment guide.* Guilford Press.

St. Clair, M., & Wigren, J. (2004). *Object relations and self psychology: An introduction.* Cengage Learning.

Sandage, S. J., Rupert, D., Stavros, G. S., & Devor, N. G. (2020). *Relational spirituality in psychotherapy.* American Psychological Association.

Santelli, R. (2012). *This land is your land: Woody Guthrie and the journey of an American folk song.* Running Press.

Santelli, R. (2013) Interview with Bruce Springsteen: Grammy.com, February 7. In C. Phillips and L. P. Masur (Eds.), *Talk about a dream: The essential interviews of Bruce Springsteen* (pp. 421–428). Bloomsbury.

Shafranske, E. (1996). *Religion and the clinical practice of psychology.* American Psychological Association.

Shultz, F. L., & Sandage, S. J. (2006). *Transforming spirituality: Integrating theology and psychology*. Baker Academic.

Siebert, D. C., Mutran, E. J., & Reitzes, D. C. (1999). Friendship and social support: The importance of role identity to aging adults. *Social Work, 44*(6), 522–533. https://doi.org/10.1093/sw/44.6.522

Smith, M. N. (1992). Sexual mobilities in Bruce Springsteen: Performance as commentary. In A. DeCurtis (Ed.), *Present tense: Rock & roll and culture* (pp. 197–218). Duke University Press.

Snyder, C. R. (1994). *The psychology of hope*. Free Press.

Snyder, C. R. (2000). *Handbook of hope: Theory, measures, & applications*. Academic Press.

Snyder, C. R., & Lopez, S. J. (Eds.). (2009). *Oxford handbook of positive psychology*. Oxford University Press.

Sperry, L. (2012). *Spirituality in clinical practice: Theory and practice of spiritually oriented psychotherapy*. Routledge.

Sperry, L., & Shafranske, E. P. (Eds.). (2005). *Spiritually oriented psychotherapy*. American Psychological Association.

Springsteen, B. (2011). Bruce Springsteen's eulogy for Clarence Clemons. In *Eulogy*. http://www.eulogyspeech.net/famous-eulogies/Bruce-Springsteen-Eulogy-for-Clarence-Clemons.shtml

Springsteen, B. (2016). *Born to run*. Simon & Schuster.

Springsteen Boston College. (2020). Read: Bruce Springsteen's message to the Boston College class of 2024. *America: The Jesuit Review*. https://www.americamagazine.org/arts-culture/2020/09/11/read-bruce-springsteens-message-boston-college-class-2024-covid-19

Strauss, N. (1995). Interview with Bruce Springsteen: *Guitar World*, October. In C. Phillips and L. P. Masur (Eds.), *Talk about a dream: The essential interviews of Bruce Springsteen* (2013, pp. 170–181). Bloomsbury.

Streight. I. (2019). Interview with Martyn Joseph. In J. D. Cohen & J. S. Sawyers (Eds.), *Long walk home: Reflections on Bruce Springsteen* (pp. 135–142). Rutgers University Press.

Stuckey, H. L., & Nobel, J. (2010). The connection between art, healing, and public health: A review of current literature. *American Journal of Public Health, 100*(2): 254–263. https://doi.org/10.2105/AJPH.2008.156497

Sutcliffe, P. (2006) Mojo—January 2006. In C. Phillips and L. P. Masur (Eds.), *Talk about a dream: The essential interviews of Bruce Springsteen* (2013, pp. 300–319). Bloomsbury.

Swirsky, C. (2014). Fandom as a modern popular religion [unpublished manuscript].

Symynkywicz, J. B. (2008). *The gospel according to Bruce Springsteen: Rock and redemption, from Asbury Park to magic*. Westminster John Knox Press.

Tasca, G. A., Mikail, S. F., & Hewitt, P. L. (2020). *Group psychodynamic-interpersonal psychotherapy*. American Psychological Association.

Tedeschi, R. G., & Calhoun, L. G. (2004). Posttraumatic growth: Conceptual foundations and empirical evidence. *Psychological Inquiry, 15*(1), 1–18. https://doi.org/10.1207/s15327965pli1501_01

Wallin, D. J. (2007). *Attachment in psychotherapy*. Guilford Press.

Walsh, F. (Ed.). (2012). *Normal family processes: Growing diversity and complexity* (4th ed.). Guilford Press.

Wampold, B. E. (2001). *The great psychotherapy debate: Models, methods, and findings*. Lawrence Erlbaum.

Wampold, B. E. (2010). *Basics of psychotherapy*. American Psychological Association.

Wampold, B. E. (2018). *The basics of psychotherapy: An introduction to theory and practice*. American Psychological Association.

Wise, S. (1990). Sexing Elvis. In S. Frith, & A. Goodwin (Eds.), *On record: Rock, pop and the written word* (pp. 390–398). Routledge. (Reprinted from Wise, S., "Sexing Elvis" (1984), *Women's Studies International Forum*, 7(1), 13–17. http://dx.doi.org/10.1016/0277-5395(84)90077-3.)

Woge, S. (2011). Evangelism from E Street: Brother Springsteen's salvation show. In D. G. Izzo (Ed.), *Bruce Springsteen and the American soul* (pp. 142–151). McFarland.

Wolff, W. I. (2018). *Bruce Springsteen and popular music: Essays on rhetoric, social consciousness, and contemporary culture*. Routledge.

Wurtzel, E. (1994) *Prozac nation*. Mariner Books.

Yalom, Irvin D. (1980). *Existential psychotherapy*. Basic Books.

Yalom, I. D., & Leszcz, M. (2020). *The theory and practice of group psychotherapy* (6th ed.). Basic Books.

Zitelli, L. (2012). "Come to the Door, Ma": Mothers, women and home in Springsteen's *Devils and Dust*. In K. Womack, J. Zolten, & M. Bernhard (Eds.), *Bruce Springsteen, Cultural Studies, and the Runaway American Dream* (pp. 79–96). Ashgate.

DISCOGRAPHY

Jackson, M. & Richie, L. (1985). We are the world. (Song). On *We are the world.* Columbia Records.

Springsteen, B. (1973). New York City serenade. (Song). On *The wild, the innocent, and the E Street shuffle.* Columbia Records.

Springsteen, B. (1975). *Born to run.* Columbia Records.

Springsteen, B. (1975). Born to run (Song). On *Born to run.* Columbia Records.

Springsteen, B. (1975). Jungleland (Song). On *Born to run.* Columbia Records.

Springsteen, B. (1975). Thunder road (Song). On *Born to run.* Columbia Records.

Springsteen, B. (1978). *Darkness on the edge of town.* Columbia Records.

Springsteen, B. (1978). Badlands (Song). On *Darkness on the edge of town.* Columbia Records.

Springsteen, B. (1980). *The river.* Columbia Records.

Springsteen, B. (1980). Independence Day (Song). On *The river.* Columbia Records.

Springsteen, B. (1980). The river (Song). On *The river.* Columbia Records.

Springsteen, B. (1980). Ties that bind (Song). On *The river.* Columbia Records.

Springsteen, B. (1980). Hungry heart (Song). On *The river.* Columbia Records.

Springsteen, B. (1980). Point blank (Song). On *The river.* Columbia Records.

Springsteen, B. (1984). *Born in the U.S.A.* Columbia Records.

Springsteen, B. (1984). I'm on fire (Song). On *Born in the U.S.A.* Columbia Records.

Springsteen, B. (1986). Fire. (Song). On *Live/1975–85.* Columbia Records.

Springsteen, B. (1987). *Tunnel of love.* Columbia Records.

Springsteen, B. (1987). Tougher than the rest (Song). On *Tunnel of love.* Columbia Records.

Springsteen, B. (1987). Tunnel of love (Song). On *Tunnel of love.* Columbia Records.

Springsteen, B. (1992). Better days (Song). On *Lucky town.* Columbia Records.

Springsteen, B. (1993). Red headed woman (Song). On *In concert/MTV plugged*. Columbia Records.

Springsteen, B. (1995). *Greatest hits*. Columbia Records.

Springsteen, B. (2002). *The rising*. Columbia Records.

Springsteen, B. (2002). Waitin' on a sunny day (Song). On *The rising*. Columbia Records.

Springsteen, B. (2002). Further on up the road (Song). On *The rising*. Columbia Records.

Springsteen, B. (2005). Reno (Song). On *Devils & dust*. Columbia Records.

Springsteen, B. (2009). Working on a dream. (Song). On *Working on a dream*. Columbia Records.

Springsteen, B. (2012). Wrecking ball. (Song). On *Wrecking ball*. Columbia Records.

Springsteen, B. (2012). Land of hope and dreams (Song). On *Wrecking ball*. Columbia Records.

Springsteen, B. (2019). *Western stars*. Columbia Records.

Springsteen, B. (2019). Sleepy Joe's Café. (Song). On *Western stars*. Columbia Records.

Springsteen, B. (2020). *Letter to you*. Columbia Records.

Springsteen, B. (2020). One minute you're here. (Song). On *Letter to you*. Columbia Records.

PERMISSIONS

"New York City Serenade." Copyright 1973 Sony Music Publishing (US) LLC and Eldridge Publishing Co. All rights administered by Sony Music Publishing (US) LLC, 424 Church Street, Suite 1200, Nashville, TN 37219. All rights reserved. Used by permission.

"Jungleland" and "Born to Run." Copyright 1975 Sony Music Publishing (US) LLC and Eldridge Publishing Co. All rights administered by Sony Music Publishing (US) LLC, 424 Church Street, Suite 1200, Nashville, TN 37219. All rights reserved. Used by permission.

"Badlands." Copyright 1978 Sony Music Publishing (US) LLC and Eldridge Publishing Co. All rights administered by Sony Music Publishing (US) LLC, 424 Church Street, Suite 1200, Nashville, TN 37219. All rights reserved. Used by permission.

"Point Blank" and "The River." Copyright 1980 Sony Music Publishing (US) LLC and Eldridge Publishing Co. All rights administered by Sony Music Publishing (US) LLC, 424 Church Street, Suite 1200, Nashville, TN 37219. All rights reserved. Used by permission.

"I'm on Fire." Copyright 1984 Sony Music Publishing (US) LLC and Eldridge Publishing Co. All rights administered by Sony Music Publishing (US) LLC, 424 Church Street, Suite 1200, Nashville, TN 37219. All rights reserved. Used by permission.

"Thunder Road." Copyright 1986 Sony Music Publishing (US) LLC and Eldridge Publishing Co. All rights administered by Sony Music Publishing (US) LLC, 424 Church Street, Suite 1200, Nashville, TN 37219. All rights reserved. Used by permission.

"Tougher Than the Rest" and "Tunnel of Love." Copyright 1987 Sony Music Publishing (US) LLC and Eldridge Publishing Co. All rights administered by

Sony Music Publishing (US) LLC, 424 Church Street, Suite 1200, Nashville, TN 37219. All rights reserved. Used by permission.

"Better Days." Copyright 1992 Sony Music Publishing (US) LLC and Eldridge Publishing Co. All rights administered by Sony Music Publishing (US) LLC, 424 Church Street, Suite 1200, Nashville, TN 37219. All rights reserved. Used by permission.

"Red Headed Woman." Copyright 1993 Sony Music Publishing (US) LLC and Eldridge Publishing Co. All rights administered by Sony Music Publishing (US) LLC, 424 Church Street, Suite 1200, Nashville, TN 37219. All rights reserved. Used by permission.

"Land of Hope and Dreams." Copyright 2001 Sony Music Publishing (US) LLC and Eldridge Publishing Co. All rights administered by Sony Music Publishing (US) LLC, 424 Church Street, Suite 1200, Nashville, TN 37219. All rights reserved. Used by permission.

"Wrecking Ball." Copyright 2012 Sony Music Publishing (US) LLC and Eldridge Publishing Co. All rights administered by Sony Music Publishing (US) LLC, 424 Church Street, Suite 1200, Nashville, TN 37219. All rights reserved. Used by permission.

INDEX

ABOUT THE AUTHORS

LORRAINE MANGIONE, Department of Clinical Psychology at Antioch University New England, focuses on women in many aspects of who they are; creativity and artistry; group therapy; spirituality and religion; aging, loss, and grief; Italian American culture; mentoring; and #MeToo in her clinical and research work and publications. She is the coauthor of *Daughters, Dads, and the Path through Grief: Tales from Italian America,* as well as articles integrating Springsteen and psychology.

DONNA LUFF is a British-born writer and sociologist, an educator at Boston Children's Hospital, and faculty at Harvard Medical School. She has published on gender, sexuality, and health care innovations and taught widely on qualitative research practice. She is author of several personal essays, as well as articles on Springsteen, and coauthor of a prior chapter on Springsteen's women fans.